TREASURES OF
ISLAM

ARTISTIC GLORIES OF
THE MUSLIM WORLD

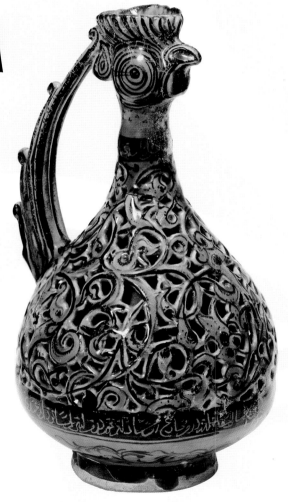

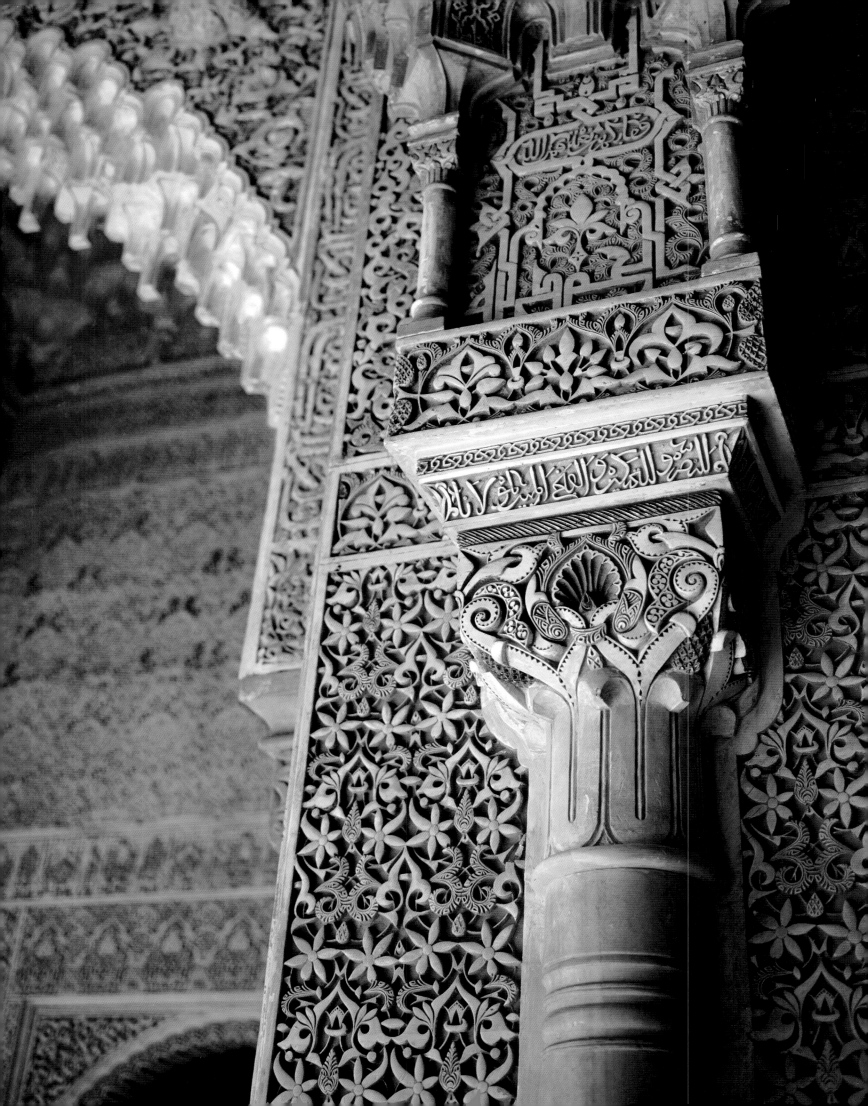

TREASURES OF
ISLAM

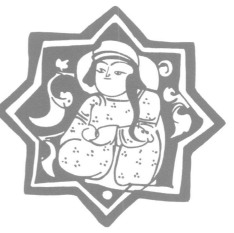

ARTISTIC GLORIES OF
THE MUSLIM WORLD

dbp

DUNCAN BAIRD PUBLISHERS

LONDON

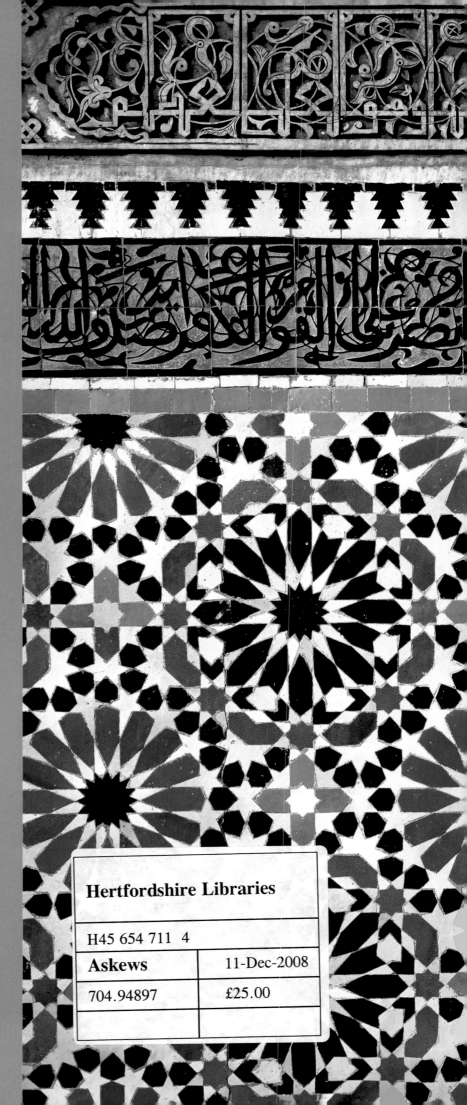

TREASURES OF ISLAM

Bernard O'Kane

First published in the United Kingdom and Ireland in 2007 by
Duncan Baird Publishers Ltd
Sixth Floor
Castle House
75–76 Wells Street
London W1T 3QH

Conceived, created and designed by Duncan Baird Publishers
Copyright © Duncan Baird Publishers 2007
Text copyright © Bernard O'Kane 2007
Artwork copyright © Duncan Baird Publishers 2007
For copyright of photographs see page 223, which is to be
regarded as an extension of this copyright

Editor: Peter Bently
Designer: Luana Gobbo
Picture Editor: Julia Ruxton
Managing Editor: Christopher Westhorp
Managing Designer: Manisha Patel
Commissioned Artwork: Map by Gary Walton,
site plans by Sailesh Patel

British Library Cataloguing-in-Publication Data:
A CIP record for this book is available from the
British Library
ISBN: 978-1-84483-446-4

10 9 8 7 6 5 4 3 2 1

Typeset in Perpetua and Optima
Colour reproduction by Scanhouse, Malaysia
Printed in Singapore by Imago

Captions for pages 1–3
Page 1: Underglaze-painted stonepaste ewer from
Kashan, Iran. Seljuk period, early 13th century.
Page 2: Stucco decoration in the Court of the Lions, the
Alhambra, Granada, Spain; second half of the 14th century.
Page 4: Decorative details from the Saadian necropolis,
Marrakesh, Morocco. From top to bottom: a Kufic
inscription in stucco; a reciprocal pattern of crenellations in
tile mosaic; a *naskhi* inscription in sgraffito tiles; and a star
pattern in tile mosaic. Late 16th century.

DEDICATION
To Paul and Maeve

CONTENTS

INTRODUCTION

ART AND FAITH

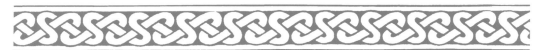

Islam originated one of the world's great artistic traditions. It covers an enormous span of geography and time, from Spain to Indonesia and from the seventh century to the present. "Islamic art" is generally used to describe the art produced in this area, but the term is relatively recent, first used by European scholars in the late nineteenth century. The artists who created the examples in this book probably identified themselves as belonging to a particular city or perhaps a province, but none would have considered that they were making "Islamic", or even "Mamluk" or "Ottoman" art.

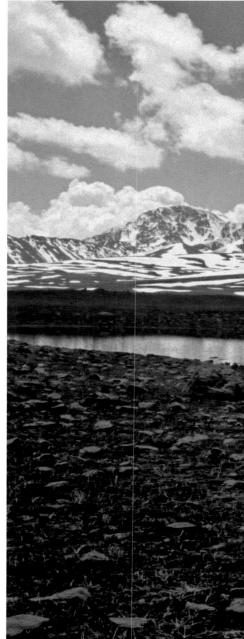

Even in modern art historical parlance, "Islamic art" is used in a very different sense from Christian or Buddhist art. Unlike Christianity, which draws a distinction between art for religious and non-religious purposes, Islam purports to encompass all aspects of society, which is why the term has been applied to the entire artistic creations of the Islamic lands. As usual, however, practice differs from theory, and even in Islam's first century, art was produced within a secular context that would be objectionable on strictly religious grounds. It would also be wrong to think of Islam over this vast period and area as a monolith: just as the modern theocracies of Iran and Saudi Arabia have different doctrinal interpretations, so earlier dynasties varied in the extent to which, for instance, they permitted figural images on mosques or madrasas.

But there are features shared within the whole of the Islamic realm. A tall tower will frequently beckon Muslims to a place of worship; beside it the mosque will probably be decorated in Arabic calligraphy displaying verses of the Quran. Domes, while not exclusive to Islam, are associated with many of its major monuments. Other common building forms rarely found except in Islamic monuments include *iwan*s and *muqarna*s.

To most Westerners, mention of the Middle East conjures up images of sandy deserts. The reality can be very different, with rivers such as the Nile, Tigris and Euphrates supporting extensive agriculture. The plateau of Iran receives little rainfall and does incorporate two major deserts, but its 3,300-feet (1,000m) altitude also makes it subject to winter snows. The dissimilarity of the Iranian climate to that of the Arabian

While not the landscape usually associated with Islamic lands, this snow-covered vista of the Tianshan range in Kyrgyzstan, seen from the Alabel Pass at an altitude of 10,170 feet (3,100m), is typical of many mountain ranges on the Silk Road between China and the Near East, an important route for the transmission of Islam.

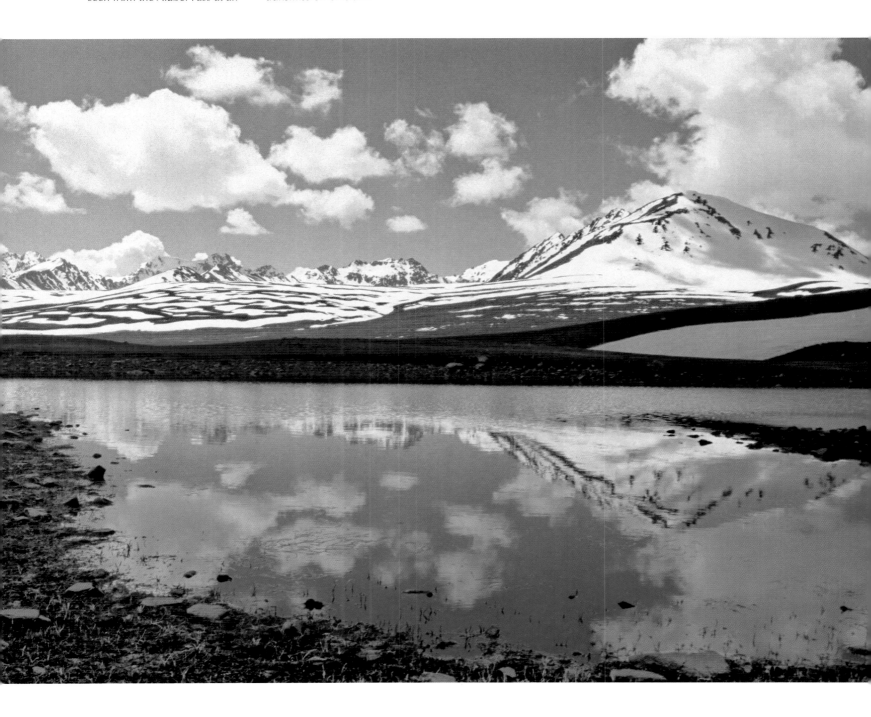

BELOW AND INSET
Map of the Islamic world,
showing locations of major
artistic centers and monuments.
Islam expanded from its early
heartlands (inset) as far as
Spain and Indonesia. Today
most Muslims actually live to
the east of Iran, an area that
includes four of the world's
most populous nations,
Pakistan, India, Bangladesh,
and Indonesia.

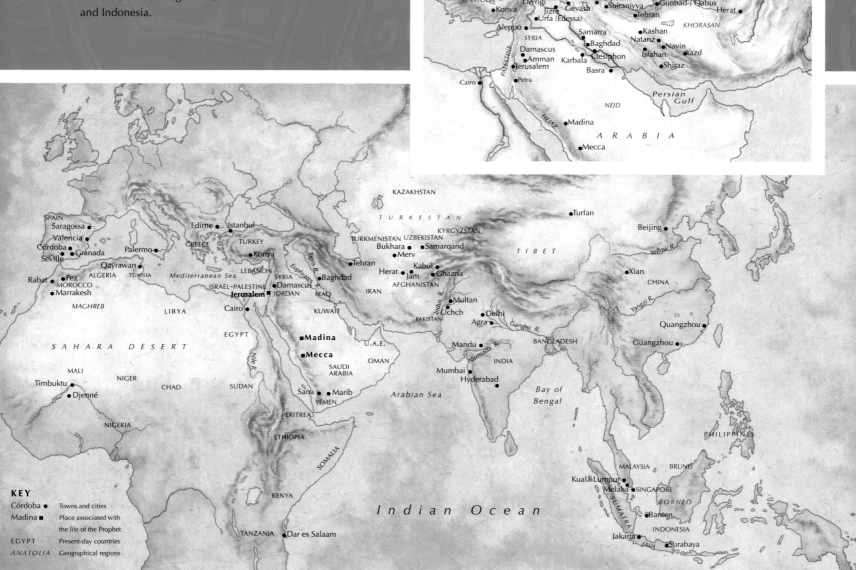

KEY

Córdoba ●	Towns and cities
Madina ■	Place associated with the life of the Prophet
EGYPT	Present-day countries
ANATOLIA	Geographical regions

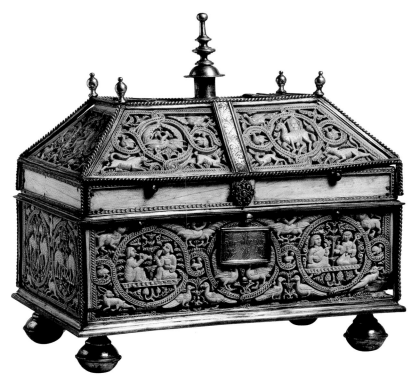

peninsula may be one reason why, in comparison to other areas, Arabs in the early period may have settled there in smaller numbers. As a result Persian (albeit laden with Arabic loan words) continues to be spoken by the majority of Iranians, unlike in Syria, Egypt and North Africa, where respectively Aramaic, Coptic and Berber were supplanted by Arabic.

The disparities of these territories are significant, but the account of one of the world's great travellers, Ibn Battuta, shows how homogenous much of this area was, at least in social terms. He left his native Morocco in 1325, journeying as far as China before returning in 1354. On his travels he was often able to find accommodation through the enormous network of Muslim religious institutions, especially in *khanaqah*s, monasteries for Sufis (Islamic mystics). Despite his poor Persian (the spoken language of the court) he was able to find employment even in distant Delhi, where he was appointed the city's chief judge.

The huge physical and climatic variations had obvious effects on the development of art and architecture. Where stone was easily quarried it was the material of choice for building and for decoration, as monuments in Egypt, Syria, Anatolia and India demonstrate. In other areas, such as Iraq and Iran, brick was employed, and in order to enliven it glazed tiles played an increasingly important role from the eleventh century onward. The rain-drenched climates of Indonesia and the Caspian littoral demanded buildings with sloping roofs instead of the flat ones prevalent elsewhere.

The vast span of Islamic art mentioned earlier means that in a book of this size it is impossible to do more than highlight some of the major historical and artistic trends and dwell on a few of the finest examples. The first chapter of the book outlines the origins and formative years of Islam. Chapter 2 deals with the period of political unity, or near unity, under the early empires of the Umayyad and 'Abbasid caliphs. Chapter 3

ABOVE

Luxury for the bourgeoisie. The workmanship on this ivory box is close to others probably made in Córdoba in the early 11th century. Its lack of a dedicatee makes a princely origin less likely, although the inscriptions could have been removed when it acquired its metal reinforcements in the 18th century. Muslim rule in Iberia lasted some 780 years, from 711 to 1491.

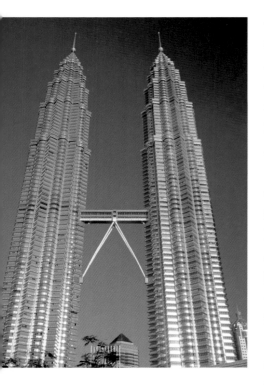

Erected in 1998, the Petronas
Towers in Kuala Lumpur
(designed by Cesar Pelli)
were briefly the world's tallest
buildings. Their stellate plan
echoes Delhi's Qutb minaret
(see page 182), similarly
designed to display the might
of Islamic civilization.

examines the rival dynasties that grew up in their wake, notably the Fatimids, Ayyubids, and Mamluks, with their focus on Egypt. The phenomenon of Islam in Iberia and the Maghreb is discussed in Chapter 4, while Chapter 5 focuses on the Turkish and Iranian dynasties of the eastern Islamic heartlands. The Turks are again the center of Chapter 6, on the Seljuks of Anatolia and their Ottoman successors, founders of the last great Islamic empire. The final chapter looks at Islam on the Indian subcontinent and in East Asia, where the majority of today's Muslims live.

Many illustrations here represent types on which whole books have been written, and can be seen as pointers to further exploration. The material discussed is mainly from before the nineteenth century, but that does not mean that there has not been later interesting material. After 1800, however, the increasing invasion of media and communications meant that it was difficult for any artistic tradition to evolve without being aware of trends formerly outside it. This has recently become a matter of increasing urgency as Muslim patrons, particularly of architecture, debate the attributes of Islamic buildings and the ways in which they might be elucidated to enhance Muslim society.

One of the world's most able and famous contemporary architects is Zaha Hadid, an Iraqi-born British citizen who has worked exclusively in the West. Is she an Islamic architect? The question is not an easy one to answer, but perhaps this should be a matter for celebration. The Aga Khan Award for Architecture (on whose juries Zaha Hadid has served more than once), which has been presenting awards to buildings for the Muslim community for a quarter of a century, has given prizes to Western architects as well as local Muslim ones for their work in Islamic countries. When a woman brought up in a Muslim culture, even one who has made a career of defying convention, can blur boundaries to reach such a position, then perhaps one can cheer the intermingling of artistic traditions on the world stage which will enable Islamic art and architecture both to reach a broader audience and reinvigorate itself with the carefully selected adaptations that characterized its first appearances.

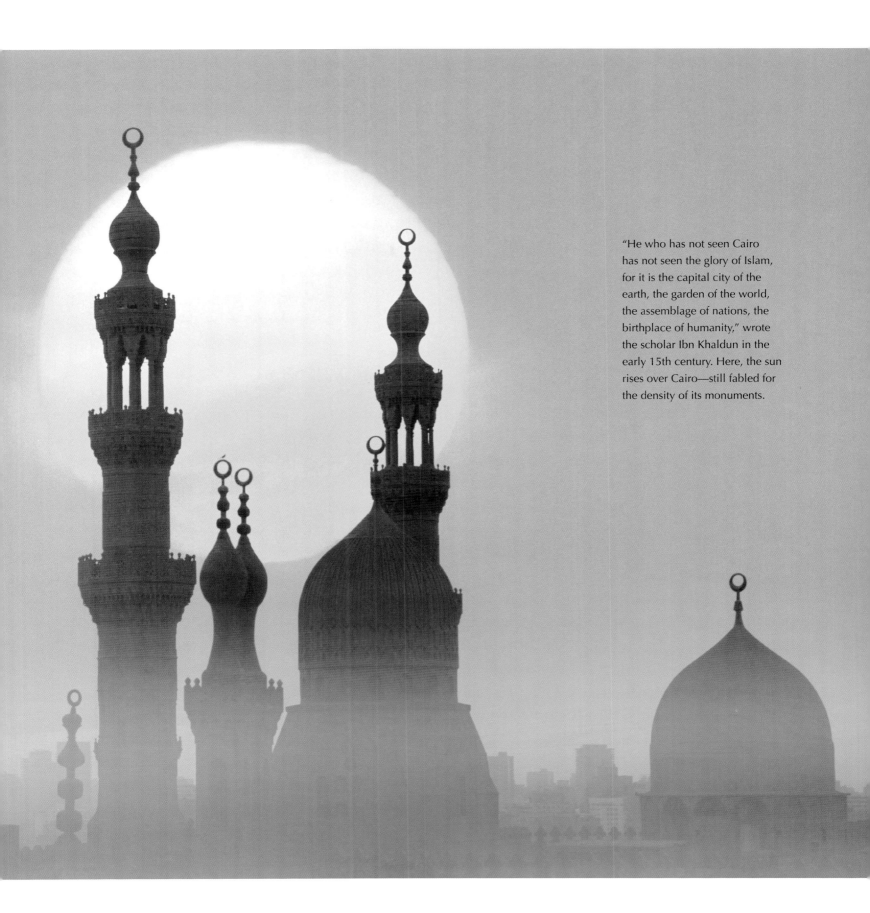

"He who has not seen Cairo has not seen the glory of Islam, for it is the capital city of the earth, the garden of the world, the assemblage of nations, the birthplace of humanity," wrote the scholar Ibn Khaldun in the early 15th century. Here, the sun rises over Cairo—still fabled for the density of its monuments.

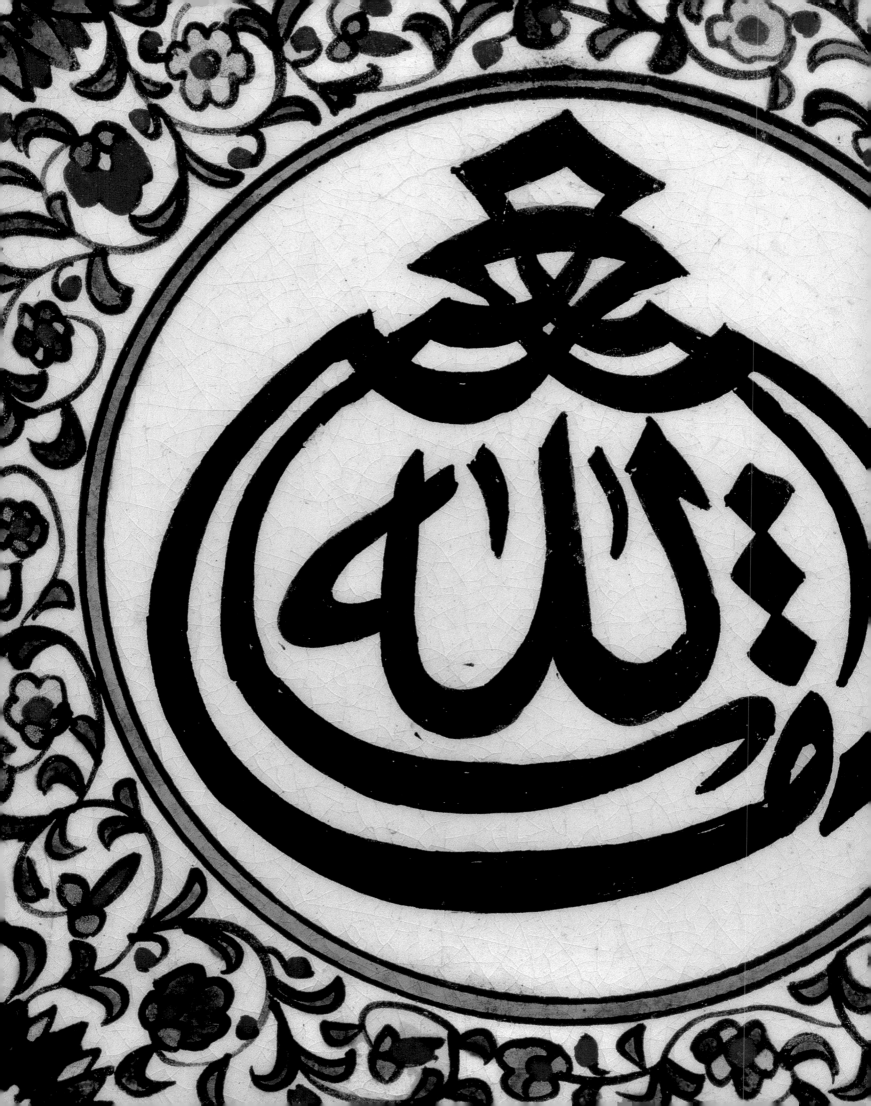

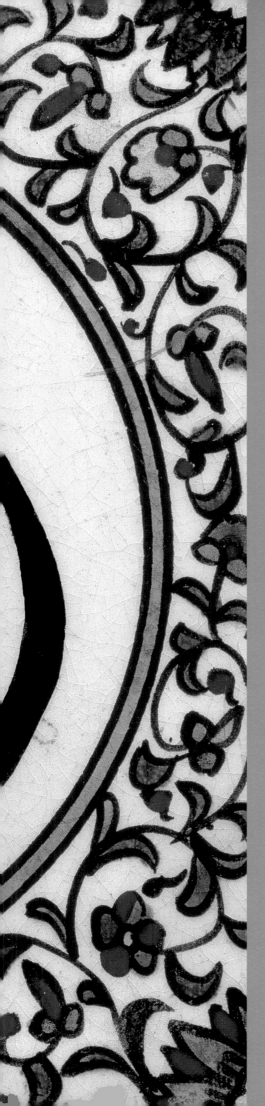

chapter I

ORIGINS:

A GIFT FROM GOD

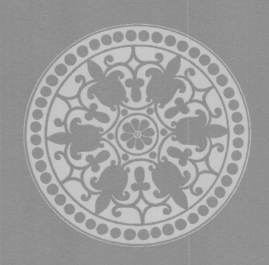

THE CRUCIBLE

THE AGE OF THE PROPHET

OPPOSITE

The Deir, Petra's largest building, is now thought to be a *triclinium*, a hall with benches around its sides, for banquets in honor of King Obodas. He was deified soon after his death in 86BCE, but the hall probably dates from the 1st century CE.

BELOW

The Sasanian king stabs a stag, having already dispatched another. From the 4th century, when this plate was made, the hunt was a standard motif on Sasanian silver, symbolizing the king's prowess and invincibility.

For many centuries before the coming of Islam, Rome and its descendant, the Byzantine empire, had been the major power in the Mediterranean. In 313 the emperor Constantine had issued an edict that tolerated Christianity as an official religion within the empire; it soon became the state religion. In 330, he transferred the imperial capital from Rome to Byzantium, later named Constantinople in his honor. As the capital of "Rum" ("Rome"), Islam's oldest foe, the city was the supreme prize for Muslim armies until it finally fell in 1453. The Byzantine empire was at its height under Justinian (ruled 527–65), who built Constantinople's magnificent Haghia Sophia cathedral (see page 23), which still inspired Muslim architects ten centuries later (see, for example, pages 176–179).

The cities and craftsmen that the Muslims encountered in Syria, where they established their first capital outside of Arabia, were largely the product of Byzantine civilization, and much of the decoration of the earliest Islamic monuments is thus of Roman or Byzantine origin, as are the forms of some buildings (see pages 30–32).

THE SASANIANS

The implacable enemies of Rome and Byzantium were the Sasanians, the dynasty founded in Iran upon the defeat of the Parthians in 224. By the start of the seventh century, the constant warfare between the Byzantines and Sasanians had seriously weakened both empires, making the subsequent Arab conquests that much easier.

The Sasanians adhered to Zoroastrianism, an essentially monotheistic faith that worshipped Ahura Mazda as the supreme being, but also emphasized his struggle with an evil spirit over whom he would eventually prevail. The Sasanians built temples in which a fire was kept burning as a symbol of purity. The inner core of these fire temples had an arched entrance on each of their four sides, a form reinterpreted in early Islamic Iran. The dome of the temples was supported on a

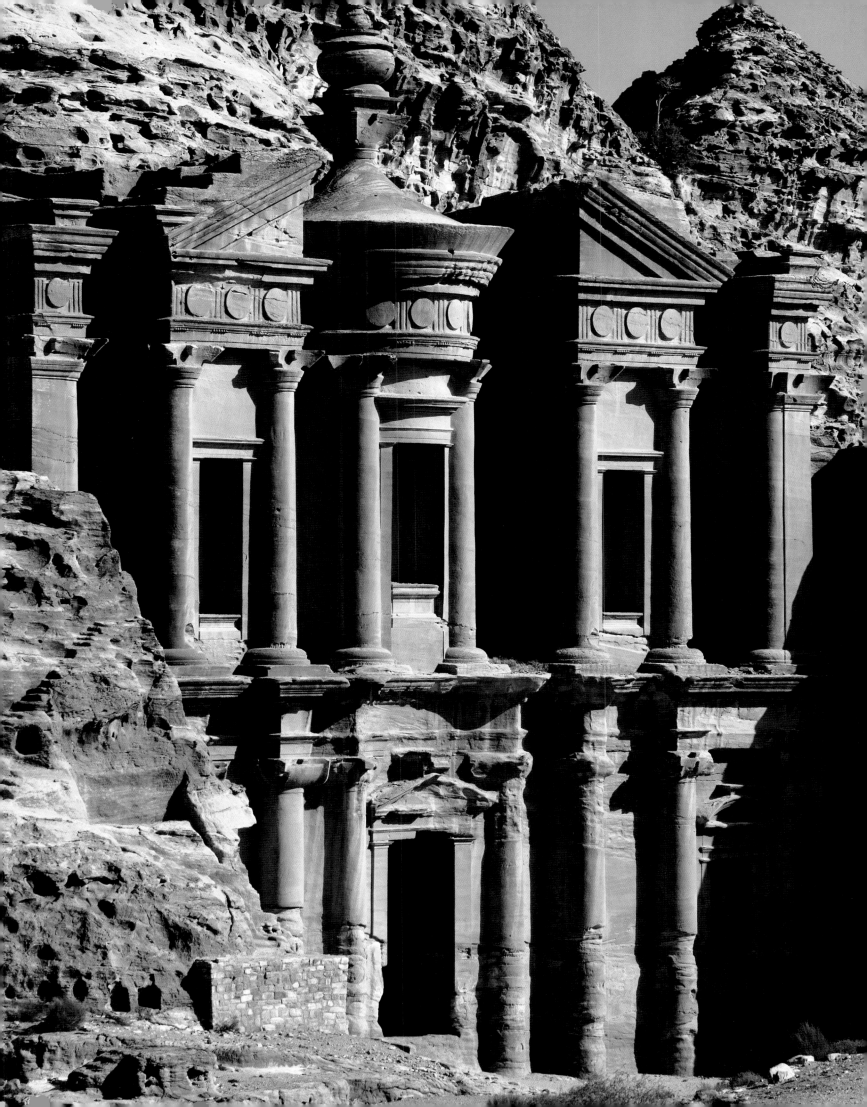

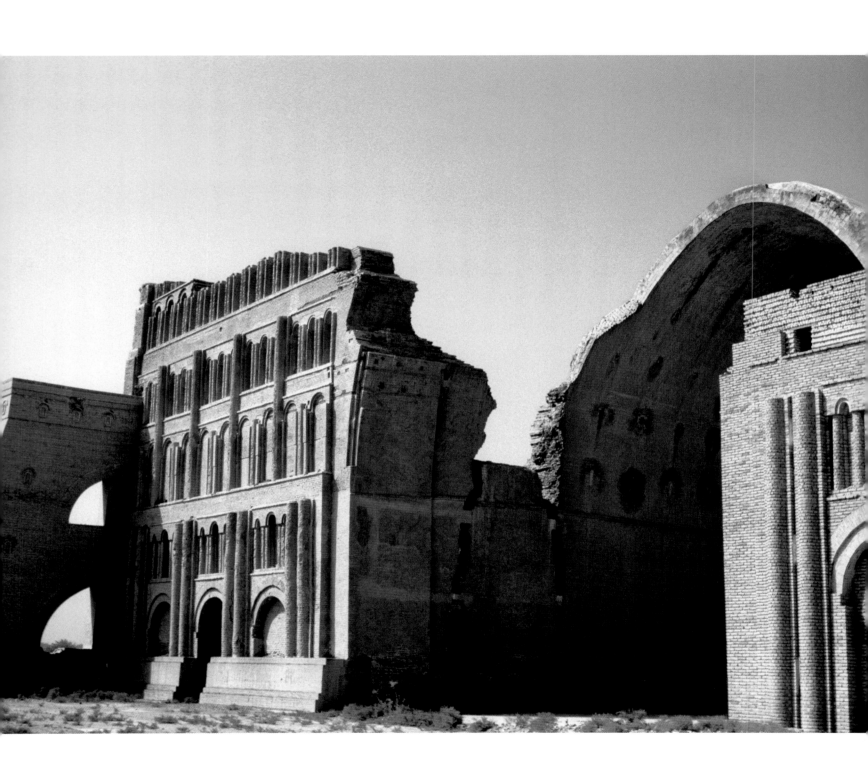

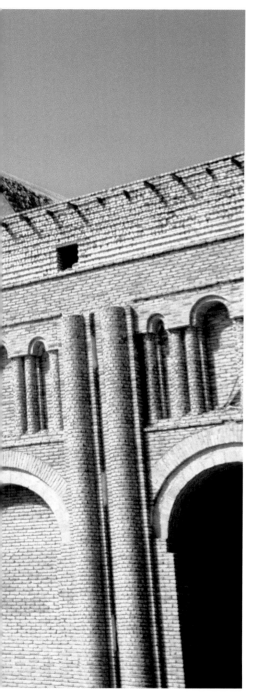

squinch, a Sasanian method of bridging the space between a lower square and a dome that became the focus of many later innovations in Iranian Islamic architecture. The *iwan*, a rectangular hall closed on three sides, had been used by the Parthians, but attained its ultimate expression in the Sasanian palace at Ctesiphon. Its brick arch is still the largest in the world, and later Islamic patrons strove to outdo it (see page 127).

The Sasanians decorated their buildings with stucco (carved plaster), which proved to be one of the favorite decorative techniques in Islamic architecture. Textiles and metalwork (see page 14) were two media whose portability ensured that many aspects of Sasanian style and iconography were reflected in early Islamic art.

Alongside these superpowers there were early centers of Arab civilization. The Nabateans, with their capital at Petra (see previous page), flourished for several centuries on the trade route between the Red Sea and the Mediterranean. Petra was eclipsed in the second century by Palmyra in the Syrian desert. Under Roman rule since the first century, one of its rulers, Queen Zenobia, (267–74), briefly rebelled and even invaded Egypt. In southern Arabia, the Sabeans had ruled a large kingdom (modern Yemen) for most of the first millennium BCE, centered on their capital of Marib. Their realm, which has been identified with the biblical Sheba, prospered from the spice trade.

MUHAMMAD AND THE COMING OF ISLAM

Mecca in the lifetime of the Prophet was a wealthy town whose income, like that of the ancient Marib before it, derived mainly from the trade in spices. These would be landed in Yemen on the southern coast of Arabia and brought by land up the western coast on their way to the Mediterranean. Mecca was also important as the site of the Ka'ba, a rectangular building that was the object of pagan pilgrimage among the local Arab tribes.

Muhammad (ca. 571–632) was from a mercantile family, but when after 610 he began to preach the message of Islam, submission to God, the doctrine of equality that it espoused aroused resentment from the wealthier merchant families of Mecca. As a result,

OPPOSITE

The first mosque. The sanctity of the place at Madina where the Prophet led prayers and was buried in 632CE has attracted pilgrims for centuries. Its greatly enlarged state is shown in this commemorative tile dated 1729, from the Ottoman period.

in 622 he and his followers migrated north to Madina. The date of the *hijra* (migration) is considered the foundation of the first Muslim community, and is so important that it marks the start of the Muslim calendar.

The buildings of that first community have been greatly enlarged in the past century to accommodate the increase in pilgrims, and in order to envisage them as they were one has to rely on historical sources. The most important building in Madina associated with the Prophet had a large open courtyard with shade on the side facing Mecca provided by two rows of palm trunks thatched with palm leaves. Around or adjacent to the courtyard were houses in which the Prophet and his wives lived. The exact configuration of the surrounding rooms is unknown but important since, depending on the configuration, the building has been interpreted as the Prophet's house or mosque. The most recent thinking suggests the latter, which would help to explain why so many early mosques adopt the plan of a courtyard building with a roof on columns on the side facing Mecca.

After the migration Muhammad's influence grew rapidly, and when in 630 he marched on Mecca at the head of an army of ten thousand, the city offered virtually no resistance. The Ka'ba at Mecca was henceforth dedicated to Allah (God), and became the destination of Muslim pilgrims. At the time of his death in 632 about two-thirds of Arabia had become Muslim. Under the four leaders, or caliphs (*khalifa*, successor), who followed him, Muslim territory expanded at a phenomenal rate. The Byzantines in Syria were defeated in several battles between 636 and 641, the Sasanians, who controlled Iraq, in 637 and again in 642. By the time of the assassination of the fourth caliph, 'Ali, in 661 Muslim rule extended from Armenia and Iran in the north to Libya in the west.

In the early Islamic community a split arose over the caliphate, or succession to Muhammad. One group, the Shi'i (or Shi'a) considered 'Ali to be the first rightful caliph, and his descendants to be his successors. This split with Sunni, or orthodox, Islam, had important religious, artistic, and of course political consequences.

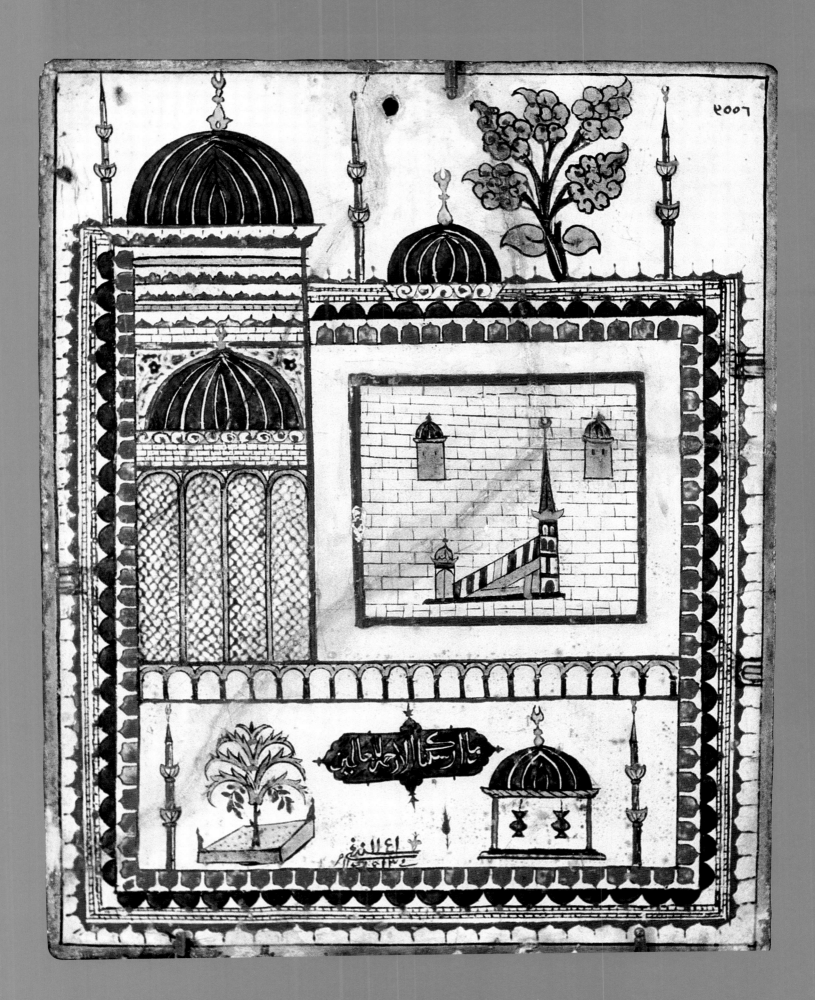

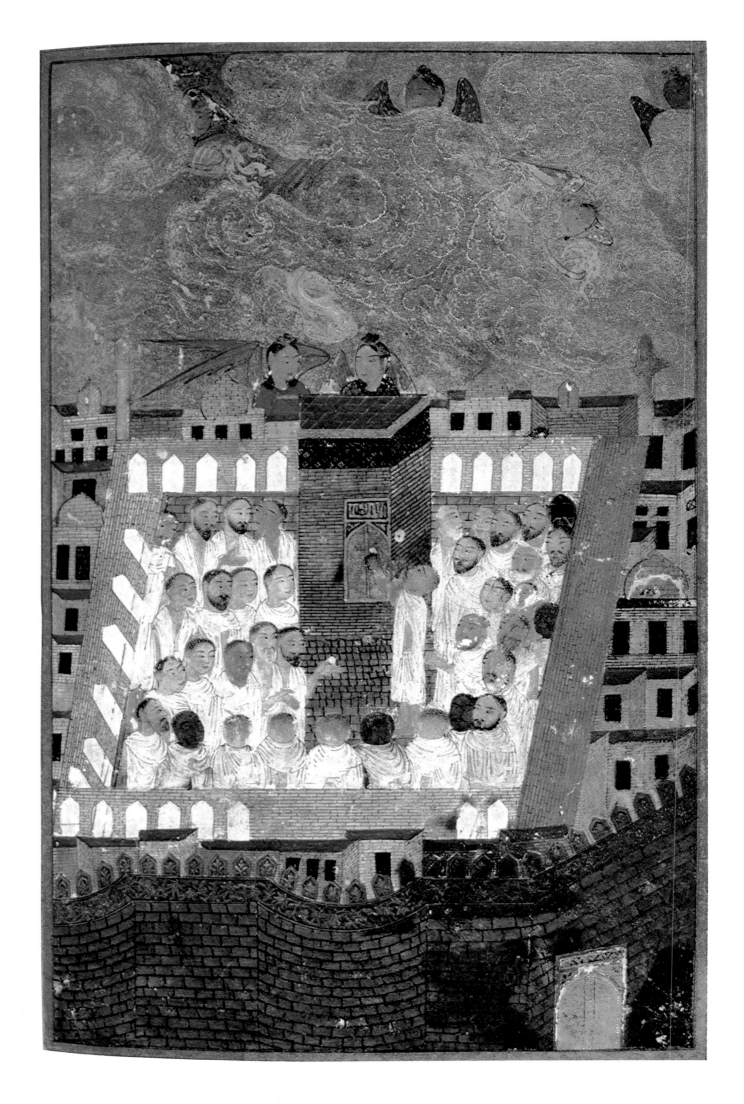

NO DEITY BUT GOD

THE FAITH OF SUBMISSION

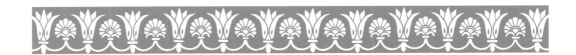

LEFT

A duty watched over by angels. Pilgrims circumambulate the Ka'ba at Mecca. From an *Anthology* written in 1410 for Iskandar Sultan, ruler of Shiraz on behalf of his father Shah Rukh, the son of Timur.

BELOW

The veneration of God. The inscription reads, in large letters, "Allah" (God), followed by "may His glory be exalted." Carved and painted wood, Ottoman, 19th century.

The foundation of Islam is its holy book, the Quran ("Recitation"), revealed to Muhammad and written down from 610 onward (see pages 60–63). The act of copying the text is highly meritorious, and helps explain the primacy of calligraphy in the canon of Islamic art. The importance of the Quran in Muslim life is also reflected in the ubiquity of Quranic texts, in the original Arabic, on religious and secular buildings from Spain to China. The Quran contains few pronouncements on the arts, although idolatry is clearly prohibited. Where God might be represented in Christian art by an image, for Muslims the Quran, the eternal uncreated word of God, has similar value as a symbol of the Divine.

THE FIVE PILLARS

Some of the basic tenets of Islam are traditionally described as the "Five Pillars." The first pillar is the *shahada*, bearing witness that there is but one God and that Muhammad is his Prophet. Not surprisingly, this is one of the commonest inscriptions on monuments.

The second pillar is the requirement to pray five times a day. The centrality of prayer is reflected in the preponderance of neighborhood and congregational mosques in the Islamic world. Muslims are encouraged to pray together, but this is obligatory only at the noon prayer on Fridays. It was desirable that a mosque should be able to accommodate all of the local inhabitants, so clearly there was a need for large buildings in many towns. Their form is not specified in the Quran. However, washing is necessary to achieve a state of ritual purity, so ablutions facilities were a normal adjunct to mosques. The call to prayer was given by the sound of the human voice, originally from the rooftop. The benefit of tall towers for this purpose, both to aid the dispersion of the call and to advertise the presence of mosques, soon led to minarets becoming standard features of larger mosques. In congregational mosques a sermon

OPPOSITE

The emperor Justinian's
rebuilding of the cathedral
of Haghia Sophia in
Constantinople (532–37)
has excited admiration for
its immense dome since its
foundation. Converted into a
mosque after the conquest of
the city in 1453, it was finally
turned into a museum in 1935.

(*khutba*) preceded the prayer, during which the *imam* sat on a *minbar* (pulpit); these, usually of wood, attracted some of the finest craftsmanship (see page 69).

Almsgiving is the third pillar. The distribution of wealth was a means of self-purification, and many wealthy patrons fulfilled this obligation by erecting religious monuments such as mosques and madrasas; or water dispensaries for the community at large. The fourth pillar is fasting. In the month of Ramadan, Muslims engage in a total fast from dawn to dusk. This was both a means of inculcating self-discipline and of reminding the faithful of their duties to the less fortunate who did not have enough to eat.

The fifth pillar is the *hajj*, the pilgrimage to Mecca, enjoined upon all of those who could afford it at least once in their lifetime (see pages 19–20). This convergence of Muslims upon one location had important consequences for Islamic art, since it encouraged the mobility of craftsmen and the exchange of artistic ideas. The Muslim world covers an enormous expanse; one fascination of Islamic art is to see which local elements were copied in other areas, and to understand why they became popular.

SUFISM

Sufis, or Islamic mystics, first emerged in the late tenth century. Initially solitary individuals, by the eleventh century they usually banded together in orders following the teachings of a founder, and frequently lived communally in a specially constructed building (*khanaqah*). The *ulama*, the orthodox religious leaders, sometimes censured Sufis for their use of *dhikr*, the repeated invocation of the word of God, often sung. However, by the fifteenth century Sufism was so popular that, for instance in Mamluk Egypt and Timurid Iran, studies of Sufism became the norm even in madrasas, the orthodox religious colleges. Persian poetry and Sufism are inextricably linked in Iran, and the works of some of the finest poets were often illustrated. The intricate symbolism in these texts should lead us to expect a similar iconography in the visual arts; scholarship in this field is relatively recent, and promises exciting findings in the future.

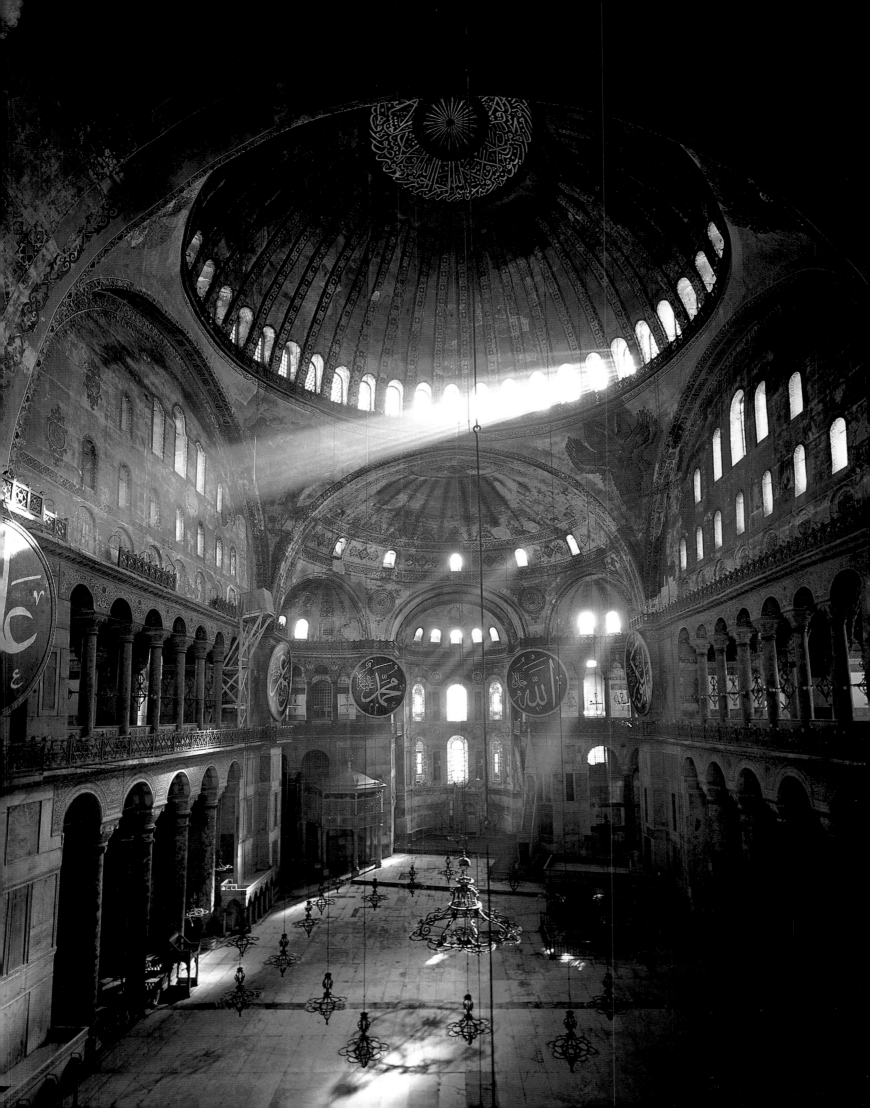

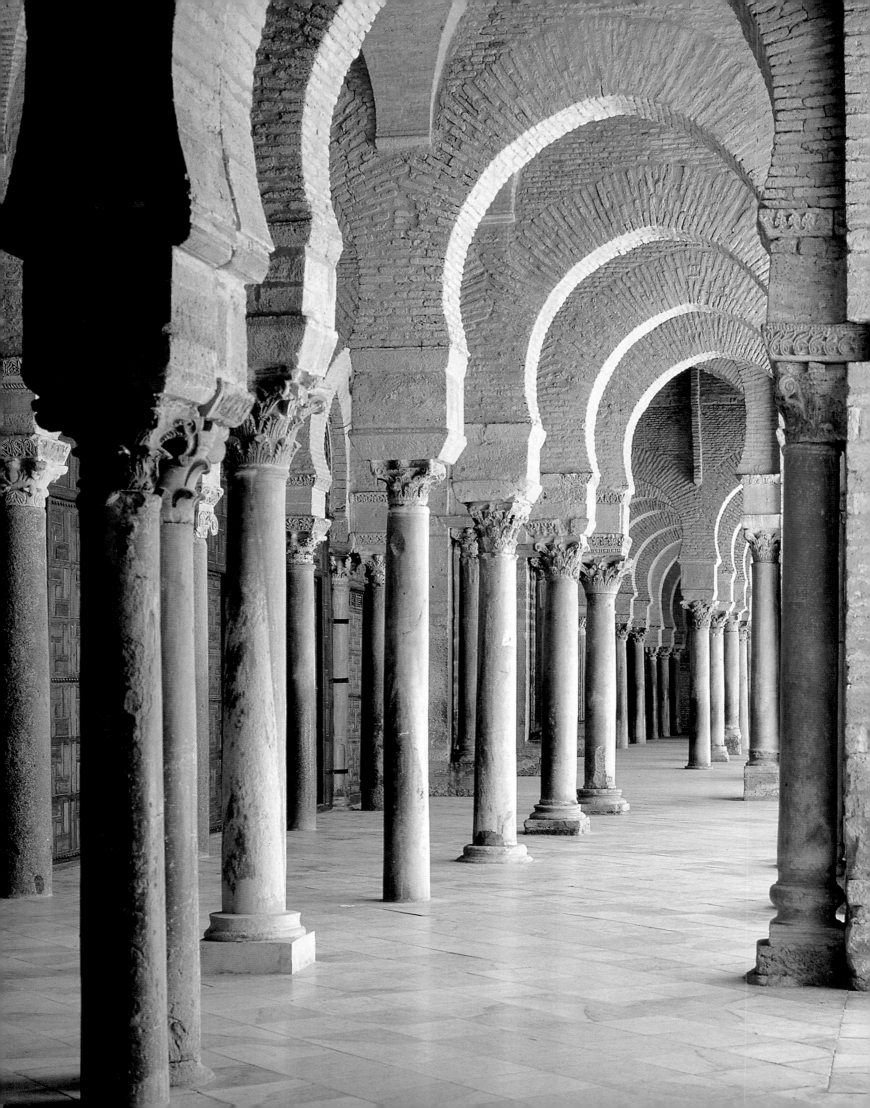

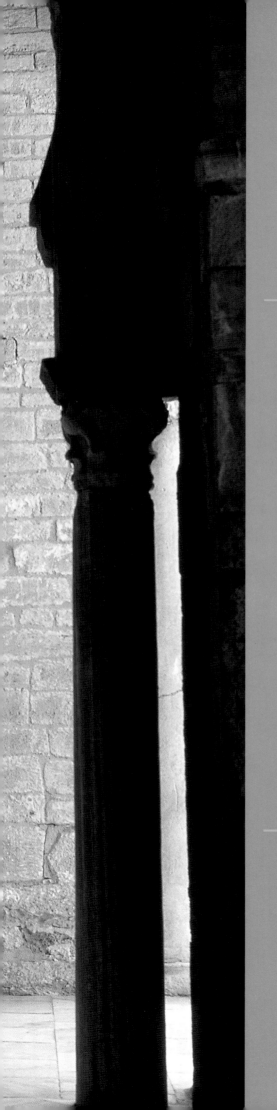

chapter 2

THE EMPIRE OF ISLAM

THE UMAYYADS AND 'ABBASIDS

INHERITORS OF BYZANTIUM

THE UMAYYAD CALIPHATE

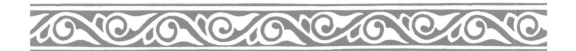

OPPOSITE

The domed transept of the Great Mosque of Damascus towers over the adjacent courtyard. It was built by the Umayyad caliph 'Abd al-Walid (705–15) on the precincts of the former Roman temple of Jupiter. The colonnaded courtyard adjacent to the basilical prayer hall is inspired by the model of earlier Roman and Byzantine forums, and Byzantine skill and influence are also seen in the mosaics, although the absence of figures reflects Islamic strictures on their depiction in a sacred context.

The transfer of power to the Umayyad dynasty, initially based in Damascus, marks a turning point in the evolution of the Islamic state. Mu'awiya—from whose great-grandfather, Umayya, the dynasty takes its name—had been governor of Syria for twenty years before he became caliph in 661, ensuring that that province, with its Classical and Byzantine legacy, would play a major part in shaping Islamic art and architecture.

Four Umayyad caliphs had relatively long reigns, Mu'awiya (661–80), 'Abd al-Malik (685–705), 'Abd al-Walid (705–15) and Hisham (724–43), and not surprisingly it was they who provided the impetus for the evolution of the Islamic state. Mu'awiya was an able delegator, but made no attempt to unify the administrative system, which still retained the bureaucrats and practices of the earlier Byzantine and Sasanian empires. However, the increasing confidence of the new rulers is shown by 'Abd al-Malik's decision to change the coinage from the previous overstamped Byzantine and Sasanian issues to one that used only inscriptions, was completely in Arabic, and served as a model for the next 500 years. This was accompanied by administrative and fiscal reforms that led to more centralized control. This confidence is also reflected in 'Abd al-Malik's patronage of the earliest surviving example of Islamic architecture, and one of Islam's finest masterpieces: the Dome of the Rock in Jerusalem (see pages 34–37).

THE GREAT MOSQUE OF DAMASCUS

'Abd al-Malik's son al-Walid is also remembered as a great builder. The Great Mosque of Damascus is one of only two Umayyad religious monuments that survive in a state recognizable to their builders, the other being the Dome of the Rock. Until the reign of al-Walid, Christians and Muslims in Damascus had shared a space within the enclosure of the former Roman temple of Jupiter, in whose western section the Christians had built a church dedicated to St. John the Baptist. After negotiations, al-Walid destroyed the church and completely rebuilt the interior of the former temple. The exterior

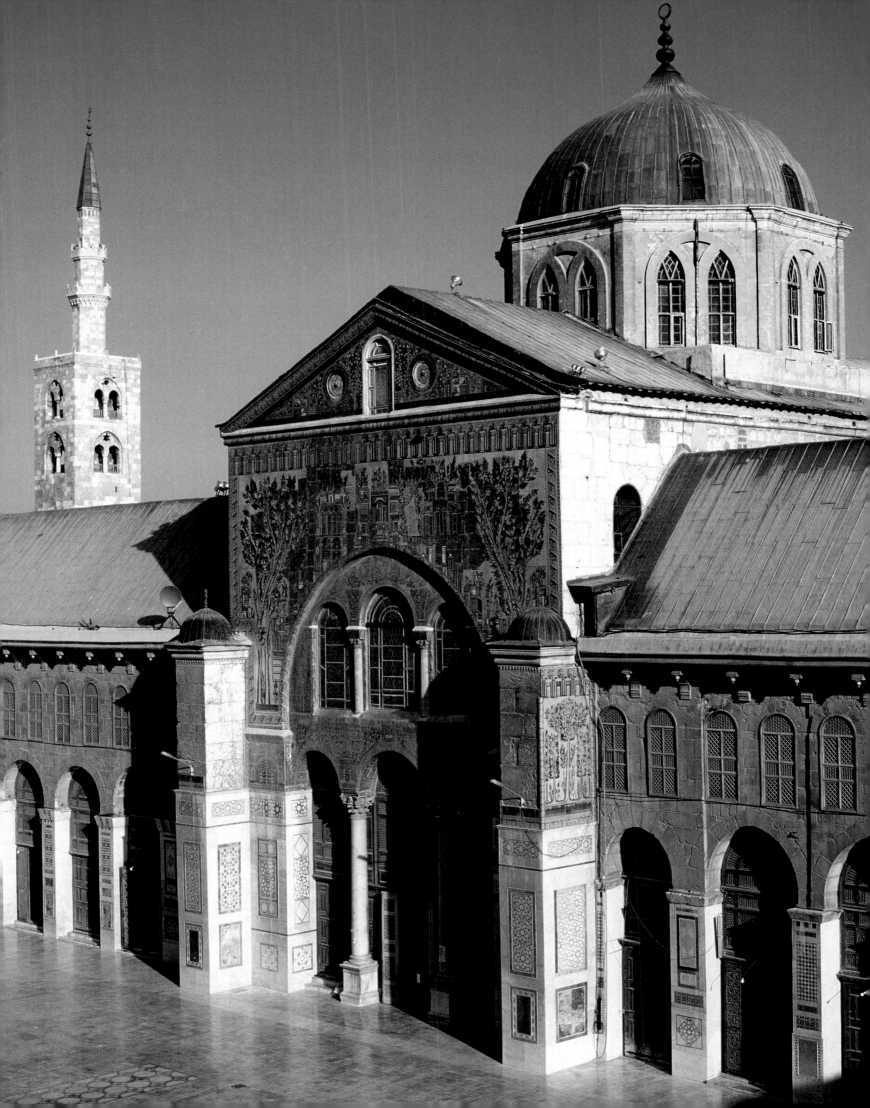

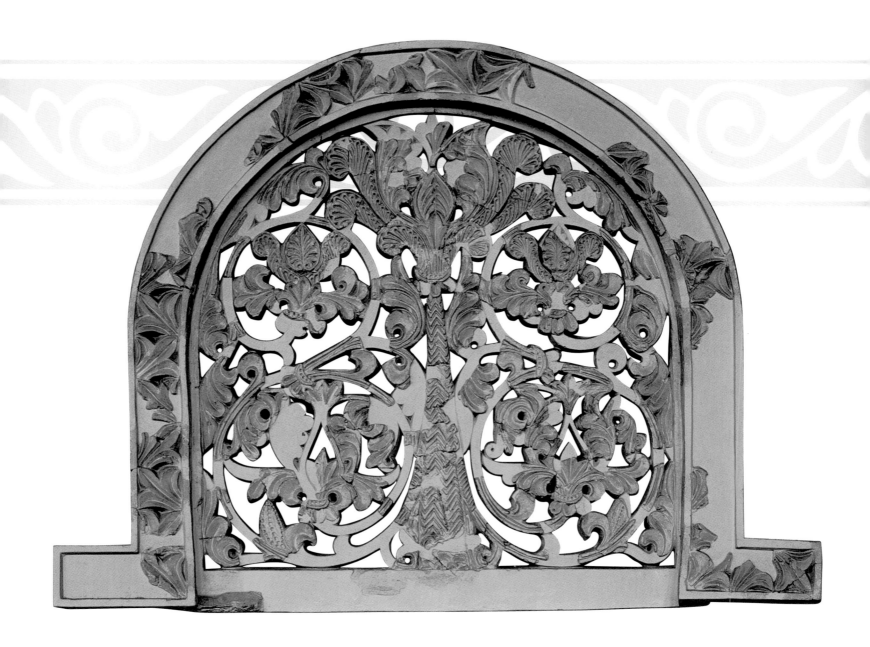

The birth of the arabesque. The swirling leaves and symmetry of this stucco window grille are typical of the mastery of vegetal ornamentation by early Muslim artists. The abstract tree is adapted from Sasanian design. From the palace of Qasr al-Hayr West, Syria, 727.

walls of the Roman temple were thus a defining element of the mosque, and within them, rather than following most earlier mosque plans, al-Walid built a structure that was essentially basilica-like rather than hypostyle, using columns that were not evenly spaced but which formed a definite axis, in this case parallel to the *qibla* wall.

The combination of basilical hall and adjacent arcaded courtyard occurred frequently in Roman forums, and another borrowing, this time from a Byzantine palace, can be seen in the triple-arched transept that bisects the prayer hall. The recombination of elements however, with the prayer axis on the long side of the basilica, is a distinctively

Islamic creation, and such was its prestige that it was used as a model for centuries to come in Syria and adjacent areas. Part of this prestige came from its decoration, the quartered marble and mosaics that formerly covered almost all of its interior wall surfaces. Although a fire at the end of the nineteenth century destroyed the mosaics in the prayer hall, a major part of the original has survived along the western wall of the courtyard. It depicts riverside landscapes filled with tall trees interspersed with palatial structures and humbler dwellings. Conspicuous by their absence are figures, a clear sign that Muslim opinion had already rejected their suitability for a religious context.

The landscapes are often called the "Barada Panel," after the river flowing through Damascus, but some medieval chroniclers saw in them cities from all over the Muslim world, one mentioning a representation of the Ka'ba above the *mihrab*. A paradisial interpretation has also been suggested, reinforced by the mention of heaven and the last judgment in the Quranic verses originally on the *qibla* wall. These interpretations need not be mutually exclusive—the various messages of the mosaics of the near-contemporary Dome of the Rock suggest that a similar overlapping of ideas was intended here.

THE MOSQUE OF THE PROPHET

Al-Walid undertook major restorations of other important early mosques, including the Mosque of the Prophet in Madina. It too was provided with mosaic decoration of trees and fine marble paneling on the *qibla* wall. But it had three elements that, given the prestige of this mosque, proved to be extremely significant for the design of mosques all over the Islamic world. First of all it was provided with a *mihrab*, an arched niche in the wall facing the direction of the Ka'ba. In almost all mosques this is in the center of the *qibla* wall, but here it was displaced to one side, evidently because, when the mosque was expanded unequally on each side, it marked the place where Muhammad had originally led prayers. This makes it more likely that in later buildings it commemorated the Prophet, rather than being a *qibla* marker. Secondly, the building had a shallow shell-shaped dome in the bay in front of the *mihrab*. Domes in this location were frequently erected in later mosques, and the importance of the Madina mosque, usually visited in addition to Mecca at the time of yearly pilgrimage, must have been one reason why it was copied so often. Likewise, it had a transept, as did the Great Mosque of Damascus, giving the arcade leading up to the *mihrab* a special emphasis.

PALACES OF PEACE AND PLEASURE

The variety of Umayyad residential and commercial buildings is remarkable, ranging from small caravanserais (Qasr al-Hayr West in Syria) to large trading and agricultural settlements (Qasr al-Hayr East), and from small but exquisite retreats (Qusayr 'Amra in Jordan) to giant uncompleted follies (Mashatta, also in Jordan, 744CE). The earlier view that Umayyad desert palaces were exclusively retreats for hedonistic pleasures has been revised in recent decades as the extent of the agricultural activity associated with them has begun to be understood. Some were indeed havens from urban pressures, although the whine of jets at Amman airport beside Mashatta, or the drone of trucks on the transnational highway alongside Qusayr 'Amra, may now make this difficult to appreciate.

Those palace complexes that actually were residences of caliphs, or of heirs

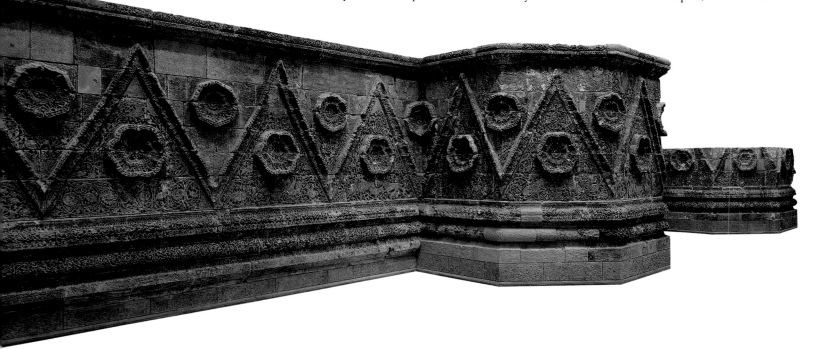

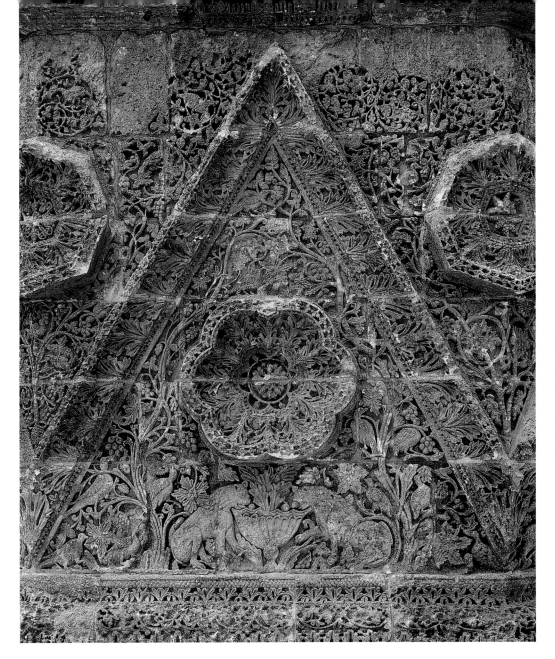

apparent such as al-Walid II, shared several features. The main palace was roughly modeled on a Roman frontier fort, with one main entrance, although the large defensive corner towers gave way to purely symbolic versions, since invaders were unlikely at the heart of the Umayyad empire. At the entrance, benches were often provided for those seeking an audience with the caliph. Both exterior and interior often had elaborate decoration. This could be of traditional Roman or Byzantine carved stone, glass mosaic or wall painting, or the newly introduced technique of Sasanian stucco, used both for sculpture in the round and for shallow reliefs.

Many palaces had nearby baths, none more spectacular than those of Khirbat al-Mafjar, near Jericho in the Jordan valley, built by the pleasure-loving al-Walid II,

the heir apparent of his uncle, the caliph Hisham. The prominent niche near the top
of the projecting entrance portal (based on a Roman triumphal arch) was empty until
al-Walid's accession in 743, after which it displayed a statue of him modeled after Sasanian
emperors, staring confidently straight ahead, sword in hand, wearing a pearl-bordered
tunic, on a pedestal supported by Roman lions flanking a Sasanian royal rosette. Stucco
rams, also Sasanian symbols of kingship, appeared on either side of the lower arch.

The interior of the bath was covered by a lofty dome surrounded by a Byzantine
quincunx plan, comprised of four domes at the corners with barrel vaults between
them. Further apsidal recesses surrounded this. The apse opposite the entrance was
graced with a stone hat hanging on a stone chain from the roof, a parody of the massive
gold crown suspended from the roof of the Sasanian royal palace at Ctesiphon.

This part of the bath hall would hardly have been a place for solemnity, since its
mosaic floors would have been constantly splashed by revelers using the bathing pool
that takes up one-sixth of the interior space. However, one domed room in the corner
of the building probably was used for formal audiences. It marshals a variety of images
into an elaborate iconographic representation of power and pleasure: winged horses on
the four pendentives have connotations of ascension and apotheosis; partridges at the
base of the dome mark the realm of the heavens; and the heads of six handsome young
males and females surrounded by luxuriant acanthus vegetation at the apex of the dome
represent the delights of paradise. A raised apse opposite the entrance has the finest
mosaic in the ensemble, displaying a fruit-laden tree with two grazing gazelles on one
side and a lion attacking another gazelle on the other (see illustration, right).

When al-Walid II finally succeeded as caliph in 743 his profligate reputation
preceded him and after only fourteen months he was murdered by opponents of his
immoral lifestyle. Just six years later, the Umayyad caliphate itself came to an abrupt
and bloody end at the hands of a new dynasty, the 'Abbasids.

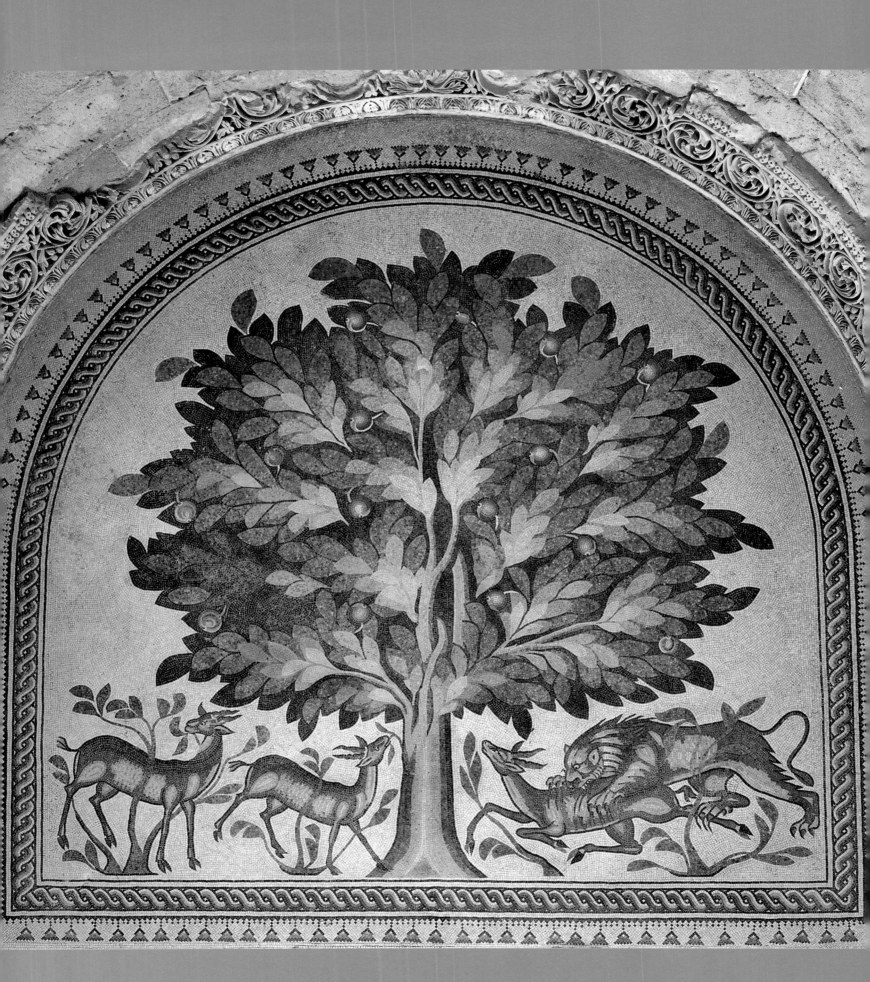

THE DOME OF THE ROCK

A MYSTERIOUS MASTERPIECE

More has been written about the Dome of the Rock in Jerusalem than any other Islamic building. The reason is clear: even though its patron and date are known (the Umayyad caliph 'Abd al-Malik, 692), its original function is not. It is mentioned in no historical sources dating from the period of its erection or even shortly after. The building's purpose, or purposes, have to be deduced from its location, form and decoration, including its inscriptions.

The location is of course most significant, in the center of the Temple Mount (or the Noble Sanctuary, *al-Haram al-Sharif,* as it is known to Muslims). This was the great enclosed platform upon which the Temple of Solomon had once stood until it was destroyed by the Romans in 70CE. The enclosure is also graced with an earlier Islamic building, the Aqsa mosque, that in its first state was probably built by one of 'Abd al-Malik's caliphal predecessors.

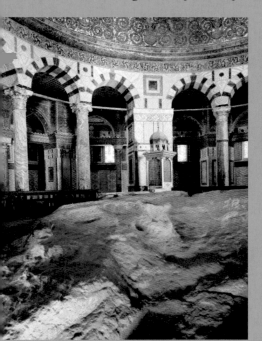

The Dome of the Rock's plan of a circular core surrounded by one or more ambulatories, themselves either octagonal or circular, is shared by three earlier buildings in Jerusalem: the Church of the Ascension, the Tomb of the Virgin Mary, and the Church of the Holy Sepulcher (the tomb of Christ). Each of these buildings has an important commemorative function, and it is likely that the builder of the Dome of the Rock wanted it to be immediately recognized as having a similar purpose.

Competition with these earlier Christian monuments also played a part in the design of the Dome. The size of its inner dome is just a little bigger than that of the Church of the Holy Sepulcher, and the ninth-century historian Muqaddasi relates how the Umayyads deliberately made buildings such as the Damascus and

LEFT, BELOW

The core of the Dome of the Rock is the circle of piers and columns surrounding the rock. Above that is part of the acanthus scroll that decorates the drum below the dome. A combination of factors doubltess motivated the building's construction. Its site suggests its patron wished to be remembered as a wise ruler, like Solomon. The decoration and inscriptions proclaim Islam to be the culmination of earlier religion, and the building consciously rivals Jerusalem's great Christian monuments. Otherwise its form suggests it to be a commemorative monument—but of precisely what still remains a mystery.

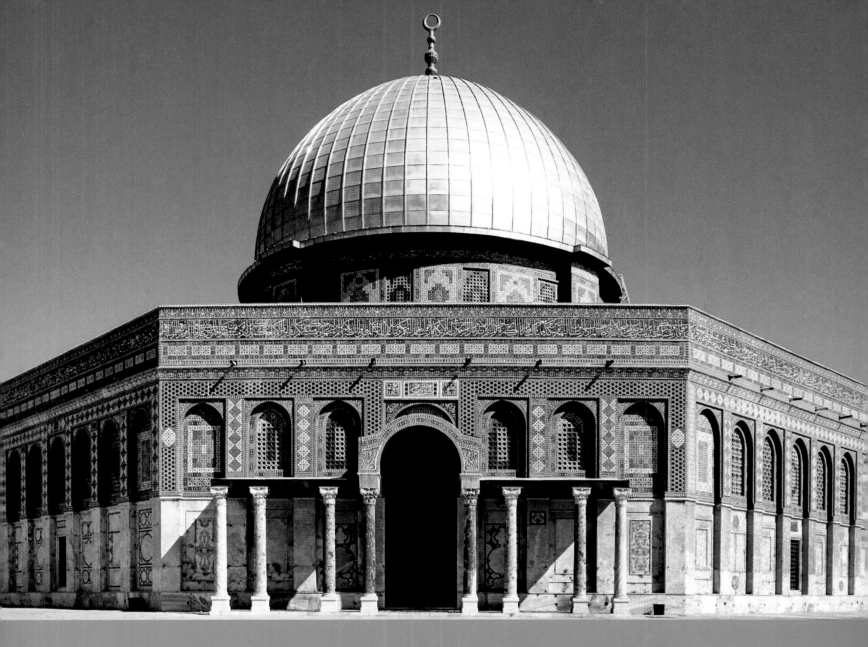

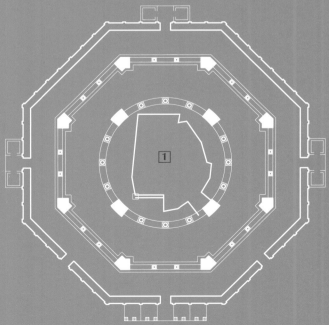

LEFT
The Dome of the Rock has a circular core supporting a tall double-shelled dome, some 66ft (20m) wide and nearly 108ft (33m) high. This is surrounded at a lower level by two octagonal ambulatories covered with a sloping roof. At the heart of the building is the rock (1) for which it is named (see opposite page).

ABOVE
The exterior of the Dome of the Rock was originally covered in mosaic similar to that which adorns the building's interior (see illustrations opposite and on the following page). The outside was redecorated (1545–52) in tiles by the Ottoman sultan Suleyman the Magnificent, although these were replaced by modern copies in the 1960s.

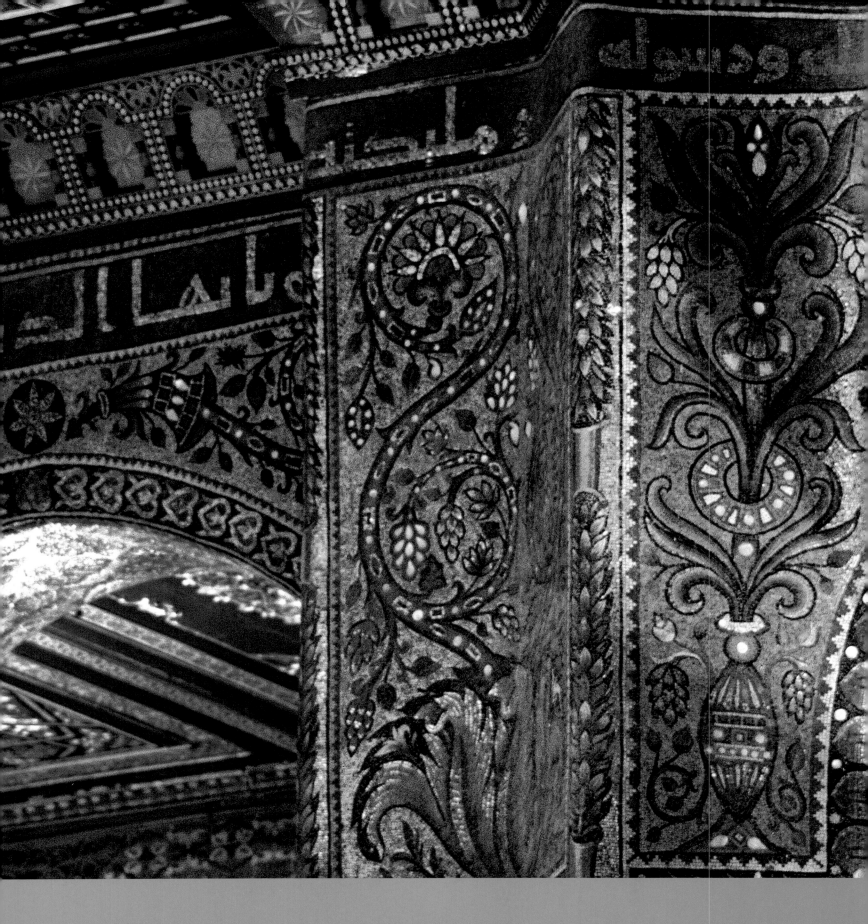

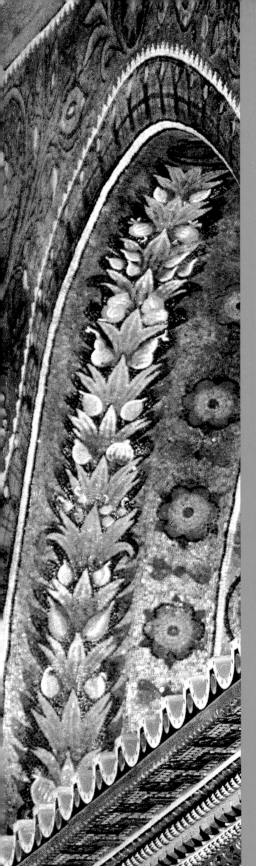

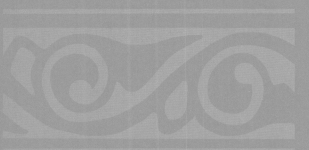

Aqsa mosques and the Dome of the Rock as luxurious as possible in order to stop Muslims being led astray by the "enchantingly fair" churches of Syria, such as that of the Holy Sepulcher.

A WEALTH OF MOSAIC

The interior of the Dome of the Rock is notable for its extensive use of mosaic. Amidst the predominantly vegetal decoration are images of Sasanian and Byzantine crowns, mostly facing inwards. It had earlier been the custom to display the trophies of defeated enemies inside the Ka'ba in Mecca, and these images of crowns can also be seen as symbolically paying homage to the new power in the region. Some of the trees are bejeweled, recalling those of Solomon's palace.

The inscriptions consist mostly of Quranic extracts. They emphasize three themes: the basic tenets of Islam, the role of Muhammad as the culmination of Prophets, and the relation of Christianity to Islam. Jesus is revered as an earlier prophet, but Christians are warned against regarding him as divine and the error of the Trinity. It is not likely that Christians had access to the building when it was erected, so these verses are more likely to have had some special significance to recent converts.

One of the earliest theories of the Dome of the Rock's purpose revolved around the civil war in the Muslim community at the time of its erection. Mecca then was held by a rival of 'Abd al-Malik, and it was suggested that 'Abd al-Malik built the Dome as a substitute for the Ka'ba. However, this was first mentioned in histories of the Abbasids, arch-enemies of the Umayyads, and was a slander, as such an action would be contrary to the basic tenets of Islam. The most popular current explanation is that the Dome commemorates the Prophet's night journey (*mi'raj*) and tour of heaven in the company of the angel Gabriel. However, the lack of reference to the *mi'raj* in the Dome's inscriptions would argue against this, as would the presence beside the Dome of the Rock of a much smaller thirteenth-century domed structure named the Dome of the Mir'aj.

THE GOLDEN AGE

THE 'ABBASIDS AND THEIR VASSALS

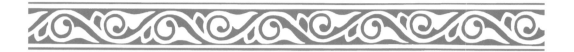

Several factors contributed to the success of the 'Abbasid revolution. The profligacy of the later Umayyad caliphs was notorious, but a more general feeling of inequity within the Muslim polity was probably of greater importance. Converts to Islam (*mawali*) felt that they not were treated as equals by fellow Muslims. They were most numerous in the eastern empire, and it was there that an emissary of the clan of al-'Abbas, an uncle of the Prophet, was able to recruit followers most easily. He captured the eastern province of Khurasan in 747 and within three years most of the Umayyads had been killed and the capital of the caliphate had moved eastward, nearer the supporters of the new régime, to the new Madinat al-Salam (City of Peace), later known as Baghdad.

The move to Iraq had important artistic consequences. The lack of stone quarries there meant that brick became the main building material, with stucco the preferred form of decoration. The vast scale of 'Abbasid palaces is reminiscent of Sasanian examples, and this may also reflect a societal change whereby the caliph distanced himself from most of his subjects by becoming more monarchical. Baghdad's original circular plan has long disappeared under modern sprawl, so the excavations at Samarra, 75 miles (125km) upstream, are our main source for 'Abbasid architecture.

SAMARRA: CITY OF THE CALIPHS

Samarra was a new capital created in 836 by the caliph al-Muta'sim (reigned 833–42). The reasons given by contemporary historians are friction between the caliph's huge army of Turkish slave-troops and citizens of Baghdad, and the caliph's adherence, in opposition to the *ulama*, to the rationalist Mutazalite movement. However, given the scale of construction at Samarra, the caliph's desire to immortalize his name through a magnificent new foundation could well have been uppermost. For the next fifty-six years a variety of caliphs vied in outdoing one another in architectural projects, until in 892 the decision was made to abandon it and return to Baghdad.

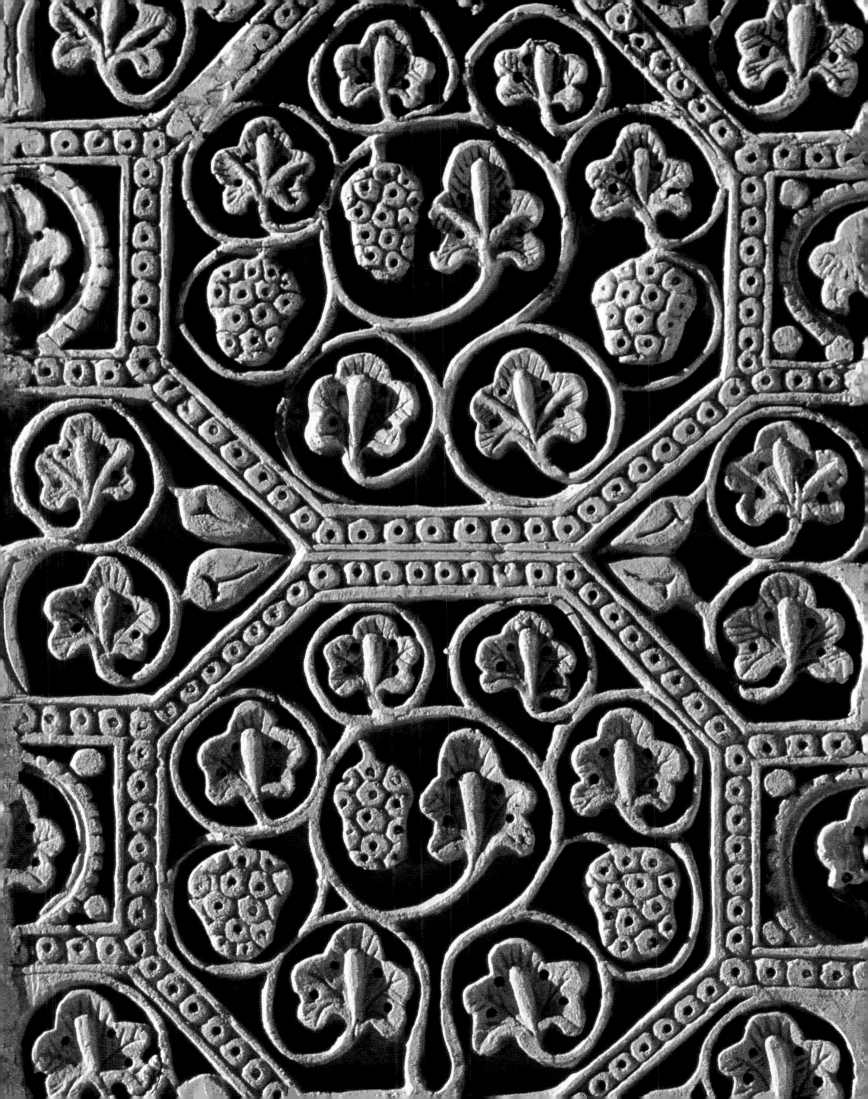

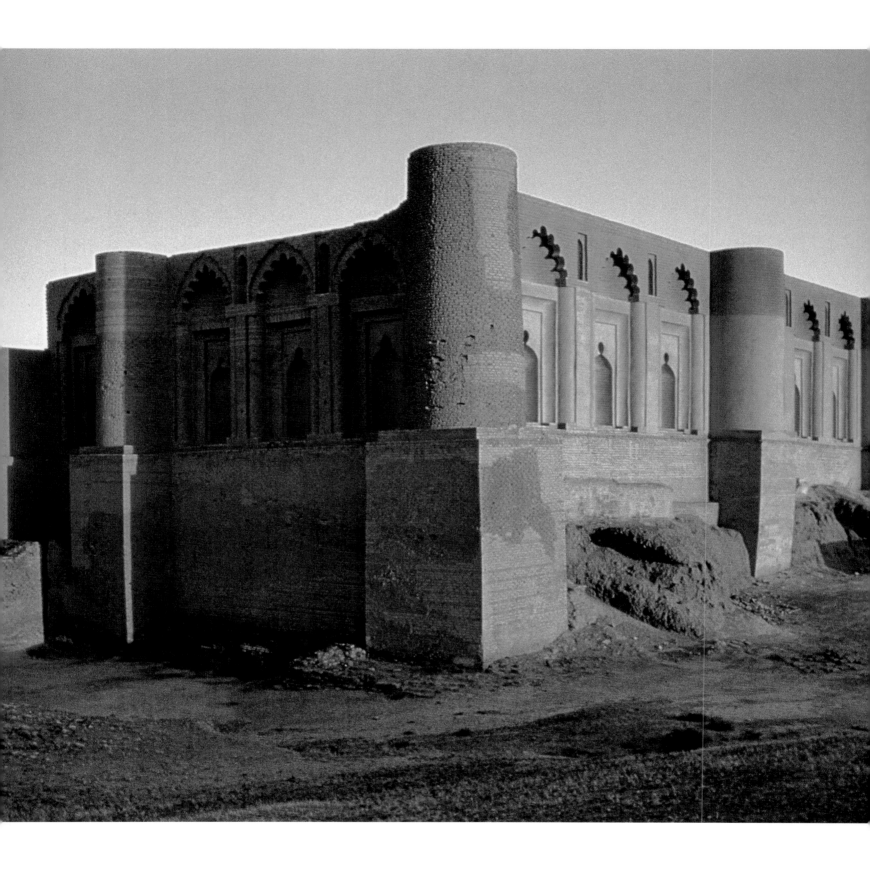

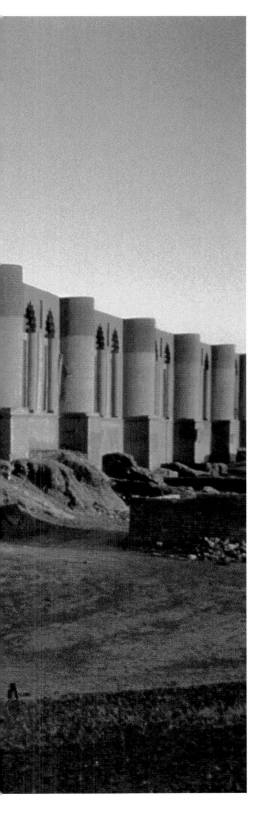

Samarra's main caliphal residence, the Dar al-Khalifa, is not so much palatial as urban, such is its scale. Its lack of fortifications has been explained by the garrisoning nearby of Turkish troops. The main entrance was the triple-*iwan* Bab al-'Amma (Public Gate), which could be approached through a quadripartite garden between it and the river. Many other such gardens featured in other palaces, a reminder of the increasing influence of Persian prototypes. The main gate led toward the throne hall, a dome chamber surrounded by four axial triple-aisled basilicas, another merging of Roman and Sasanian elements. Further away from the river were more gardens, the main axis culminating in polo grounds and a pavilion that overlooked, beyond the palace grounds, a bottle-shaped racetrack that ran three miles (5km) out into the desert steppe and back. Like today, keeping stables was expensive, but the twelve polo grounds and five racetracks found at Samarra indicate their popularity.

The main decoration of the monuments at Samarra was in stucco, but in a quite new stylization of natural forms that was closer to Iranian than Roman sources. Vine leaves do appear in one style, but more common are abstract vegetal motifs, framed within geometric compartments. The most original form is often described as beveled (cut at a slant), but in fact it was rounded, enabling a smooth transition from foreground to background and a consequent ambiguity between the two. This form also employed abstract motifs and was the most common, probably because its rounded forms would have enabled it to be applied by molds, greatly speeding up work on the vast surfaces available for decoration.

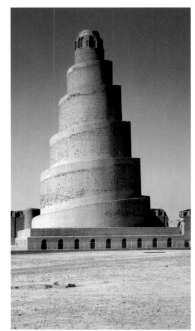

Two enormous mosques were built at Samarra (the Great and Abu Dulaf mosques), each on an

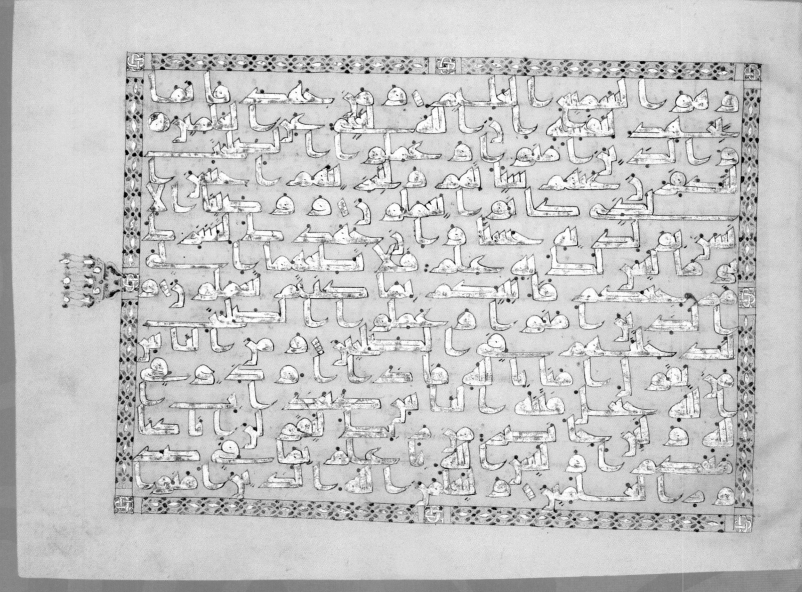

unprecedented scale. The cost of transporting materials for the Great Mosque was reduced by employing three elephants for the heaviest materials. The mosque was surrounded by further immense courtyards, or *ziyada*s, the long side of the largest enclosure being almost 0.3 miles (0.5km) in length. These huge extra spaces were probably necessary to provide stabling and other amenities, since the court, accompanied by the infantry and cavalry, proceeded to the mosque on horseback.

Each mosque had a novel form of minaret with a spiral ramp leading to the top. The founder of the Great Mosque, the caliph al-Mutawakkil (ruled 847–61), used to enjoy the view from the top after riding up on a donkey. The later mosque, Abu Dulaf, had extra arcades added onto the outer walls, indicating that even its huge interior could not accommodate the masses in attendance at Friday prayer.

THE IBN TULUN MOSQUE, CAIRO

The well-preserved mosque of Ibn Tulun at Cairo (876–79) can give us a better idea of the spatial qualities of the now dilapidated Samarra mosques, for it is in many ways a replica of them, if on a slightly smaller scale. Samarra was the town where Ahmad ibn Tulun was raised, before he was sent to Egypt as 'Abbasid vice-governor in 868. He subsequently established a rival dynasty that ruled Egypt for a century before the 'Abbasids re-established control. Like the Samarra mosques, that of Ibn Tulun has no single prominent doorway—this feature did not become common in the Islamic world until at least a century later. On venturing through any of these doorways one is first confronted, as at the Samarra mosques, by a *ziyada*, here a corridor which surrounds it on three sides. In this case we know that the additional space was used for ablutions and also had a dispensary with a resident physician and aides who provided for those who might be injured in the crush on Fridays.

Further similarities to the mosques of Samarra—all of them novelties for Egypt— such as the rectangular piers, the stucco decoration of the arcades, and the spiral form

OPPOSITE

The exceptional luxury of this 9th-century Quran leaf written on parchment is seen not only in the gold used for the calligraphy, but also in the ornamental border that graces every page.

of the minaret, indicate that Ibn Tulun probably imported an architect from Iraq to design his mosque (although the present partially spiral Mamluk minaret is only a loose copy of the original). Moving further inside, the great size of the building is revealed in endless vistas that spring up simultaneously in multiple directions through the arcades. From within, it is apparent that the *ziyada* still fulfills its function of isolating the prayer area from the noise of the surrounding urban area. The resulting stillness enhances the sense of quiet contemplation that imbues the building.

CLOTH OF SILK AND GOLD

Although relatively few textiles have survived from this period, it is as well to remember the importance that they had in contemporary life. "Waste on your back, but save on your stomach," runs an ancient Near Eastern maxim, meaning economize on food but not on clothing. In every era, government textiles factories (*tiraz*) were busy producing robes of honor, both for the ruler's personal use and for distribution to courtiers and distinguished visitors. The most sumptuous clothing was made of silk interwoven with silver and gold threads, although its very luxury frequently led to its demise when it was realized that burning would recover the precious metals within it.

'Abbasid domestic interiors had no furniture within them. Instead, people reclined on cushions and bolsters, slept on portable bedding, and ate from tablecloths spread on the carpets or matting that covered the floor. Two Umayyad mosaics may have been based on textile designs. One, the finest of the numerous Khirbat al-Mafjar mosaics (in the domed reception room of the bath hall; see page 33), depicts tassels around the edge, while at Khirbat al-Minya (in Israel) one panel has a pattern of lozenges surrounded by several borders, strikingly similar to the flatweave patterns of many Near Eastern nomads. A medieval author wrote that "a house full of cushions is like a garden full of flowers," revealing that cushions were both ubiquitous and extremely colorful. Curtains also were used with more versatility than they generally are in modern life.

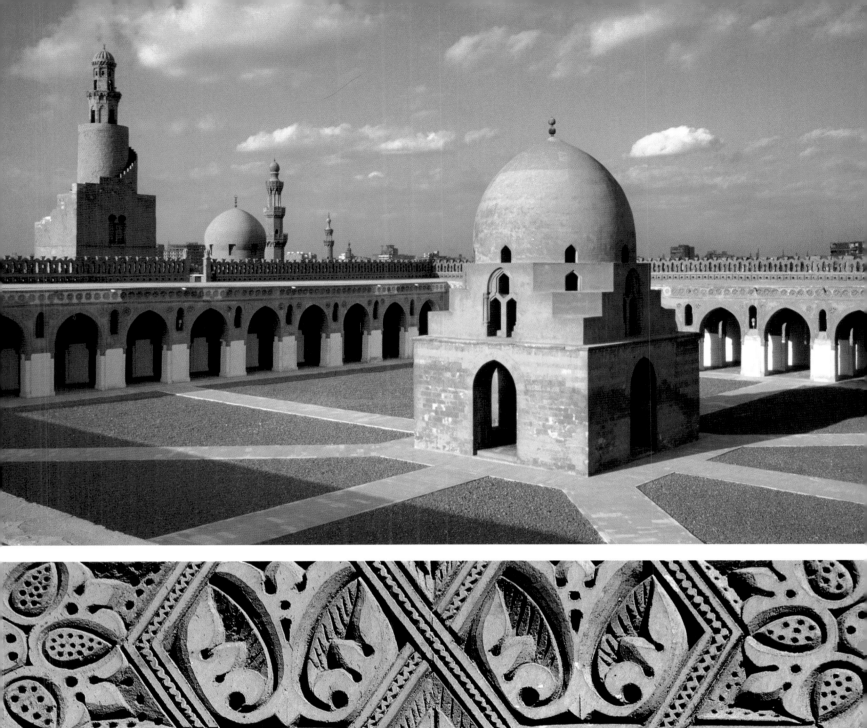

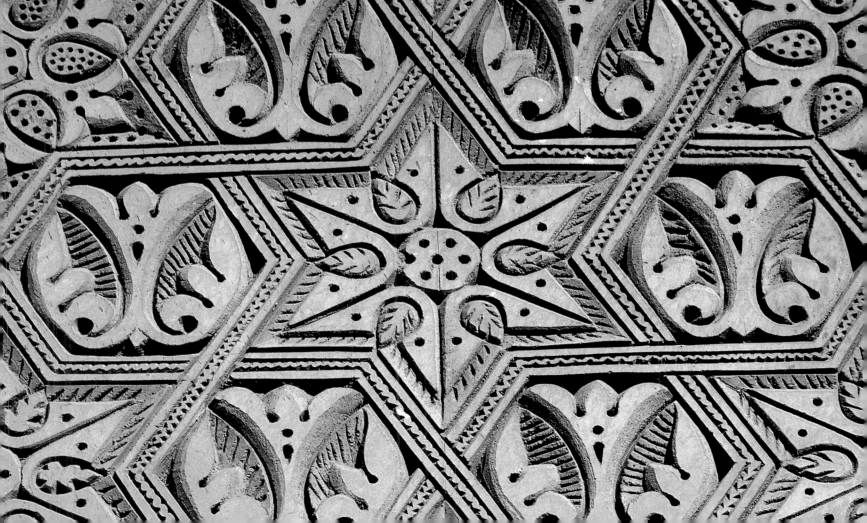

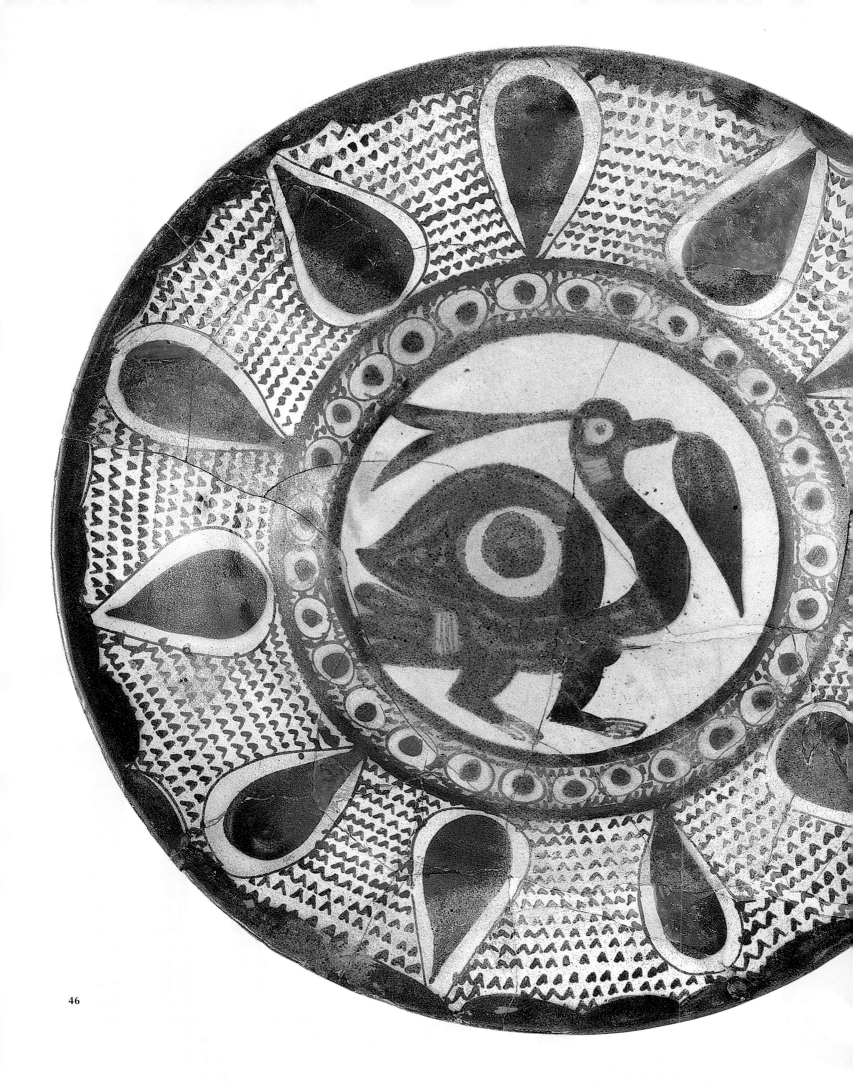

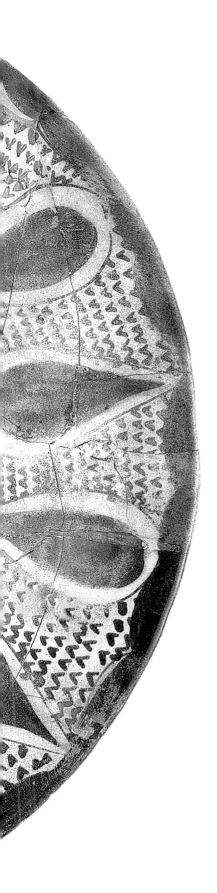

They usually took the place of wooden doors inside the house, and were also suspended in front of niches. Curtains could be used to divide a room for privacy (for example, for women), or simply hung on the wall for decoration.

GENIUS IN CLAY: 'ABBASID CERAMICS

The best preserved body of 'Abbasid decorative arts is ceramics. 'Abbasid pottery used to be attributed to Samarra, the place where most excavated examples of it were found, but owing to modern analysis of the ceramic body we now know that it was made at Basra in southern Iraq. Not only the scale of production, but the quality and variety of types represent an astonishing breakthrough. This sudden burst of inspiration is usually attributed to the new arrival of Chinese imports, a theory supported by the first appearance of ceramics with an opaque white body, made from a tin glaze, since kaolin, the clay used to make the porcelain body of the Chinese originals, is not found in the Middle East. Rather than leave the surface bare, Muslim artists added decorative details of vegetal forms or inscriptions in cobalt blue, which softly merged with the white base, spreading like ink on blotting paper. It was probably from the export of these wares to the East that Chinese potters were in turn inspired to imitate the blue and white color scheme, which came to be synonymous with the word "china".

The most luxurious 'Abbasid pottery type was luster, the product of two firings, producing a metallic sheen imperceptible to the touch. On some pieces the luster is a deep ruby red, a color not duplicated by later dynasties. It was on luster that figural decoration became common (see illustration, opposite).

The 'Abbasid caliphate diminished in prestige following the sovereignty established over Baghdad by the Buyids (in 945) and Seljuks (in 1055), but experienced a resurgence of power in the late twelfth and early thirteenth centuries. This ended abruptly in 1268 when the Mongols captured Baghdad and assassinated the last 'Abbasid caliph, after which they became purely nominal heads of state under the tutelage of the Mamluks in Egypt.

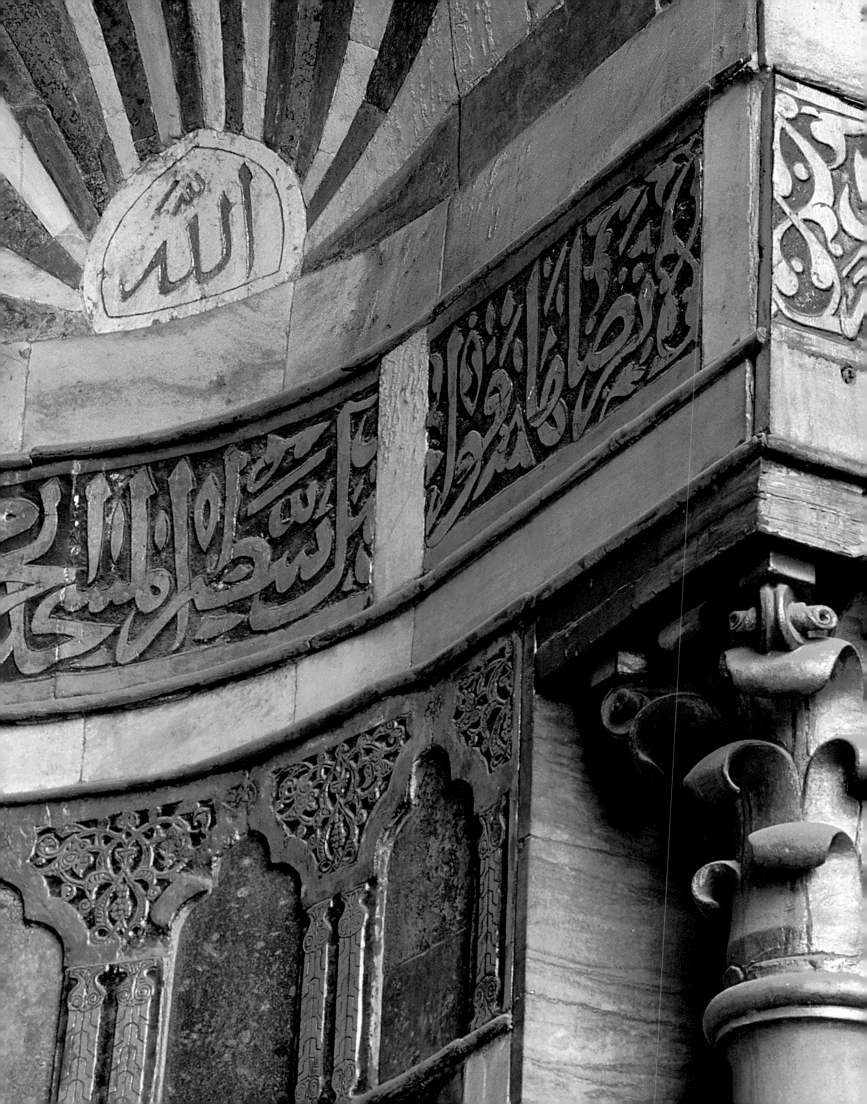

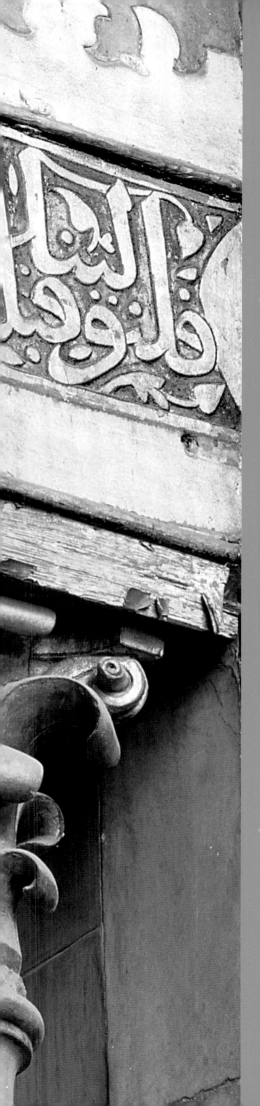

chapter 3

IMAMS, PRINCES, AND SULTANS

RIVALS OF THE 'ABBASIDS

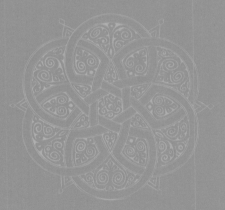

SHI'ISM TRIUMPHANT

THE FATIMID CALIPHATE

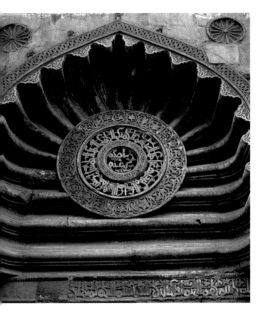

A substantial body of Muslims, the Shi'i, believe that the first rightful caliph was not Abu-Bakr, but 'Ali, the cousin and son-in-law of the Prophet, and that 'Ali's descendants, the Imams, were divinely guided. Prior to the coming of the Safavids in Iran (see Chapter 5), the Fatimids (909–1171) established the most extensive Shi'i state in the Middle East. They claimed descent from the Prophet's daughter Fatima, the wife of 'Ali, the first Imam, and the mother of his sons Hasan and Husain, the second and third Imams. The Fatimids recognized seven Imams in all, the last being Isma'il, hence the name Isma'ilis, by which the Fatimids were also called.

Although incapable of winning support in Syria, where they originated, the Fatimids were able to convert the Berbers of Tunisia to their cause and establish their leader, 'Abd Allah al-Mahdi, as ruler there in 909. Al-Mahdi (the Rightly-Guided One) declared himself caliph in opposition to the 'Abbasids, putting an end to the semblance of political unity that until then had prevailed in the Muslim world. He built a new capital on a well-defended coastal promontory, naming it Mahdiyya after himself.

The Fatimids were never satisfied with Tunisia and made probing raids toward a much richer prize, Egypt. In 969 they finally overcame the 'Abbasid governors there, and consolidated their position by expanding into Syria. Their prestige also greatly increased when they subsequently took control of the holy cities of Mecca and Madina.

LORDS OF CAIRO

In Egypt the Fatimids founded a new princely city, naming it al-Qahira (the Triumphant), from which its names in English (Cairo) and other European languages are derived. At the center of the city were the royal palaces, facing each other across a square, and nearby on the southeast was the mosque of al-Azhar (972). Over the centuries this mosque has both benefited and suffered from being the main one of the city. Numerous restorations have destroyed much original work but have also left an important legacy

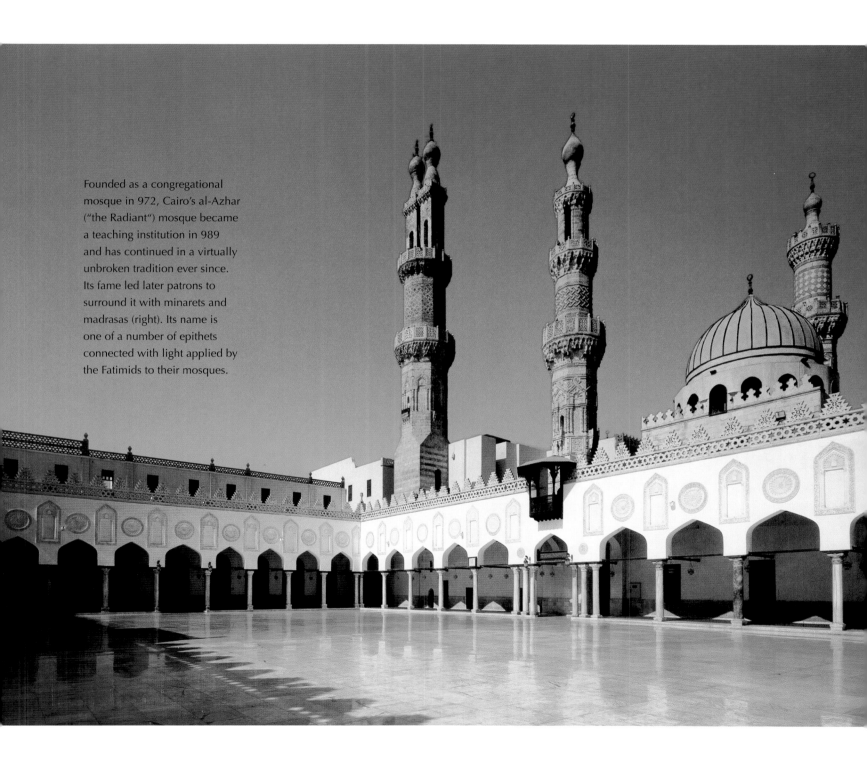

Founded as a congregational mosque in 972, Cairo's al-Azhar ("the Radiant") mosque became a teaching institution in 989 and has continued in a virtually unbroken tradition ever since. Its fame led later patrons to surround it with minarets and madrasas (right). Its name is one of a number of epithets connected with light applied by the Fatimids to their mosques.

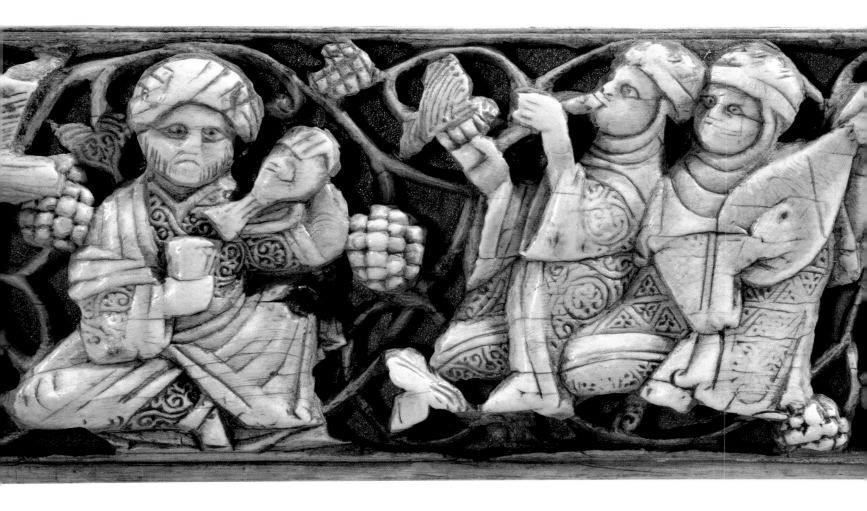

of architecture from later eras. The mosque borrowed from that of Mahdiyya doubled columns in its nave and a dome in front of the *mihrab*, although the stucco that decorates its walls is of purely Egyptian invention. In 989 a decree provided for teaching within al-Azhar, which has been maintained in an almost unbroken tradition, contributing towards al-Azhar's unrivaled prestige in Islamic education today. In Fatimid times it was important as the place where Fatimid missionaries to Sunni territory were trained.

The long reign of Caliph al-Mustansir (1036–94) saw some of the extremes of Fatimid society; beginning in great wealth, it was devastated by seven consecutive years of famine (1065–72). As a result the economy collapsed and the army, unpaid, rioted and plundered the treasury. The Fatimid governor of Syria, the Armenian Badr al-Jamali, came to the rescue, but the price to be paid was the elevation of the rank of vizier, which he subsequently assumed, to one which vied for power with that of the caliph.

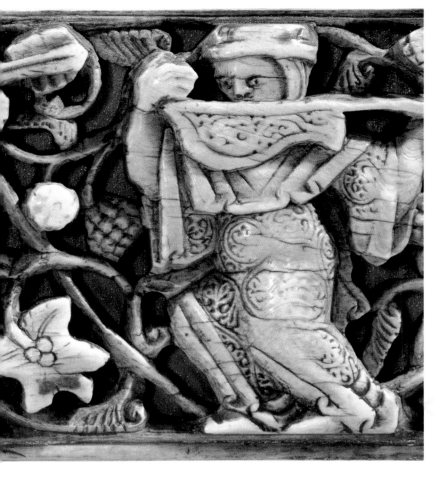

THE GREAT NORTH GATES

A symbol of Badr al-Jamali's might is the north wall of Fatimid Cairo, containing two gates, Bab al-Nasr and Bab al-Futuh, that are among the most impressive examples of military architecture in the world. Though relatively unsophisticated in terms of technology, the superb quality of the masonry has elicited wonder since medieval times. They were erected against a possible attack by the Seljuks (see Chapter 6) who had reached Baghdad by 1056 and Damascus by 1076. The Seljuks never launched their expected assault, and the gates served mainly as customs posts. Their exterior decoration is unique for Cairo: Maqrizi, the Mamluk historian, claims that the architects were from Edessa (now Urfa in Turkey). The exterior of Bab al-Nasr is decorated with images of shields, perhaps representing famous real shields in the Fatimid treasury. However, the idea that the Fatimids were the protectors of the city would also have been implied.

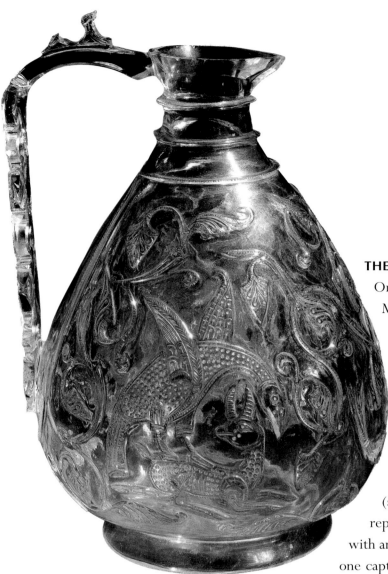

THE MOONLIT MOSQUE

One small Fatimid mosque is noteworthy, al-Aqmar (the Moonlit), built by a vizier in 1125. This was in the heart of the city, probably adjacent to the main Fatimid palace. Perhaps for this reason its façade is aligned to the axis of the street, even though the interior had to be angled to the different *qibla* direction. This was the first of many such compromises in Cairene architecture. The façade is also noteworthy for bearing, for the first time, decoration across its entire length. In addition to the two foundation inscriptions there is a variety of stylized scallop shells (see page 50), and some intriguing carved panels, one with representation of a grill and a lamp within an arch, and another with an image of a wooden door. The grill could refer to a famous one captured from the 'Abbasid palace in Baghdad and installed in the Fatimid caliphal palace next door to the al-Azhar. The door could stand for a well-known Shi'i account of the words of the Prophet Muhammad: "I am the city of knowledge and 'Ali is its gate," or, in a secular interpretation, the door could symbolize the mosque's patron, the vizier, who was Sahib al-Bab ("Controller of the Gate")—in other words, the one responsible for deciding who should be allowed access to the caliph.

ABOVE
The main motif on the side of this rock crystal ewer is a falcon attacking a gazelle, a typical symbol of royal power. Cut from a solid block, the technical feat in achieving a thickness of only 2mm, complete with relief carving, is outstanding. Fatimid, first half of the 11th century.

MEMORIALS FOR THE DEAD

The Fatimids are also notable for the many mausoleums they erected, the greatest number being in what was then the southern border town of Aswan. The strictures against building mausoleums that were debated in religious circles may have been relaxed because the buildings commemorated martyrs who died spreading the faith.

BELOW

On the feast days of Islamic saints the number of visitors at a shrine would have overflowed from the main building, hence the need for portable *mihrab*s such as this. This is decorated in what was then the most up-to-date patterns of stars surrounded by polygons, a design first developed by the Fatimids. From the shrine of Sayyida Ruqayya, Cairo, datable 1155–59.

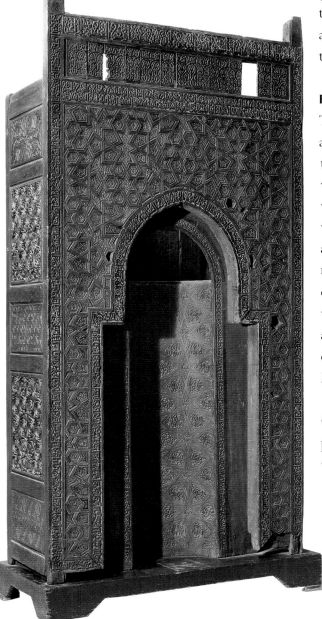

Many of the mausoleums built in Cairo were erected in honor of members of the Prophet's family, particularly those connected with the Shi'i. It was not even necessary for a body to be present. For instance, Sayyida Ruqayya, a daughter of the Imam 'Ali, is not known to have visited Egypt, but in 1133 the caliph al-Hafiz erected a mausoleum to her (with a superb stucco *mihrab*) as the result of a vision. It has been suggested that the later Fatimid caliphs were trying to inculcate Shi'i religious fervor as a distraction from the succession crises that twice caused schisms in the Fatimid community in the space of forty years.

FATIMID ART

The Fatimids were avid art collectors, as historical accounts suggest, and the availability of earlier material may have encouraged artists both to reinterpret previous styles and to incorporate figural images in their works. This is readily seen in Fatimid luster ceramics, production of which seems to have started in the second half of the tenth century, just when manufacture in 'Abbasid Basra ceased, suggesting a transfer of the atelier. A wide variety of figural subjects is found on these wares, from mounted dandies hunting in their finery to genre scenes of wrestling and cock fights. Some figures have the delicacy of line associated with Greek vase paintings. Figural images are found on many other Fatimid works of art (see pages 52–53). Wooden beams discovered in the early twentieth century had been reused, with the images turned toward the wall, in Mamluk religious buildings on the site of the western Fatimid palace.

Greatly weakened by internal schisms and the advent of the Crusaders at the close of the eleventh century, the Fatimids were ill-prepared to withstand invaders. They sought outside help, but this, as we shall see, simply hastened the dynasty's decline.

LORDS OF THE CITADEL

THE AYYUBIDS

BELOW

The inscriptions on this vase identify the patron as the Ayyubid ruler of Syria, Sultan Salah al-Din Yusuf (ruled 1237–60); its popular name of the "Barberini Vase" comes from its later acquisition by Pope Urban VIII Barberini. The medallions display hunting scenes. Copper alloy, inlaid with silver and niello.

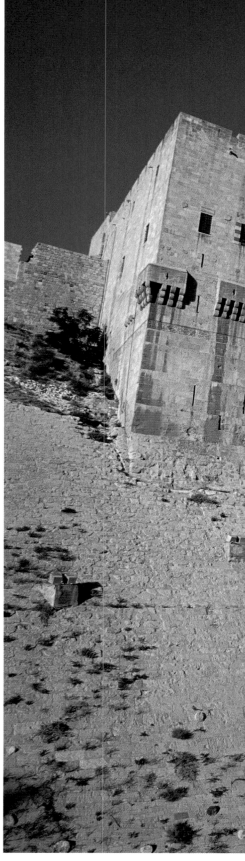

The power vacuum caused by the disintegration of the Seljuks in the second half of the twelfth century (see page 115) left a number of principalities jockeying for power. Among the most successful were the Zangids, originally based in Mosul. They expanded westward, and were notable for their victories against the Crusaders. The dynasty's founder, Zangi (ruled 1127–46), captured the Crusader city of Edessa in 1144, and his son Nur al-Din (ruled 1146–74) carried on the struggle in Syria against both the Crusaders and the Fatimids. Despite this, the Fatimids sought Nur al-Din's help in warding off Crusader attacks, and he gladly sent them Shirkuh ibn Ayyub and Shirkuh's nephew Salah al-Din, better known in the West as Saladin. Shirkuh ibn Ayyub gained control of Egypt in 1169, and Saladin deposed the Fatimid dynasty in 1171. Saladin remained in Egypt until Nur al-Din's death in 1174 enabled him to expand his power into Syria.

CITADELS: A FASHION FOR FORTRESSES

The successors of the Seljuks had established a trend, particularly in northern Mesopotamia, for building citadels, and Ayyubid ones, such as those at Cairo, Bosra, Damascus and Aleppo, remain among their most impressive buildings. It has been suggested that the Cairo citadel was built to protect the Ayyubids from

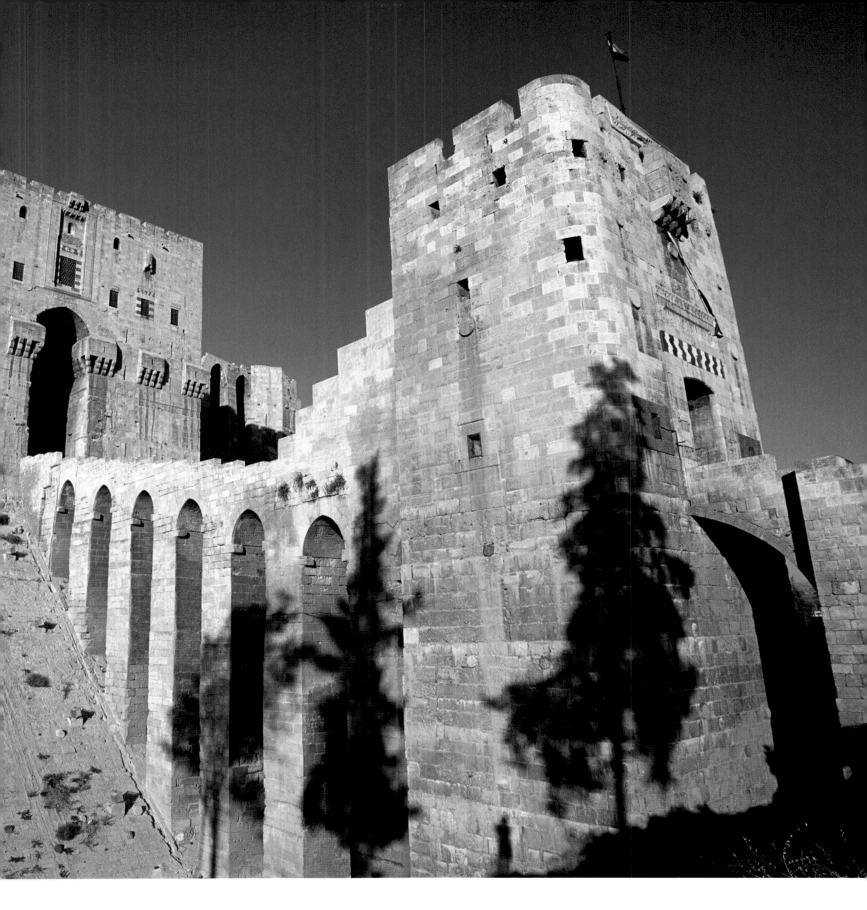

Saladin's son al-Zahir Ghazi
rebuilt the entrance to the
fortress of Aleppo in the
early 13th century with two
spectacular gateways connected
by a narrow entranceway
supported on eight arches.
The upper part of the inner
gateway is a later addition by
the Mamluks.

وَكَادَ يَنْزِعُ لِلْجِمَالِ الشَّمَرَ وَالنُّشَدَ
مَا الْحَجُّ سَيْرُكَ تَأْوِيَّا وَادْلَاجَا وَلَا اعْتِيَامَ الْجِمَالِ الْجُمْلَا وَاحْدَلَا جَا

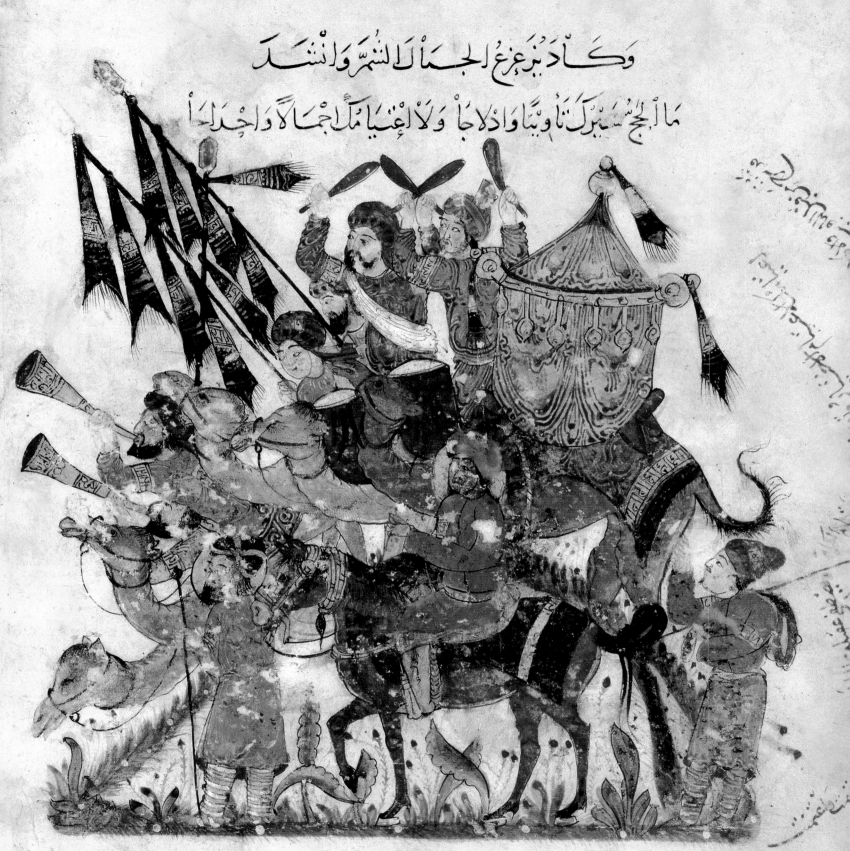

الْحَجُّ أَنْ تَقْصِدَ الْبَيْتَ الْحَرَامَ عَلَى تَجْرِيدِ لِلْحَجِّ لَا تَبْغِي بِهِ حَاجَا
وَتَقْطِي كَأَهْلِ الْإِنْصَافِ مُتَّخِذًا رَدْعَ الْهَوَى هَادِيًا وَالْحَقُّ مِنْهَاجَا

pro-Fatimid uprisings, but the fashion for fortress building must also have played a major part in the decision to erect it. Saladin's brother al-'Adil added to the Cairo citadel the strongly fortified towers which included the bent entrance passage to give attackers a disadvantage. This was a military improvement over the Fatimid gates (see page 53), even if none of the citadel entrances had decoration of comparable splendor.

More impressive was the entrance to the Aleppo citadel, rebuilt by Saladin's son al-Zahir Ghazi in 1210 (see illustration, page 57). As well as its defensive sophistication, the main gateway also provided a platform for an advertisement of the patron in the form of an inscription with his titles, such as "lord of kings and sultans, subduer of infidels and polytheists," and a display of the citadel's protective power in the form of an arch framed by intertwining dragons spouting forked tongues.

The move of the seat of sovereignty in Cairo to the citadel had the added advantage of enabling the Ayyubids to dismantle the main symbol of Fatimid sovereignty, their palaces. For the next two centuries the site of the decaying palaces was the most sought after real estate in Cairo, with successive sultans using it for properties overlooking the street on which to publicize their power and munificence.

Among the most common Ayyubid building types was the madrasa, important to help the Sunni Ayyubids counter the Shi'i propaganda of their Fatimid predecessors. Saladin built one in Cairo's vast southern cemetery, beside the tomb of Imam Shafi'i, one of the founders of the four orthodox Sunni legal schools. Ayyubid concern to champion religious orthodoxy is also seen in the mausoleum erected by Saladin's nephew al-Kamil at the site. Here was a way to gain blessings by having family members buried in close proximity to Imam Shafi'i's grave, and to make pilgrimage to the grave easier by building a spacious mausoleum to accommodate many visitors. As rebuilt it was (and remains) the largest and most conspicuous tomb in the cemetery. The many pilgrimage guides for the cemetery stressed the holiness of the graves and the efficacy of prayers uttered there; that of Imam Shafi'i now had a monument commensurate with its importance.

ILLUMINATING THE QURAN

THE GLORIOUS WORD OF GOD

For Muslims the Quran is the eternal and uncreated word of God, and therefore copies of it occupy a preeminent position in Islamic book arts. This applies both to the calligraphy that transcribes the text and the ornamentation that soon became an indispensable part of luxury manuscripts. An astonishing early example of this ornamentation is on a Quran of ca. 700 found in the Great Mosque of San'a in Yemen. Its double-page frontispiece depicts arcades hung with lamps and a larger niche, presumably a *mihrab*, flanked by trees and shrubs. Perhaps the mosque depicted had similar decoration to the mosaic trees in the Great Mosque of Damascus (see page 27), which were also added to the mosque at Madina when it was restored around the same period.

However, decoration on most early manuscripts was sparse. The Quran is divided into 114 *sura*s (chapters) with differing numbers of verses. The divisions between these elements were the first to be provided with illumination, from pyramids of simple dots to medallions and stars and, if a *sura* began on a new line, long decorated rectangles. The ends of the fifth and tenth verses were often marked in a special way. Occasionally an alphanumeric system was used, with a letter corresponding to a unit, decade or hundred.

The letter *ha* was used for the number five, and its form was later stylized into a teardrop. The use of different alphanumeric systems has been of great value in attributing provenance to some manuscripts.

THE ARRIVAL OF PAPER

The rectangular *sura* ornamentation gradually expanded to other parts of the page, with palmettes spreading into the margin, and frames surrounding the text. The Quran written and illuminated in

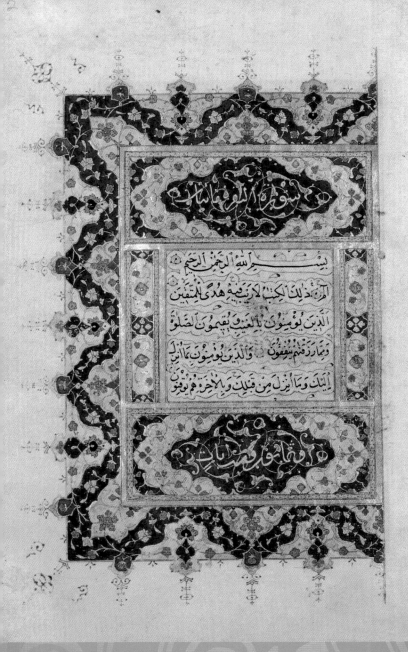
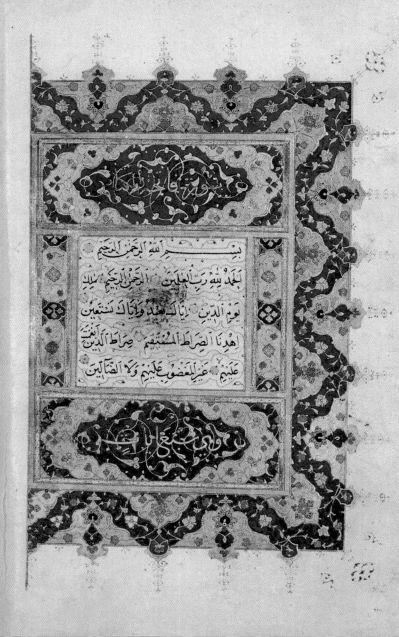

ABOVE

Fazl Allah was not only the calligrapher of this Quran, but also, according to its colophon, decorated it with colors, gold, and drawing. This example, made in Istanbul, is dated to 1493; by 1506 Fazl Allah was the head of the painting studio of the Ottoman sultan Beyazid II.

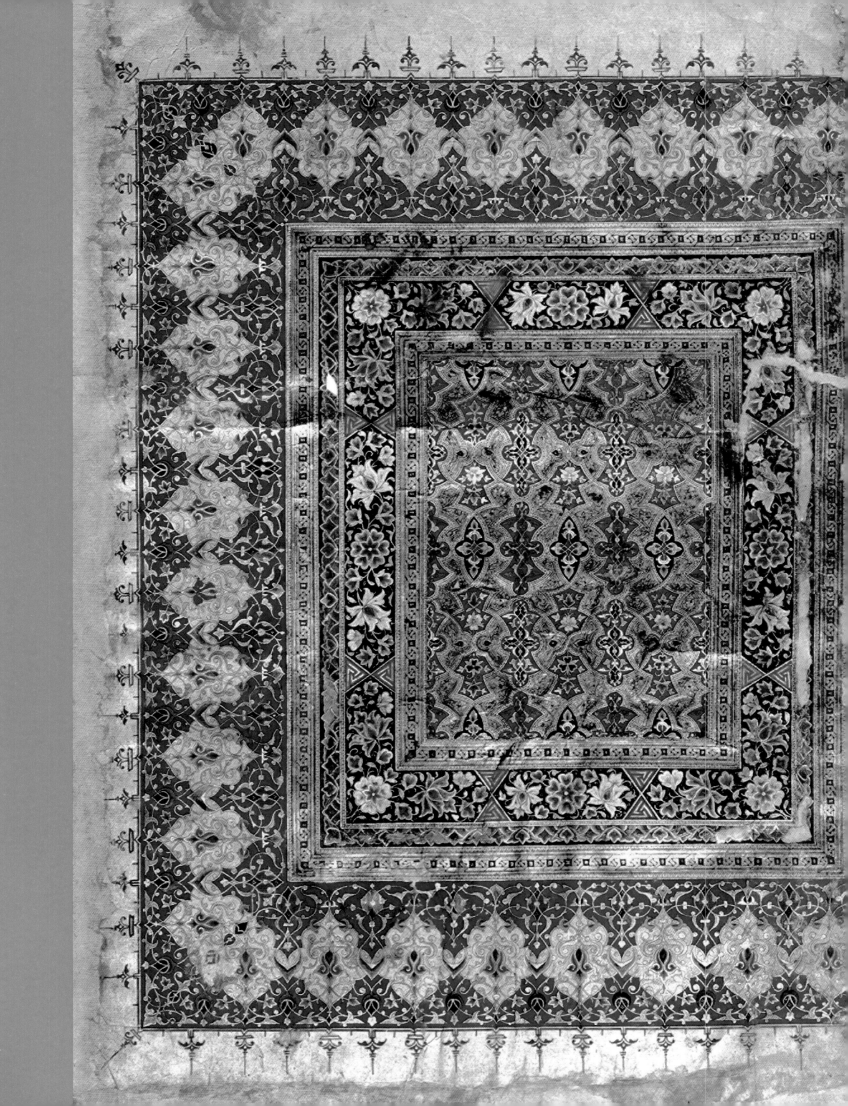

1000–1001 by one of the most famous early calligraphers, Ibn al-Bawwab, exemplifies a number of important changes. It was written on paper, a cheaper material that gradually superseded parchment following its first use for Qurans in the tenth century. Paper was more easily bound than parchment, and entailed a change from the horizontal format used by most previous Qurans to the vertical format that was easier to hold in the hand. The Ibn al-Bawwab Quran also contains a large variety of early full-page illuminations, displaying foliate designs within intersecting octagons and circles, a scheme quite different from the elongated rectangles of earlier horizontal manuscripts. This Quran was also one of the earliest to use the new more flexible and more legible cursive script instead of the previous Kufic, which had arranged the letters on a constant baseline.

Not all manuscripts changed to the cursive style immediately. A now fragmentary but spectacular thirty-volume Quran of ca. 1200 from Seljuk Iran was written in Eastern Kufic, which used tall, slender letters. With only four lines to a page, each on a fully illuminated arabesque background, it would have had a staggering 2,250 folios. Qurans in thirty volumes were common, enabling the holy text to be read in a month, one volume a day. Similarly, seven-volume copies were intended to be read in a week.

MONUMENTAL QURANS

There were a few large early parchment Qurans, probably made for mosques, but the spread of papermaking technology made large sizes more common, a feature that appealed greatly to the Mongols' love of monumentality. The largest Quran made for the Mongol Ilkhanids (ruled 1256–1336) has a bifolio of 27.5in by 39.4in (70cm by 100cm), termed a "Baghdadi" after the city in which it was made. One of the Qurans commissioned by the Ilkhanid sultan Uljaytu (1294–1304) has notations on it indicating that it arrived in Cairo and was then endowed by a Mamluk *amir* in 1326. It may have spurred the Mamluks to produce even more luxurious Qurans; in addition to their sumptuous illumination, one was as big as 29.5in by 39.4in (75cm by 100cm).

FROM SLAVES TO SULTANS

THE MAMLUKS

The Ayyubids had built up an impressive army of Turkish mercenaries (*mamluk*s, literally "owned"), recruited from the Central Asian steppes and the Caucasus. They retained an unquestioned loyalty to the ruler. However, in 1249, when the last Ayyubid ruler, al-Salih Ayyub, died fighting King Louis IX of France in the Seventh Crusade in the Egyptian Delta, a succession crisis arose. Al-Salih's death was kept secret until his son Turanshah could arrive from distant Diyarbakr. When he arrived, though, Turanshah brought with him his own *mamluk*s and it soon became apparent that he intended to eliminate those of his father. But the latter struck first, eliminating Turanshah and his *mamluk*s and putting al-Salih's wife, Shajarat al-Durr, on the throne until she was soon forced to take one of them as husband and sultan. Thus began Egypt's Mamluk dynasty.

The Mamluks preserved many of the administrative features of their predecessors, but maintained their ethnic separateness by importing young Turkish slaves. These would be freed and brought up as Muslims, and having severed all family ties would be, at least in theory, fiercely loyal to their masters. On the death of one Mamluk sultan, a nominal successor would be appointed while the main officers of the state, the *amir*s, jockeyed behind the scenes—or clashed on the streets of Cairo—to see who could gather the most support. This frequently resulted in a fast turnover of sultans, but the efficacy of the system is demonstrated by the Mamluks' lengthy tenure of over 250 years (1250–1517), during which time they were the principal power in the Middle East.

The premodern part of Cairo is today still filled with more monuments from the Mamluk period than from any other. Sultans and *amir*s vied with one another in erecting complexes containing mausoleums together with some combination of mosques, madrasas and *khanaqah*s (residences for Sufis). Crucial toward understanding this are the complex relationships that existed between the sultan and his *amir*s, the religious leaders (the *ulama*), and the practice of *waqf* (religious endowment). Although the building of mausoleums was tolerated by the majority of the *ulama*, there was a

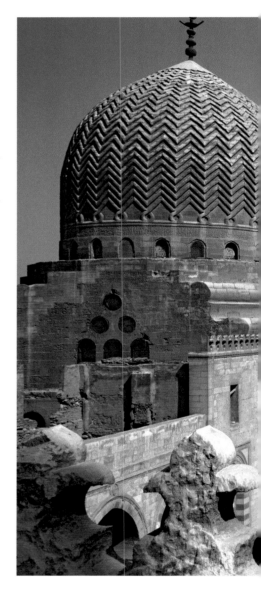

Cairo's largest stone domes
display the new fashion for
zigzag carving. Left and right
are divided between the male
and female members of the
family of the founder, Mamluk
sultan Faraj ibn Barquq, who
attached the mausoleums to his
khanaqah (1411).

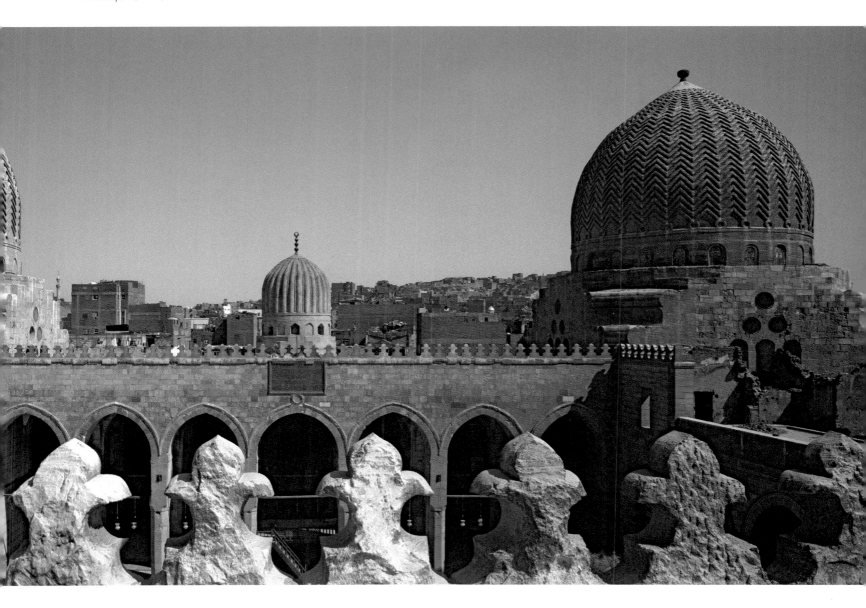

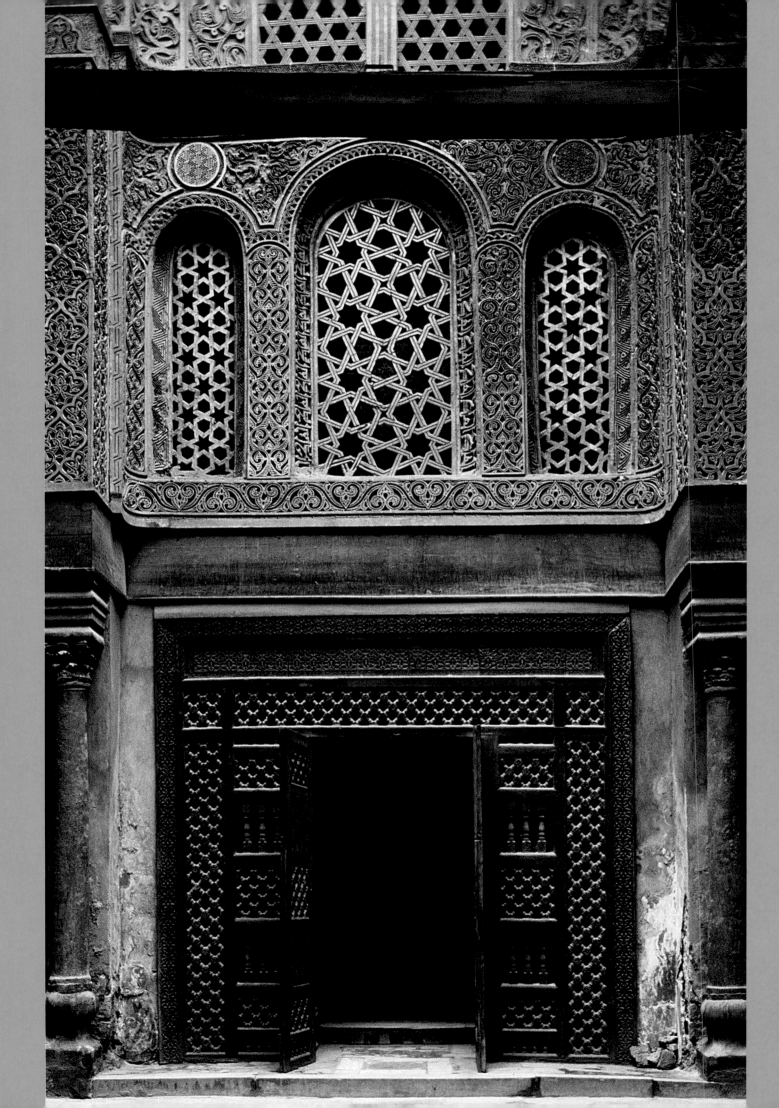

persistent minority that did not condone the practice, holding that it led to unseemly pilgrimages and inappropriate intercessionary prayers. One way to absolve oneself from criticism of this kind would be to incorporate a mausoleum within a religious complex. Islam of course encourages almsgiving, and the founders of these institutions were undoubtedly motivated by the pious intentions of bringing charitable benefits to others. But another motive is also discernible. For an *amir*, or even a sultan, life was often precarious—a coalition of unfavorable *amirs* could lead to falling out of favor and banishment, or even execution and confiscation of one's worldly goods.

However, if one's property was given as *waqf* to a religious institution it was, at least in theory, donated in perpetuity and free from the threat of confiscation. Under the family *waqf* system that operated in most of the central Islamic lands, it was possible to appoint family members as administrators of the *waqf*. The revenue from the trust would be needed to maintain the buildings and pay for the salaries of the employees, but any excess could be spent at the discretion of the administrators. Some recent quantitative studies of operating expenses for the *waqf*s of the last important Mamluk sultan, al-Ghawri (ruled 1501–16), have estimated that as much as 90 percent of the revenue of his endowments was surplus to the needs of the religious institutions.

MAMLUK ARCHITECTURE: QALAWUN AND QAYTBAY

The complex built in 1283 by Sultan Qalawun typifies many of these underlying themes. It was located in the center of Cairo and consisted of a hospital, a madrasa, and a mausoleum. The hospital was the ostensible *raison d'être* of the complex, having been built to fulfill a vow made by the sultan when he was treated at another hospital in Damascus. The concept of *baraka*, divine blessing, played an important part in the number and location of mausoleums within complexes in Cairo. It was believed that prayers offered by passers-by for the deceased could help in securing God's forgiveness for their sins. This explains the invariable siting of mausoleums overlooking one, or, if possible, two streets.

OPPOSITE

Prerogative of the powerful. Guards stationed in the vestibule of the Mamluk sultan Qalawun's mausoleum (1284) at Cairo prevented the unworthy from gaining access. The stucco is superb, but the early use of *mashrabiyya* around the door is also interesting.

The entrance to Qalawun's complex is decorated with black and white marble, one of its many features of Syrian origin. The curling ironwork of the window grille is Crusader work, either brought back as spoils from Palestine or made by one of the 300 prisoners who helped finish the complex in the short span of fourteen months.

The entrance to the mausoleum is from a small forecourt. Here a group of eunuchs served as doorkeepers, a prestigious position which they exercised by preventing anyone of lesser importance from entering. For those granted the privilege of crossing the threshold, a breathtaking sight was in store. A foretaste is given by the entrance wall, faced with some of the most elaborate stucco in Cairo (see illustration, page 66). Inside, there is a sudden contrast, the light from the dome being filtered through colored glass windows, and dappling on multicolored marble and inscriptions of gold and azure. The configuration of a dome supported on four piers and four columns within a square ambulatory is unique in Cairo. Qalawun had campaigned in Syria, and the plan of the mausoleum and its marble facing may have been inspired by the Dome of the Rock in Jerusalem, in an attempt to underline Qalawun's claims to be the spiritual heir to the glory of the Umayyads. The decoration of the *mihrab*, with marble and mother of pearl mosaic, and colonnades of arches topped by scallop shells, inspired imitations in Cairo for more than a century.

What little decoration survives in the hospital indicates that it was as sumptuous as the mausoleum. The southeast and northwest *iwan*s contain two basins, which have marble and stone inlay as fine as that of the *mihrab* of the mausoleum. Just as impressive were the provisions for running the hospital, which offered completely free treatment, including food and medicines, of in- and outpatients. On leaving, patients received a set of clothing, while any who died as patients were given a funeral befitting their standing. Such enlightened policies made Qalawun's hospital famous in the medieval Islamic world, where the study of medicine was relatively advanced compared to the West.

Although Sultan Qaytbay (ruled 1468–96) was the most important of later Mamluk architectural patrons, the type of architecture produced in his reign was markedly

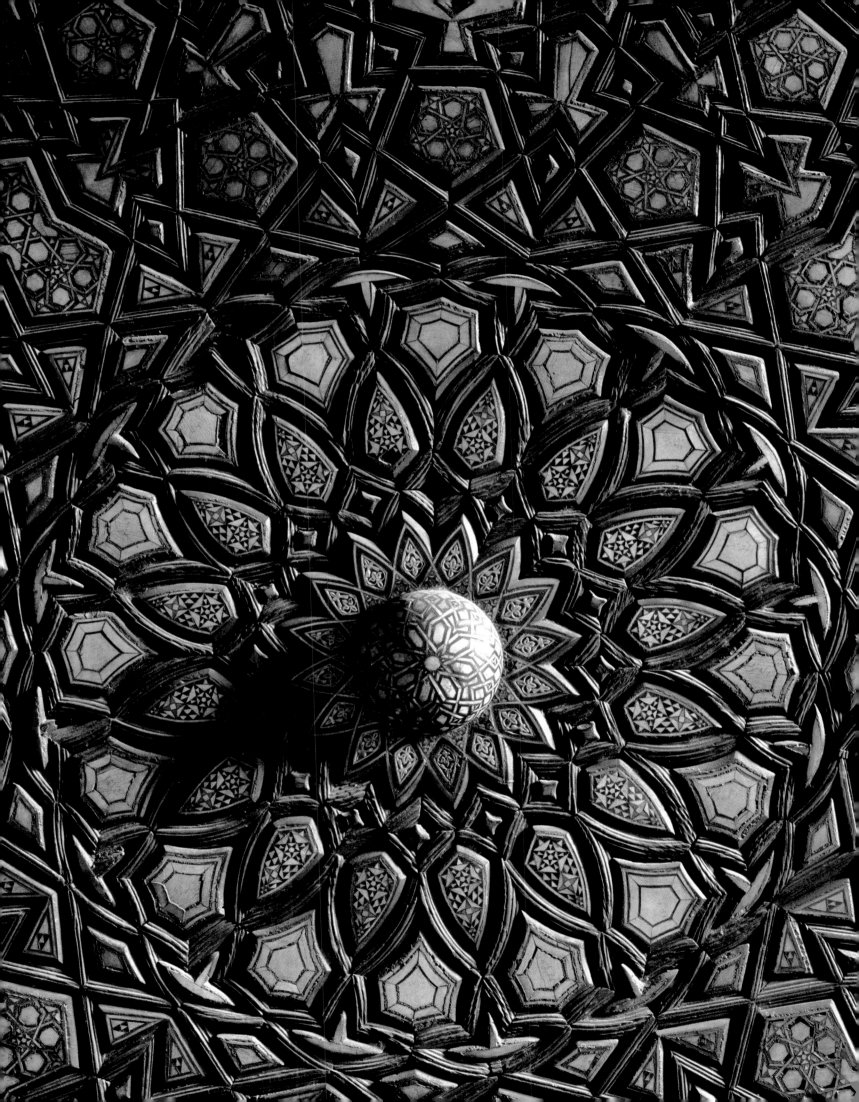

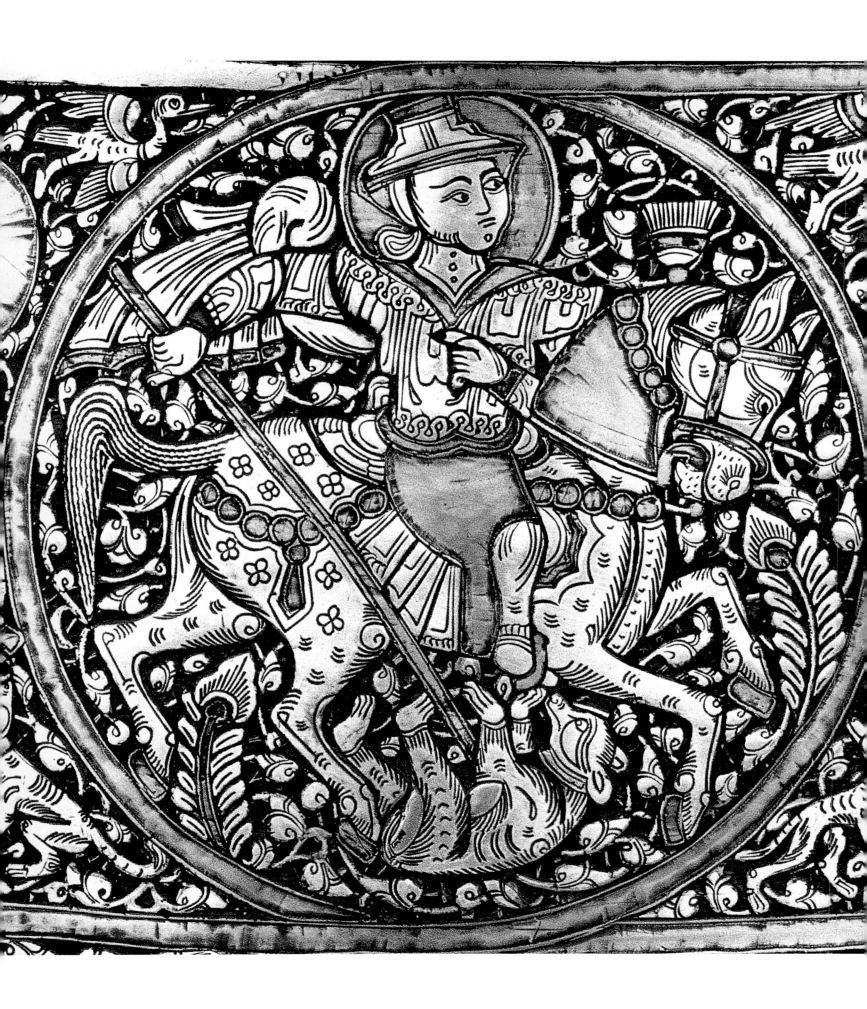

different from the Mamluk buildings of earlier centuries. The scale was considerably reduced, with his complex in the northern cemetery splitting off the student residential buildings that in earlier centuries had been attached to the main structure. However, as if to compensate, the level of ornamentation was correspondingly increased, for instance on the stone-carved domes of the period.

MAMLUK DECORATIVE ARTS

The art of inlaid metalwork was enthusiastically embraced by the Ayyubids and Mamluks. When production stopped in Herat after its conquest by the Mongols in 1221, craftsmen in Mosul developed the technique. When Mosul too fell to the Mongols in 1262, many of the metalworkers moved on to Syria and Egypt, as their signatures attest. Mamluk society was extremely hierarchical, and the metal basins, trays, vases, and candlesticks proved ideal vehicles of display for the blazons that reflected some of these social stratifications. Earlier metalwork was largely decorated with figures, but during the reign of al-Nasir Muhammad (1310–41) they suddenly disappear altogether from the repertory, presumably because of religious strictures. On the other hand, chinoiserie motifs such as the lotus appear on metalwork and buildings after 1322, indicating that trade with Mongol territories must have followed on the peace treaty made with them in that year.

Mamluk carpets are unique in both their pattern and color scheme. Some of them include composite blazons, a feature that first led to their identification as Mamluk. This origin was confirmed as recently as 1983 when a superb example was discovered in the Palazzo Pitti; according to the Medici archives it arrived in Italy from Cairo between 1557 and 1571. The compositions are usually arranged around large central octagons and surrounding geometric figures. Their even tones of cherry red, leaf green and pale blue, mingle with a subtlety that causes them to shimmer in the imagination.

RIGHT

A hexagonal table of copper alloy inlaid with silver, made in 1327 for the Mamluk sultan al-Nasir Muhammad, for the hospital that formed part of the complex built by his father, Qalawun. The craftsman, Muhammad ibn Sunqur al-Baghdadi al-Sankari, is named on the legs of the table, which is 32in (81cm) high. The other inscriptions, on the top and six sides, extol the sultan.

OPPOSITE

A detail of a Mamluk woollen carpet. The origin of these carpets is something of a mystery, emerging without precedent in the late 15th century. At the same time as Turkmen refugees from western Iran transformed Mamluk painting with Persian stylistic elements, weavers from the same area may have taken refuge in Cairo. But even if this was the catalyst, the designs are unmistakably of local inspiration.

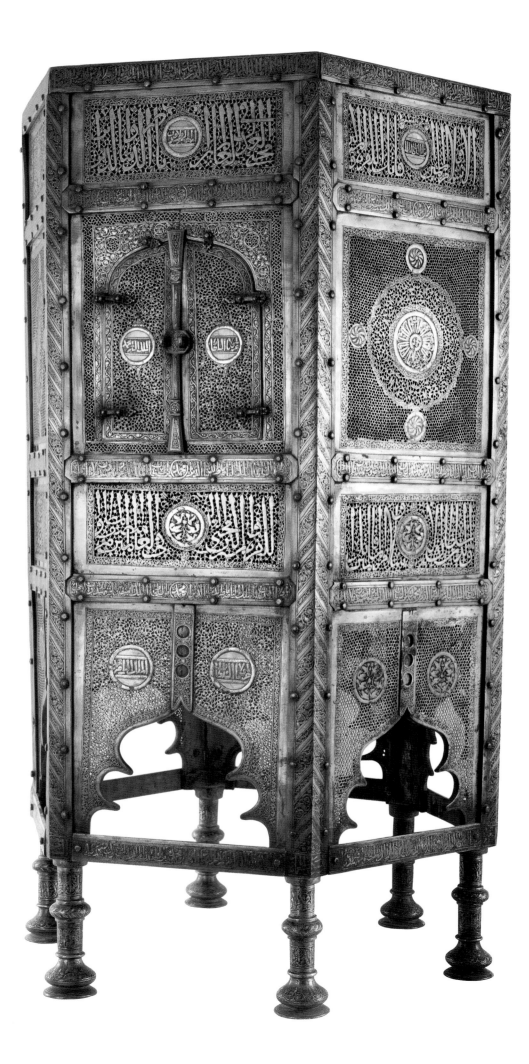

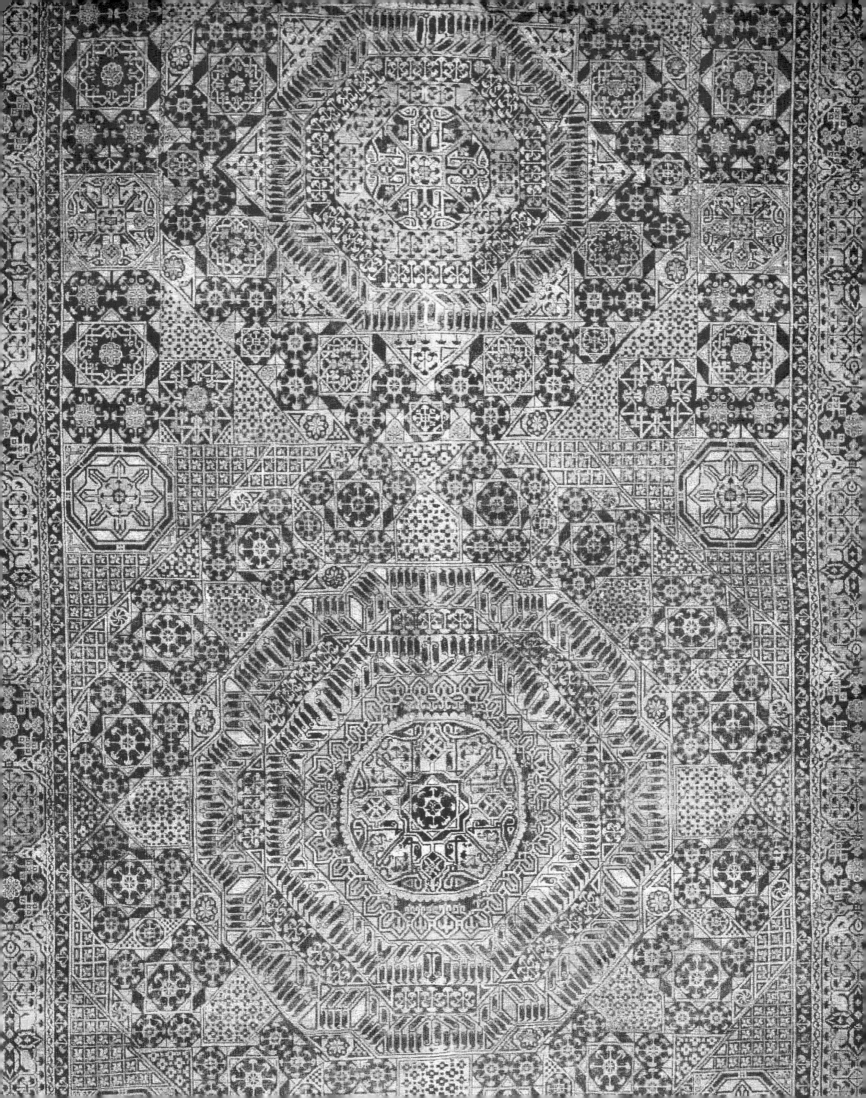

SULTAN HASAN, CAIRO

BUILDING TO IMPRESS

The complex founded by the Mamluk sultan Hasan (ruled 1347–51, 1354–61) is the single most impressive in Cairo, a city with one of the greatest concentrations of monuments in the Islamic world. Hasan—the grandson of Qalawun, who built an earlier notable complex (see pages 66–68)—was chosen sultan aged eleven, deposed and imprisoned in the harem at sixteen, then freed and enthroned again aged nineteen in 1354. He was noted for the learning he acquired in the harem, in addition to his love of women and music. His assassination at twenty-five left the partly unfinished complex as his sole major accomplishment. How did he manage to fund such a massive project? The answer seems to be that his reign coincided with the height of the bubonic plague in Egypt, when so many entire families died that their wealth reverted to the state.

Construction began in 1356 on a most prestigious site facing the square in front of the citadel. Hasan built a four-*iwan* congregational mosque; four madrasas of varying size, which were squeezed into the corners of the complex; a huge domed mausoleum behind the *qibla iwan*; and, at a lower level, a bazaar and water tower.

The exterior niches help to enhance the verticality of the exterior, leading the eye to the huge cornice of six rows of stalactites. The numerous pockmarks on the stonework facing the citadel were not caused by foreign invaders, as might first be thought, but by the cannons of the Mamluks themselves. After Sultan Hasan's death, rebels discovered that the sturdy walls provided a fine platform from which to bombard the citadel; a later sultan took the precaution of demolishing the staircases to the roof.

The entrance portal is cleverly angled so as to be visible from the citadel. Its form is based on Anatolian Seljuk models and, like these, it was planned originally to have twin minarets. However, the minarets of Anatolia are of brick and rise from beside the portal; it seems that those of Sultan Hasan were designed to be of stone and to be on the top of the portal, causing one minaret to collapse as it

RIGHT, ABOVE
The enormous mausoleum of the complex of Sultan Hasan projects into the adjacent square, making it freestanding on three sides. On the right is the neo-Mamluk late 19th-century mosque of al-Rifa'i.

RIGHT, BELOW
The *mihrab* of the Sultan Hasan mosque, constructed in white and polychrome marble and decorated with verses of the Quran in cursive script (see also page 48).

BELOW
This plan of the Sultan Hasan complex shows the entrance (1), the madrasas (2), the four *iwans* (3), the *sahn* (4) or courtyard, and the mausoleum (5).

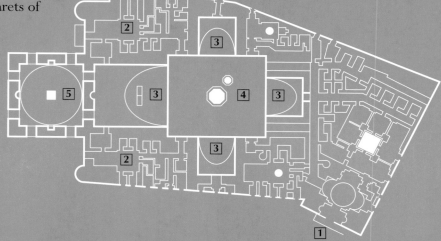

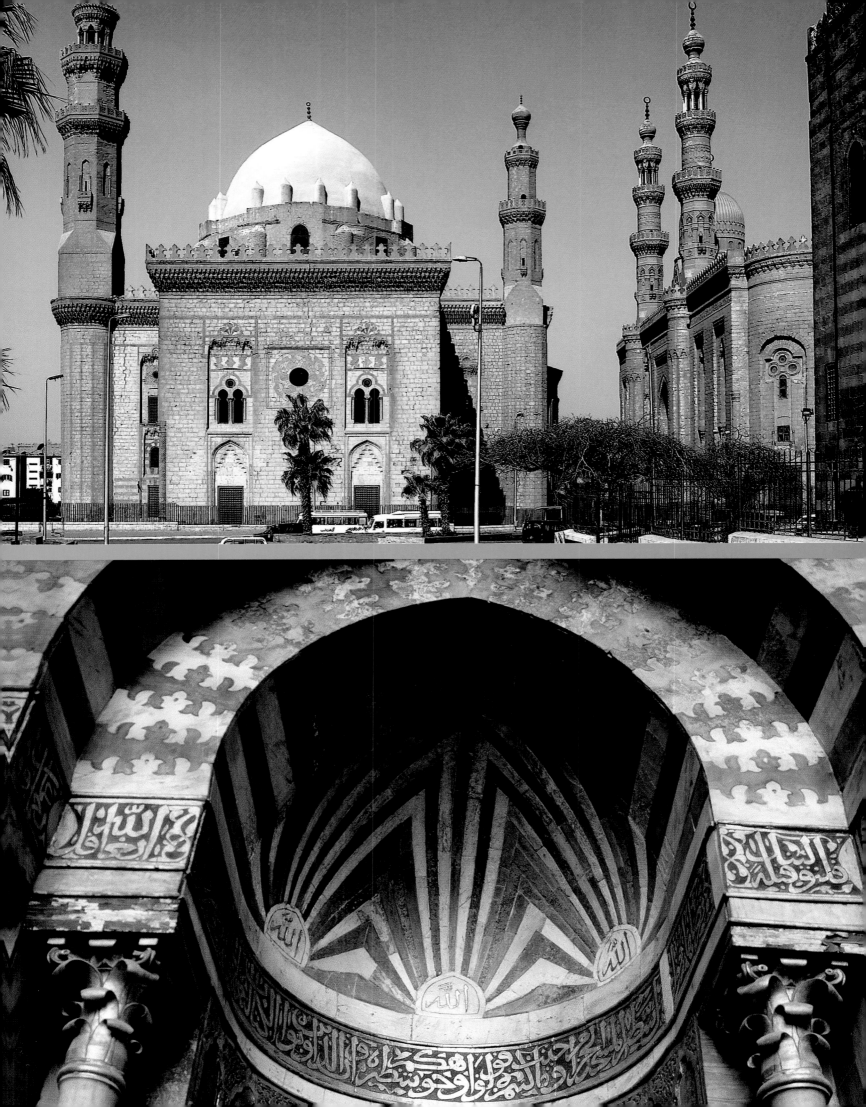

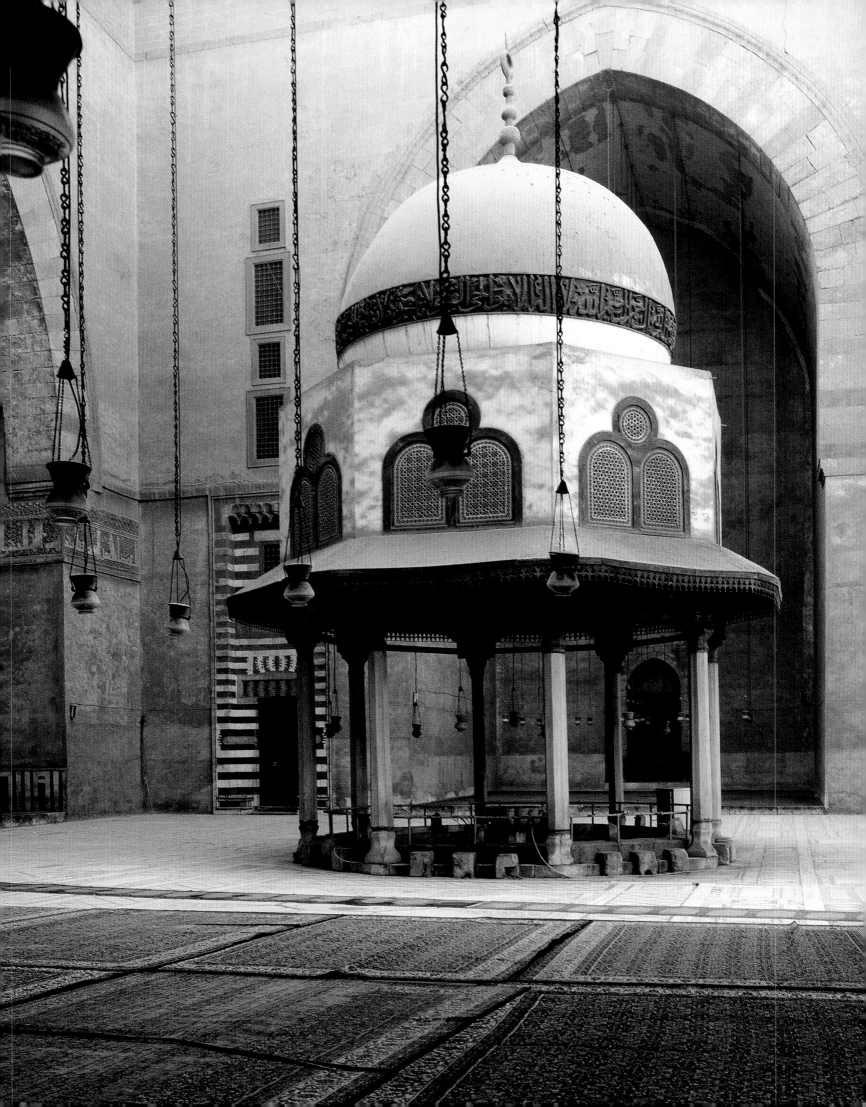

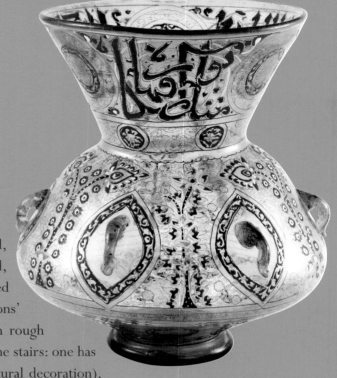

LEFT

The ablution fountain in the mosque courtyard is covered by a bulbous wooden dome; this probably echoes the shape of the original mausoleum dome, which a 17th-century traveller described as shaped like an egg (it was later restored in masonry in a different shape).

was being built, killing 300 people. The other minaret was abandoned, so the mosque today has only two of the four minarets planned, although one of these is an Ottoman replacement. The unfinished portal decoration gives valuable evidence of contemporary stonemasons' practice. Working on scaffolding, they first carved out patterns in rough outline. There are two panels of marble on both sides of the top of the stairs: one has delicately carved chinoiserie blossoms (unique in Cairene architectural decoration), while on the other the flowers were merely outlined when work stopped. The original doors to the portal are in the mosque of Sultan Mu'ayyad beside Bab Zuwayla. The most magnificent of their kind in Cairo, they were "bought" by Mu'ayyad for a paltry sum.

The huge size and elaborate decoration of the domed vestibule behind the portal are more impressive than those of many Mamluk mausoleums. A narrow corridor leads from the vestibule to the mosque courtyard, with the ablution fountain in the center.

THE HALL OF TWO HUNDRED LAMPS

The *qibla iwan* was the only one to receive decoration by the time of the sultan's death. A nineteenth-century print by David Roberts shows it in its glory, with some of the more than 200 lamps that were ordered specially for it hanging from the ceiling. The *iwan*'s vast size was no accident: the sultan specified that it be built five cubits (about 2.25m) higher and wider than the Taq-i Kisra, the Sasanian palace that was a byword for magnificence in Arabic literature (see illustration, page 16). The *iwan* is actually somewhat smaller, but the Taq-i Kisra was in Mongol territory, so it was unlikely that anyone could gather exact measurements, and what was important was that the sultan *thought* it was bigger. Historians also report that the scaffolding of the *iwan* cost as much as an ordinary mosque.

In 1261 Sultan Hasan was killed by rival Mamluks as he tried to flee Egypt. His body was never found so he was never buried in the majestic resting place he had prepared. Instead, the mausoleum contains the bodies of two of his sons.

ABOVE

Several of the 200 exquisitely gilded and enameled glass lamps that formerly hung in the *qibla iwan* of the Sultan Hasan are now preserved in Cairo's Islamic Museum, together with the original bronze chandeliers. This example, 12in (30cm) high, is notable for the blue inscription band on the neck quoting verse 35 of Sura 24 of the Quran, and medallions at the base of the neck with stylized chinoiserie lotuses. The body of the lamp is decorated with floral and lotus designs. The lower part of the lamp has inscriptions similar to those on the neck.

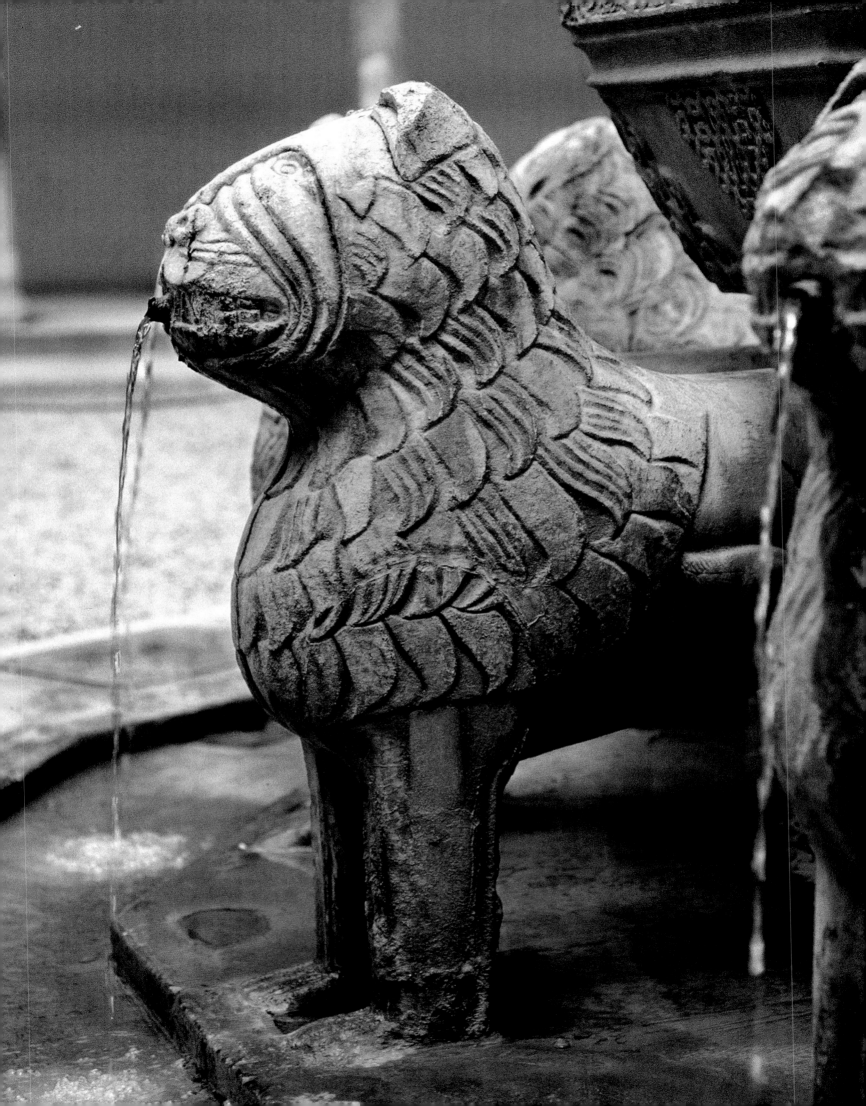

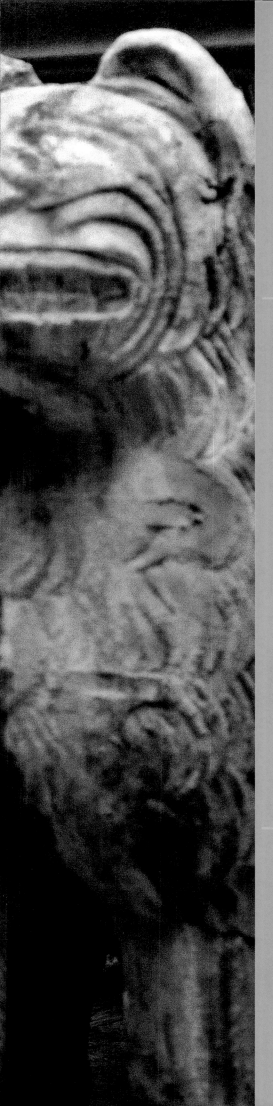

chapter 4

FUSION IN THE WEST

IBERIA AND THE MAGHREB

SPIRIT OF COEXISTENCE

THE UMAYYADS IN SPAIN

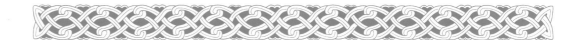

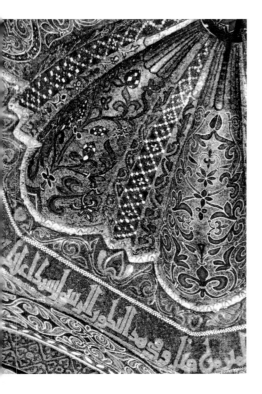

In 711 a Muslim army led by Tariq ibn Ziyad crossed the Straits of Gibraltar to the Iberian
peninsula and landed at the rock that today bears his name (Gibraltar, or Jabal Tariq—
the Mount of Tariq). The extraordinary rapidity of the Muslims' success in Iberia owes
much to the hatred of the local Christian and Jewish populations of their Visigoth rulers.
By 716 Muslim raiding parties were attacking France, but internal dissensions with the
Berber tribes who accompanied the Arab armies necessitated consolidation in Spain.
Following the bloody end of the Umayyad caliphate (see page 32), one Umayyad prince,
'Abd al-Rahman I (ruled 756–88) was able to escape his 'Abbasid pursuers and wrest
control of Iberia, establishing Córdoba as the capital of his new Umayyad emirate.

Under the Umayyads many local people converted to Islam, but a substantial
number remained Christian (the Mozarabs) and Jewish. Islam's tolerance of religious
minorities was especially notable in Iberia—a striking contrast to the Christian treatment
of Jews and Muslims after the reconquest of the peninsula was completed in 1492.

With the accession of 'Abd al-Rahman III (ruled 912–61), the Umayyads entered
a new period of prosperity, thanks in part to the stability of his long reign. The Umayyad
*amir*s previously had difficulty in establishing control over the mountainous terrain of
the Iberian peninsula; 'Abd al-Rahman not only achieved this but also, by forging links
with anti-Fatimid elements in North Africa, was able to extend his influence there. In
consequence in 929 he took the title of caliph, just as the Fatimids had done earlier,

Political ties with Baghdad were severed, but the 'Abbasid capital remained the
arbiter of taste and fashion. Córdoba tried to catch up quickly, importing musicians,
clothing, and jewelry. 'Abbasid patronage of learning was also mimicked, with poetic and
scientific manuscripts filling vast libraries—at 400,000 volumes, that of Caliph al-Hakam
II (ruled 961–76) was larger than any other in Europe at the time. As Europe's closest
Muslim neighbor, it was through Spain that Arabic translations of many Greek classics
were reintroduced into Europe, via Latin translations; and numerals and the decimal
system of counting, brought by the Arabs from India, entered Europe from Spain.

BELOW

Erected in 961 by the Spanish Umayyad caliph al-Hakam II as part of his extension of the Great Mosque of Córdoba, this vaulting of intersecting arches is based on a plan of interlacing squares which create an octagon of smaller diameter. This complexity is reflected in the intersecting arches which support the dome at the lower level. Following the fall of Córdoba in 1236, King Ferdinand III of Castile consecrated the Great Mosque as the city's cathedral.

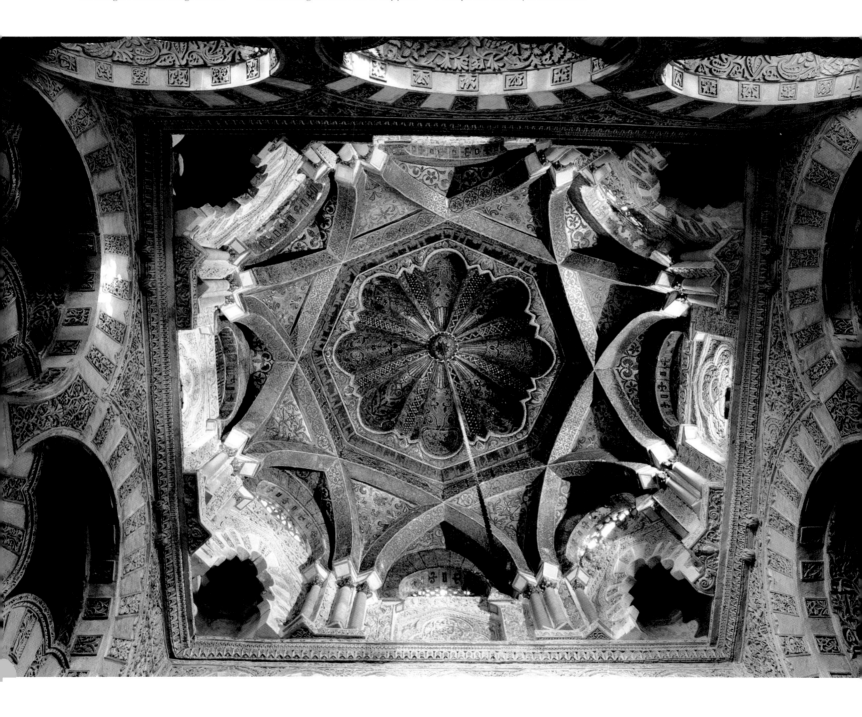

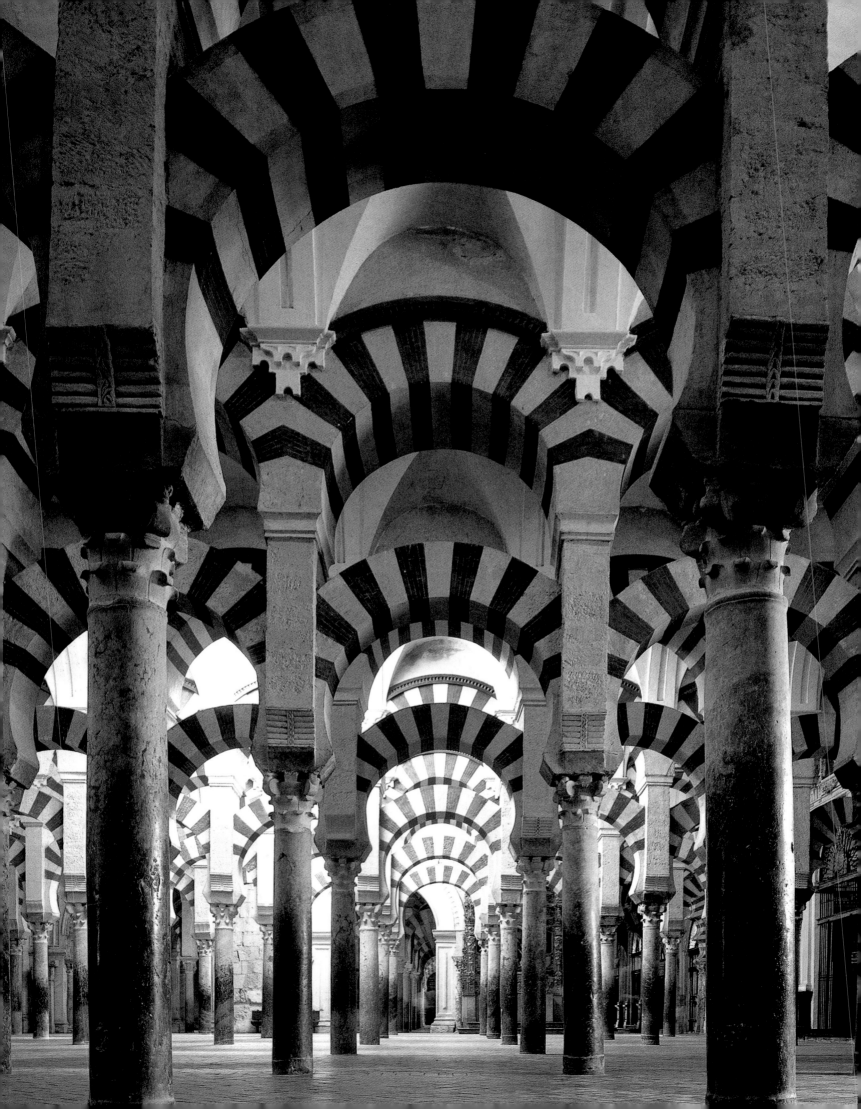

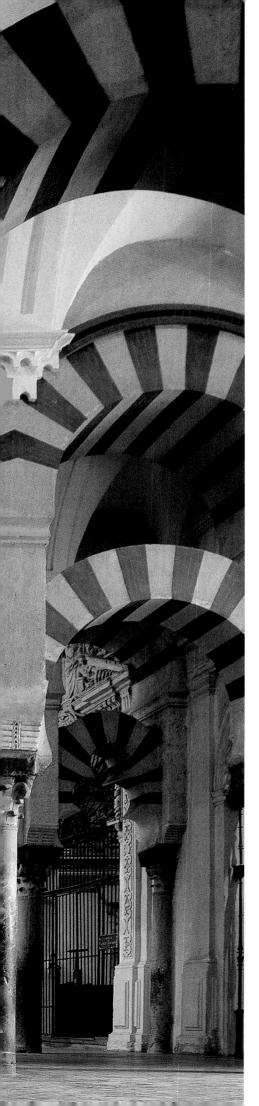

LEFT
The stunning vista of arches dwindling to infinity in the Great Mosque of Córdoba recalls the orange grove in the mosque's courtyard. In order to create a ceiling of the desired height, the reused Visigothic columns support double-tier arcades.

BELOW
The intricate stone carving of the façade of the Great Mosque of Córdoba shows stylized versions of Roman acanthus leaves, but subordinates them to other abstract forms and an overriding symmetry typical of Islamic decoration.

'Abbasid taste was also imitated in the erection of enormous palace complexes, the most celebrated being Madinat al-Zahra near Córdoba, begun by 'Abd al-Rahman III in 936 and completed during the reign of his son al-Hakam II. One-third of the revenue of the state went toward its construction, which required 1,500 beasts of burden every day. Like the 'Abbasid palaces at Samarra (see pages 38–43), this was really a caliphal city, accommodating 14,000 people as well as the mint, a zoo, a prison, textile factories, and ateliers, in addition to magnificent reception halls and living quarters.

TREASURES IN GOLD AND IVORY

One of the reasons for the prosperity of the dynasties which ruled over North Africa and Spain was their command of the gold routes between sub-Saharan Africa and Europe. Another valuable commodity that was imported by the same route was ivory. Several exquisitely carved pieces have inscriptions telling us that they were made in Madinat al-Zahra, and the names of their patrons. One piece, made for a daughter of 'Abd al-Rahman III, folds out to reveal ten circular concave compartments. Originally thought to be a container for cosmetics, it is now realized that it is a box for the game of *mancala*, still played in North Africa on similar boards. Half a dozen ivory boxes are known from the period. One has an inscription that reads: "The sight I offer is the fairest, the firm breast of a delicate girl. Beauty has invested me with splendid raiment, which makes a display of jewels. I am a container for musk, camphor, and ambergris." This tells us the purpose of these boxes,

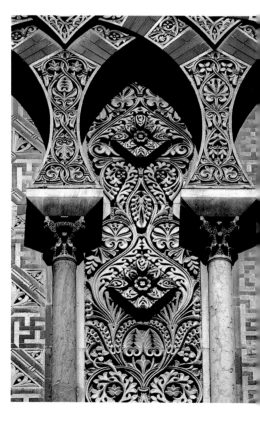

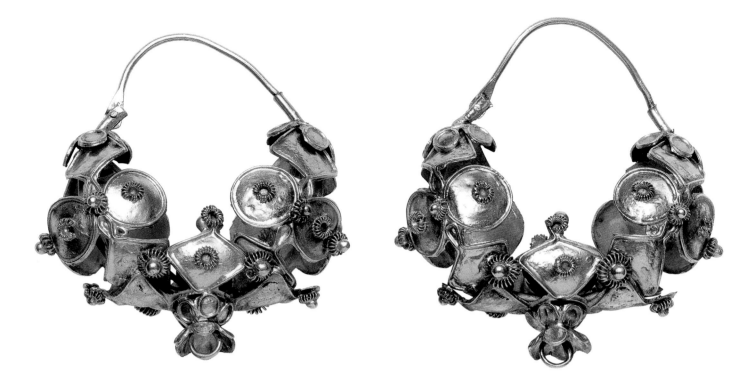

receptacles for perfume, and also suggests that precious stones mounted on pins might have filled the small holes present on them. The most splendid box was made in 968 for al-Mughira, the son of 'Abd al-Rahman III and the brother of the ruling caliph al-Hakam II. In 968 al-Hakam's son, Hisham, had not been appointed heir, and al-Mughira might have had every expectation of inheriting the throne. The royal imagery in the medallions may have been a way of implying this. The figures picking dates may at first sight look like a genre scene, but the cheetahs or bear cubs perched on the backs of the horses are no ordinary companions. The medallion also has resonances from the earliest Spanish Umayyad ruler, 'Abd al-Rahman I, who, in order to recreate a garden of his Syrian Umayyad ancestors in Rusafa, imported several plant species including the palm tree, suggesting a connection between the recipient of the box and the right to rule. As it happened, when al-Hakam died one faction supported al-Mughira, but was out-maneuvered by the chief minister al-Mansur and his lover, al-Hakam's widow, who had al-Mughira killed and enthroned the tractable child Hisham II (ruled 976–1009).

THE GREAT MOSQUE OF CÓRDOBA

The finest surviving artistic achievement of the Spanish Umayyads is the Great Mosque of Córdoba. The enlargement by al-Hakam II in 961, when the dynasty was at the height of its powers, produced the most innovative features of the building. Announcing, as it were, the beginning of the new extension, the bay south of the old *qibla* wall (now called the Villaviciosa Chapel) is domed with an entirely original system of vaulting. The

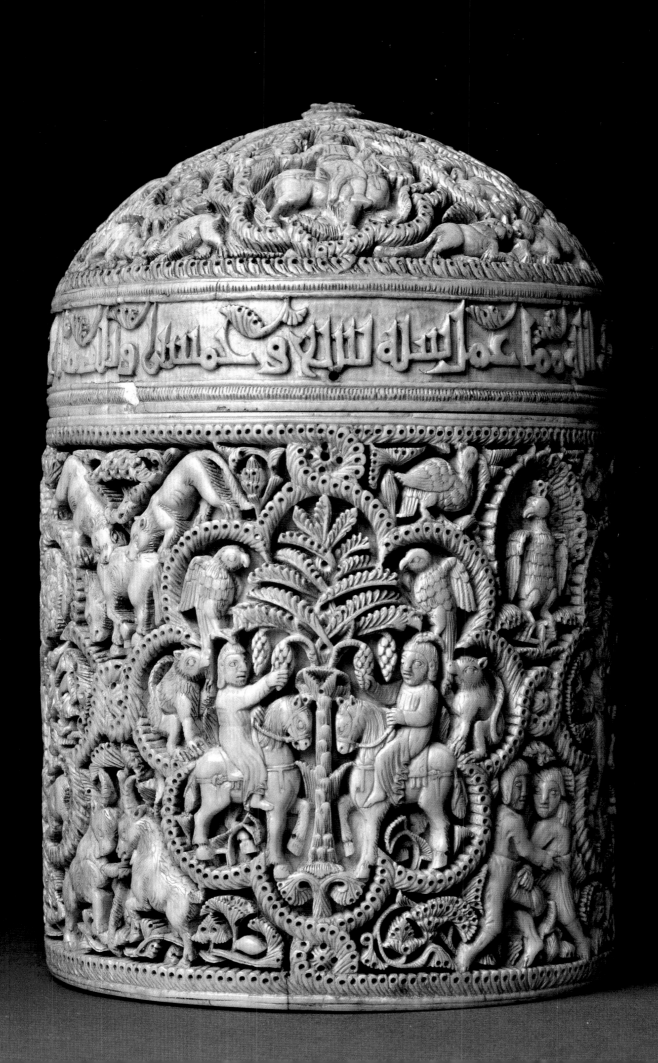

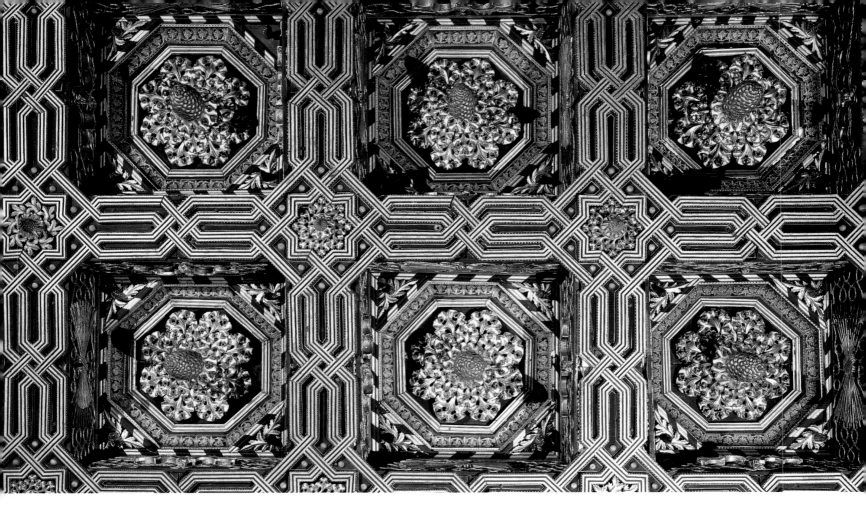

nave (see illustration, pages 82–83) is divided into three bays, and each bay now has polylobed upper and lower arches. But the retention of the two-storey arcade greatly adds to the visual complexity, for each lower polylobed arch can now be linked to a wider and taller one spanning two bays, with its apex on the upper storey, and the outer arches are in addition part of a visual span of three bays.

This complexity is a harbinger of the riches of the *qibla* area, which has three bays parallel to it, each partitioned off by polylobed arches with exquisitely carved stone decoration, a dome supported on intersecting arches arranged differently to that of the bay previously mentioned (see illustration, page 81), and an arched doorway on the *qibla* wall partially decorated in mosaic. The mosaic cubes, together with a mosaicist to train apprentices, were sent at al-Hakam II's request by the Byzantine emperor, glad to make an ally with another enemy of the Fatimids. It has been proposed that al-Hakam II deliberately aimed to imitate the Syrian Umayyad ruler al-Walid, who it was believed had once asked for Byzantine mosaicists to decorate the Great Mosque of Damascus (see page 26).

Raising the ceiling by employing a two-storey arcade let in more light from the courtyard openings, but the light inside the vast prayer hall must still have diminished rapidly as one advanced. This explains why medieval authors were struck by the

BELOW

The arcades of the inner courtyard of the Aljaferia at Saragossa (second half of the 11th century) took the style of interlacing arches pioneered at Córdoba to dizzying new levels of intricacy, subverting their ostensible role as visual support in favor of fantasy.

abundance of lights inside the building: they report that it had around two hundred polycandela (chandeliers with many openings for oil-filled glass lamps), the largest holding up to a thousand lamps and the smallest twelve. During the fasting month of Ramadan the mosque was lit all through the night and the expenditure on oil constituted half the yearly expenses. The *mihrab* with its delicate carved decoration in the extension of al-Hakam II is in the form of a windowless room, and so it must have been designed with such artificial illumination in mind.

THE TAIFA KINGDOMS

Al-Mansur's assumption of power during the regency of al-Hakam II was at first a successful strategy; he raided as far as Barcelona and sacked the Christian shrine of Santiago de Compostela. However, by usurping the caliph's power he undermined the prestige of the caliphate: if obeying the caliph was no longer necessary then anyone was free to make a bid for independence. The result was the relatively sudden collapse of the Umayyad caliphate in the early eleventh century, followed by the fragmentation of Iberia into petty kingdoms (*taifa*).

Among the most powerful of these was Saragossa in the northeast, where al-Muqtadir (reigned 1049–82) built an impressive palace fortress, the Aljaferia. As it is situated near the frontiers of the Muslim world, the outer walls display massive towers peppered with arrow slits. One could not imagine a greater contrast than the luxury of the interior courtyard, exemplified by the delicate tracery of its arcades (see illustration, right).

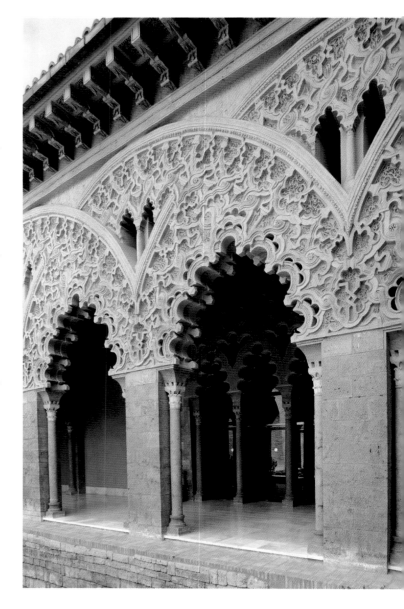

LORDS OF THE MAGHREB

ALMORAVIDS, ALMOHADS, AND MARINIDS

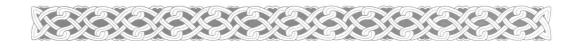

BELOW

The abandoned town of Chella near Rabat, Morocco, where this decorative detail comes from, was transformed into a necropolis at the end of the 13th century by the Marinids. The addition of two mosques, a madrasa, and other buildings in the 14th century turned it into a funerary city.

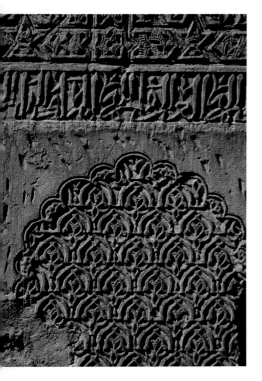

The two dynasties that burst on to the Maghreb in the eleventh and twelfth centuries had similar origins. Both the Almoravids and the Almohads were of Berber stock and were fired by the return from the *hajj* of a charismatic figure eager to promote what they believed was a purer form of Islam to counter the moral laxities of their predecessors.

The first of these dynasties, the Almoravids (al-Murabitun), were so-called because of the impetus given to their ideology by dwellers of a *ribat*, a building that in western Islam housed those who propagated the faith. The *ribat* in question may have been on the Mauretanian coast and from there followers fanned out both northward and toward the southern Sahara, where they were instrumental in spreading Islam in Senegal, Niger, and Mali. Their northern thrust was under their first ruler, Yusuf ibn Tashufin (reigned 1061–1107), who quickly gained control of Morocco and western Algeria. In 1062 he founded Marrakesh as his capital and by 1086 he had crossed into Spain, where his prestige was cemented with victories over Christian forces, enabling him both to bring the *taifa* (petty kingdoms; see page 87) under his control and even to regain territory for the Muslims.

AN ARCHITECTURE OF ASCETICISM

The Almoravids and subsequent dynasties followed the Maliki school of Islamic law, one of the more puritanical. This had several consequences for the development of Islamic architecture, since the school's hostility to Sufism meant that no *khanaqah*s were built, while its aversion to marking graves resulted in an almost complete absence of mausoleums.

In rebuilding the Qarawiyyin Mosque in Fez (1134–43), the Almoravids introduced the vaulting system of *muqarnas*. This technique had been used earlier in the eastern Islamic world, but its use here is astonishing in its variety, further embellished by stucco inscriptions and vegetal ornament. It was in this area that the Maghreb was to excel, as later dynasties pushed the concept to technical and expressive limits.

The great Maghrebi social historian Ibn Khaldun (1332–1406) was perhaps the first to formulate the theory of cycles of history, in which a desert conqueror becomes

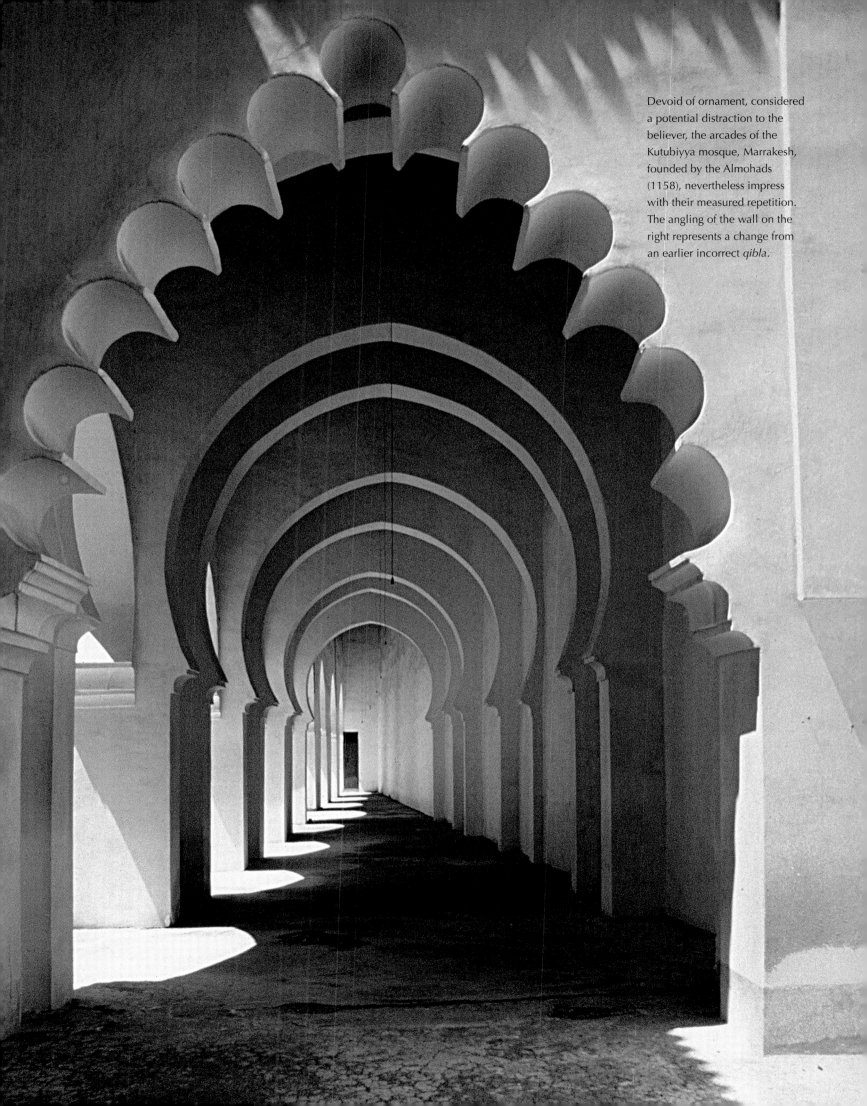

Devoid of ornament, considered a potential distraction to the believer, the arcades of the Kutubiyya mosque, Marrakesh, founded by the Almohads (1158), nevertheless impress with their measured repetition. The angling of the wall on the right represents a change from an earlier incorrect *qibla*.

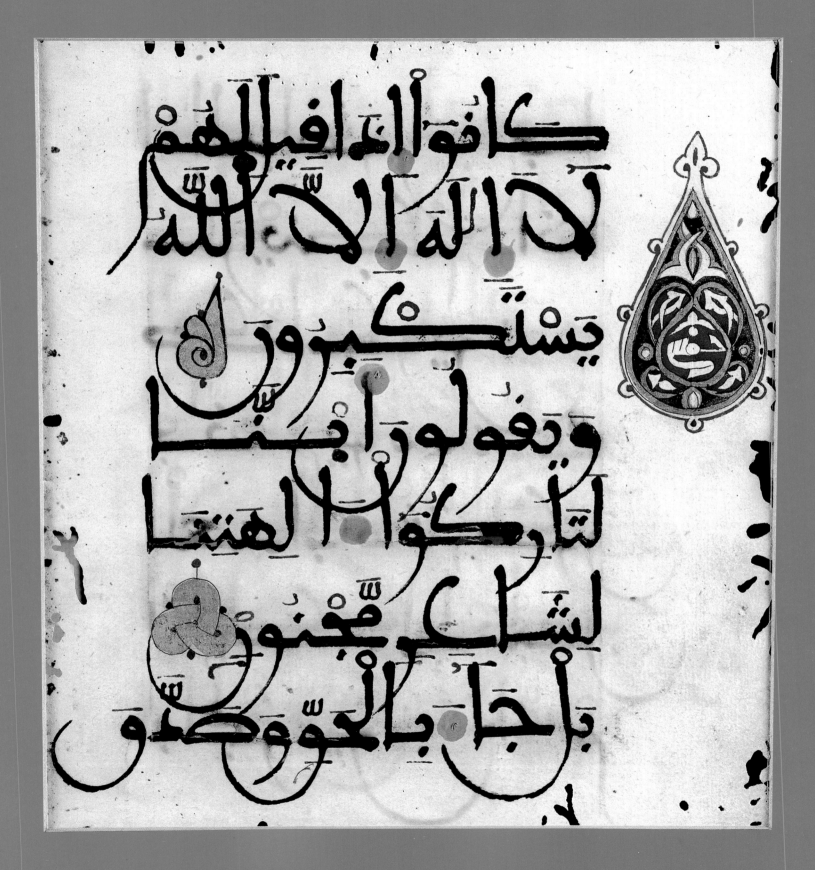

كَانُوٓا إِذَا قِيلَ لَهُمْ

لَآ إِلَٰهَ إِلَّا ٱللَّهُ

يَسْتَكْبِرُونَ

وَيَقُولُونَ أَئِنَّا

لَتَارِكُوٓا ءَالِهَتِنَا

لِشَاعِرٍ مَّجْنُونٍ

بَلْ جَآءَ بِٱلْحَقِّ وَصَدَّقَ

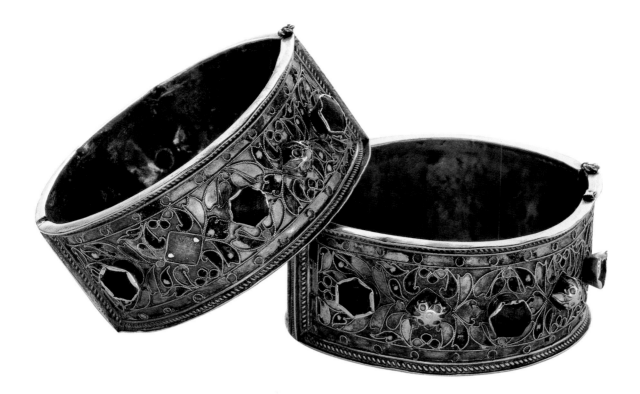

seduced by the luxuries of urban society and is replaced by another who succumbs in a similar way, and so on. His observations were undoubtedly based on the Almoravids and the Almohads (al-Muwahhidun), as the latter indeed castigated their predecessors as immoral wastrels. The Almohads' founder, Ibn Tumart (died 1130), a member of the Masmuda Berber tribe, gained favor by translating Muslim writings into the Berber language. It was only under his gifted lieutenant 'Abd al-Mu'min (ruled 1130–63) that the dynasty was able to expand from its base at Tinmal, beside Marrakesh, to capture first all of Morocco, then Spain, and subsequently all of North Africa as far as Tunis.

The repressive orthodoxy of the Almohads had unfortunate consequences for the religious minorities, as a result of which many Jews and Christians left their territory, including the Jewish philosopher Maimonides (1138–1204). Even Muslims were not exempt; upon the accession of the Almohads, the philosopher Averroes (Ibn Rushd) was removed from his position of chief judge at Córdoba.

ALMOHAD ART

Almohad asceticism extended to their art. They evidently conceived of excess ornamentation as being a distraction to prayer. In their mosque at Tinmal the *mihrab* is decorated, but with simple interlacing bands, rather than with the elaborate inscriptions and arabesques of their predecessors. At the Qarawiyyin mosque in Fez they even plastered over the carved decoration in the *muqarnas* ceilings, fortunately preserving them for us until their recent uncovering. Their main surviving mosque, in the Kutubiyya

ABOVE
Like their predecessors, the later medieval rulers of the Maghreb took advantage of the gold trade between sub-Saharan Africa and Europe. color is added to these gold bracelets in the form of green and red cloisonné enamels and by mounted cabochons alternating with enameled gold bosses. Made ca. 1500, these are among the few pieces of jewelry to survive from Tunisia in this period.

OPPOSITE
Maghrebi calligraphy is characterized by thin pen strokes and exaggerated curves of letters that swoop below the line. On this Quran page, the teardrop medallion contains the word *khams* (five), marking the passage of five verses. Marinid, 13th or 14th century.

in Marrakesh (1158), is also a mostly sober piece of work, although impressive in the repetition of its polylobed arcades. But there was a limit to Almohad asceticism, as they took the gorgeous inlaid wooden *minbar* from the Almoravid Great Mosque of Marrakesh, which they had destroyed. The *minbar* was actually made in Córdoba and reassembled in Marrakesh; the Almohads must have felt its exquisitely elaborate carving was just too skillful to be discarded.

THE RISE OF THE MARINIDS

In the thirteenth century the Maghreb produced a third Berber dynasty: the Marinids (Banu-Marin). Their origins as nomadic herders is reflected in the term used for their famous fine wool, merino. However, the Marinids were motivated less by reforming religious fervor than by political opportunism. The prestige of the Almohads declined following their catastrophic defeat in 1212 at Las Navas de Tolosa in Spain by a Christian coalition. The Marinids entered southern Morocco ca. 1215 and finally captured Fez, the town that became their capital, in 1250. Shortly afterward they acquired the prestige of calling for help in the *jihad*, holy war against the infidels, when they repulsed an attack by Christian forces that had captured Sala in northwest Morocco.

Many relatives of the Marinid sultan subsequently distinguished themselves in Spain serving in the army of the Nasrids. Rather than try to establish a permanent base in Spain, the Marinids thought it more expedient to support the Nasrids as a buffer state between themselves and Iberia's increasingly powerful Christian forces.

The most characteristic product of Marinid artistic patronage was the madrasa. Despite its much earlier popularity in the eastern Islamic lands, it took several centuries for it to become prevalent in the Maghreb, but was then embraced with an enthusiasm matched only in contemporary Cairo. However, Marinid madrasas are very different from those farther east. Their courtyards are much smaller, ranging from the largest, in the Abu'l-'Inan madrasa in Fez, which is 56ft by 60ft (17m by 20m), to as little as 20ft

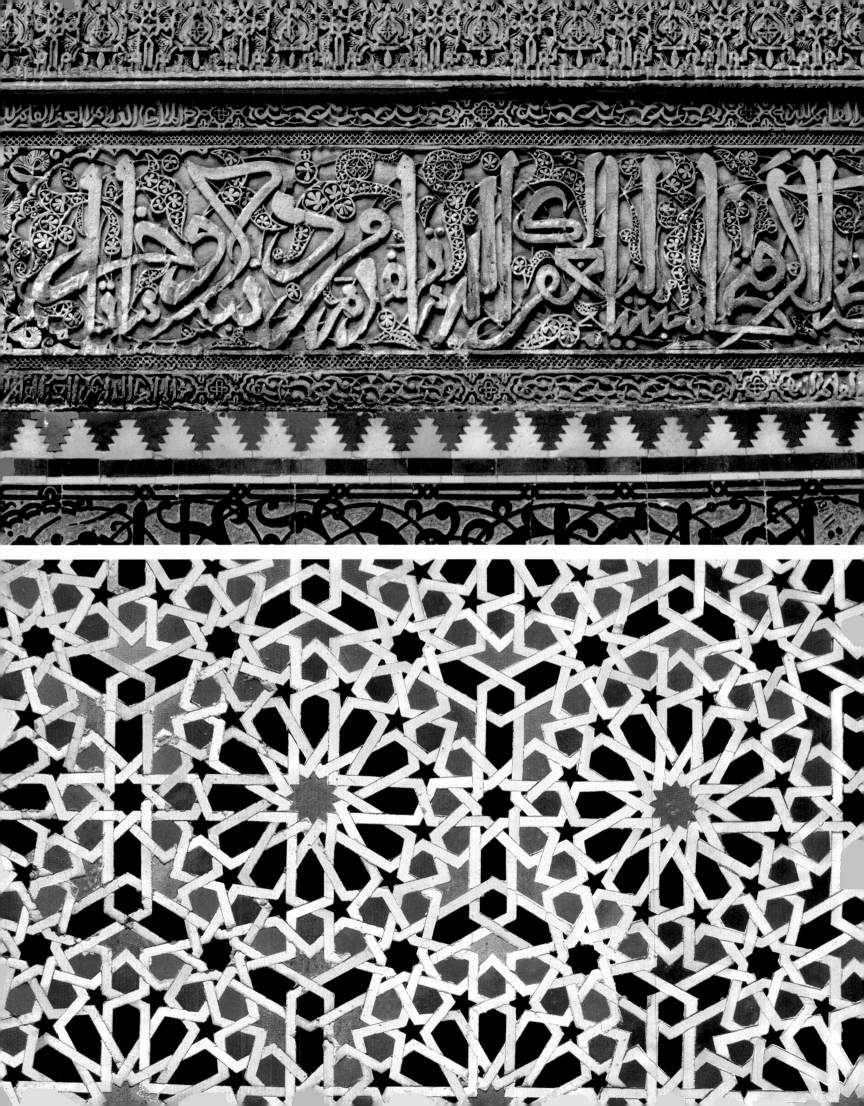

BELOW
Small-scale patterns in stucco
and wood dominate the upper
walls of the Sahrij madrasa in
Fez. The wooden screen below
provides privacy for those
within the courtyard. Marinid
period, 1321–23.

RIGHT
As if to compensate for its
smallness of scale, decoration
is lavished on every surface of
the Sahrij madrasa, even the
pavement. Fez was the capital
of the Marinids, who built
numerous madrasas there.

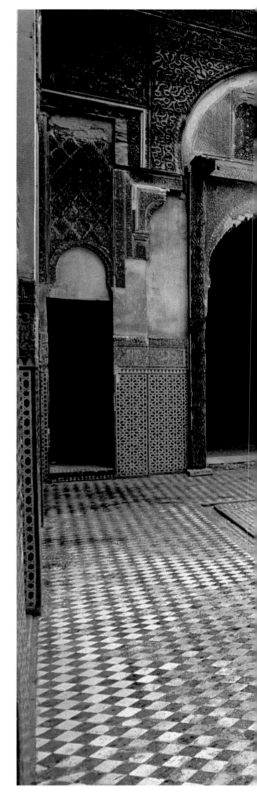

by 40ft (6m by 12m), in the Sahrij madrasa, also in Fez. The exterior of the madrasas is largely invisible, revealing only a finely decorated portal with overhanging carved wooden eaves, and frequently a door with a bronze facing. Their courtyards are usually defined by three walls with arcades (sometimes with flat arches), rather than by the *iwans* of eastern madrasas. The fourth side is almost always taken up with a prayer hall, usually occupying at least half as much space as the courtyard.

Emphasizing the role of prayer in the life of the religious students, a minaret sometimes advertised the presence of these interior mosques. Decoration within the madrasa was concentrated on the *qibla* wall of the prayer hall and on the courtyard.

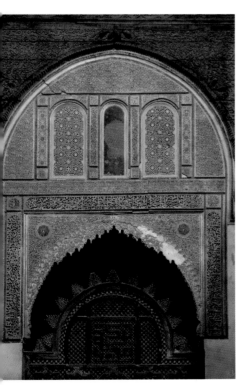

Almost all visible surfaces—tiled floors and walls, stucco arches, wooden beams and eaves—are filled with arabesques, inscriptions, and bold geometric patterns. The result is exquisite in detail, if at times overwhelming in totality.

By 1300, after the Marinids had consolidated their hold on Morocco, they felt sufficiently confident to expand eastward against two rival former clients of the Almohads, the Zayyanids in Algiers and the Hafsids in Tunisia. Under Sultan Abu'l-Hasan (ruled 1331–48) and his son Abu'l-'Inan (1348–58) the Marinids briefly ruled as far as Tunisia, only to withdraw swiftly in the face of rebellions in Morocco or their troops' dissatisfaction at being so far from home.

By the sixteenth century Ottoman rule extended as far as Algiers, but Morocco remained independent under new dynasties, the Sa'dids (1510–1659) and 'Alawids (1659 onward). But the climax of Maghrebi art had been reached with the Marinids and Nasrids (see pages 96–101); later patrons produced little to rival their mastery of ornament.

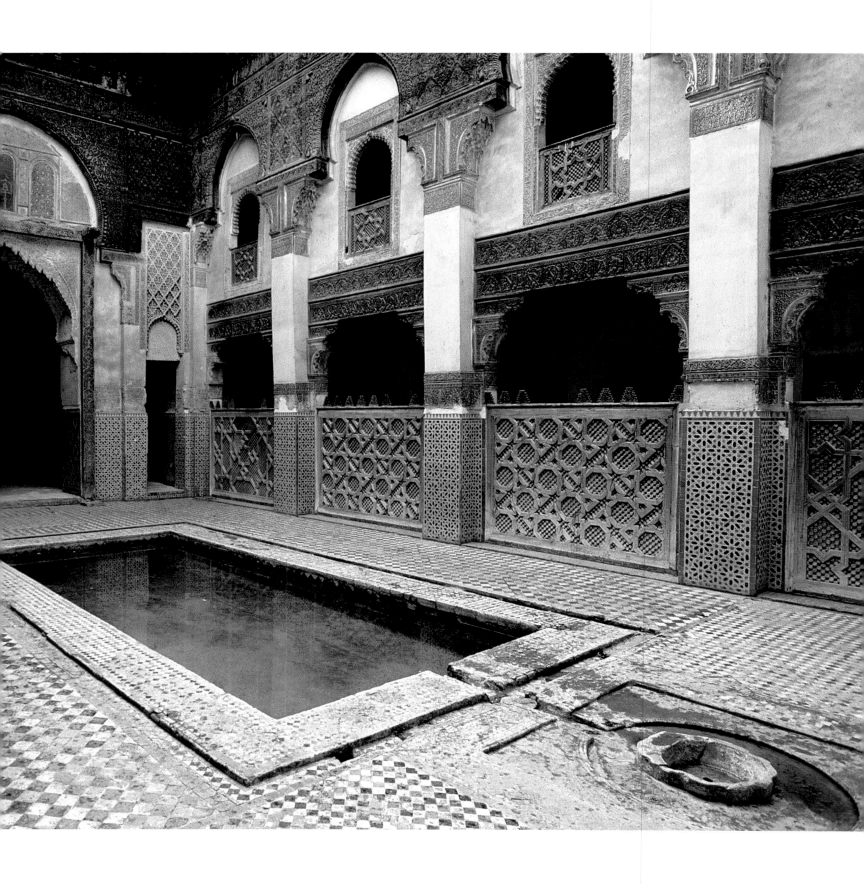

IBERIAN TWILIGHT

THE NASRIDS IN SPAIN

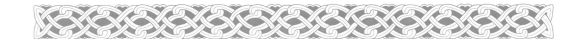

OPPOSITE

The ceramic workshops of the Mudejars (Muslims living under Christian rule) produced this earthenware bowl. Not just the difficulty of the luster technique but the assured design, with its marine motifs, make it easy to see why pottery of this kind was exported all over the Mediterranean. From Manises, Valencia, ca. 1450.

BELOW

A Mudejar tin-glazed earthenware basin decorated with a design representing palm trees. The painting in cobalt, in addition to the usual golden luster, adds interest to the design. From Manises, first half of the 15th century.

Despite the swift advance of the Christian forces into Muslim territory after their defeat of the Almohads in 1212, the local Nasrid dynasty (1232–1492) in the south of the Iberian peninsula managed to hold on to power, in part because it was easy to defend the mountainous terrain around their capital, Granada, and its neighboring provinces of Malaga and Almeria. However, even after obtaining the help of the Marinids from Morocco, the Nasrids were defeated by the combined powers of the Christian rulers of Aragon and Castile in 1340, after which the Nasrids were tolerated by their new overlords on condition that they pay an annual tribute.

Both the Christian powers of Spain and the Muslim rulers of North Africa considered the Nasrid kingdom as a useful buffer state. These neighbors helped the Nasrids to cling to power until the marriage of Ferdinand of Aragon and Isabella of Castile in 1469 united Christian Spain and spelled the end for Muslim rule in the peninsula. In 1492 the last Nasrid ruler, Abu 'Abd Allah, rather than fighting to the bitter end, negotiated a settlement whereby he was permitted to withdraw with his followers to North Africa on generous terms. The treaty of capitulation supposedly guaranteed freedom of religion for the inhabitants of Granada, but in 1499 the arrival of a fanatical cardinal spelled an end to such tolerance.

ARTS OF THE LAST SPANISH SULTANS

The luxury arts of the Nasrids are best exemplified by the Alhambra vases, imposing lusterwares so-called because it was believed they were produced to decorate the Nasrids' Alhambra palace in Granada (see pages 100–103), where two complete examples and one fragmentary one were found. Only eleven complete examples are known today. Their shape is like that of ancient Greek storage vessels, but the enormous size of the Alhambra vases, more than four feet (1.2m) tall, makes it unlikely that they were

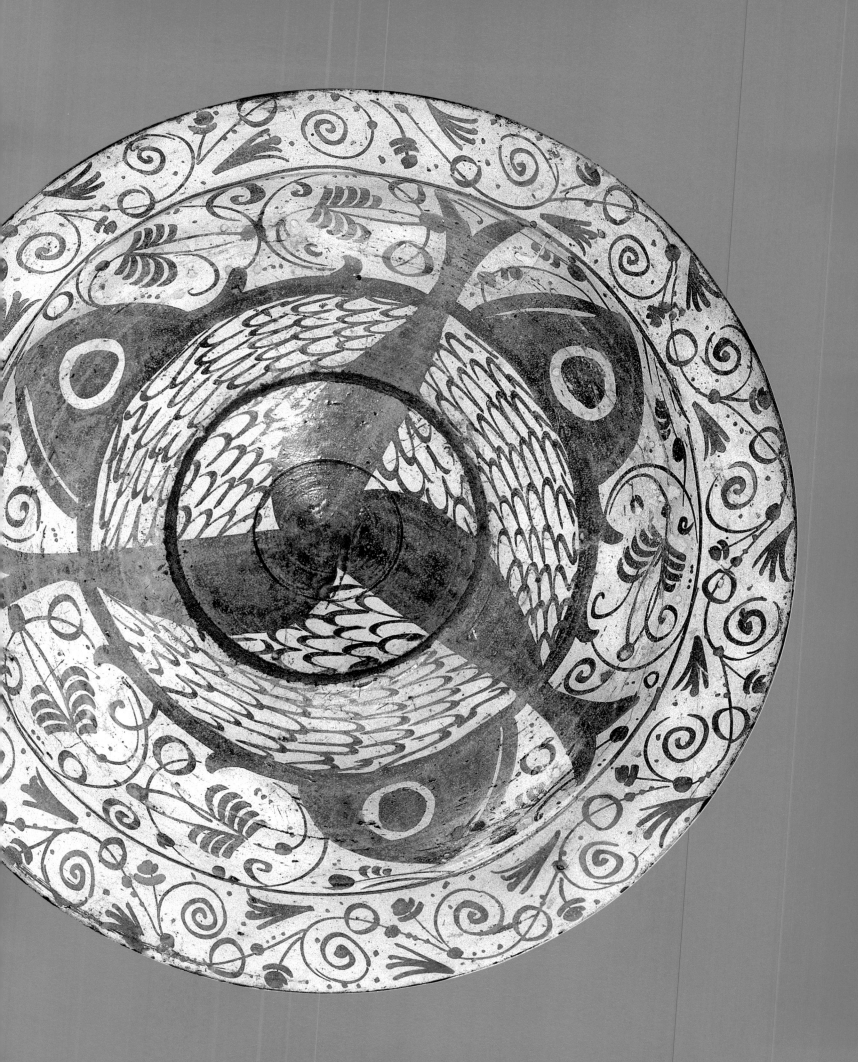

Intersecting arches are one constant of Spanish Islamic art. The closest parallel to the carving on this wooden frieze is in a 14th-century synagogue in Toledo; during this period of tolerance its original location could equally have been a mosque or monastery.

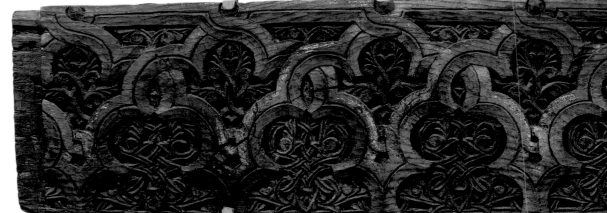

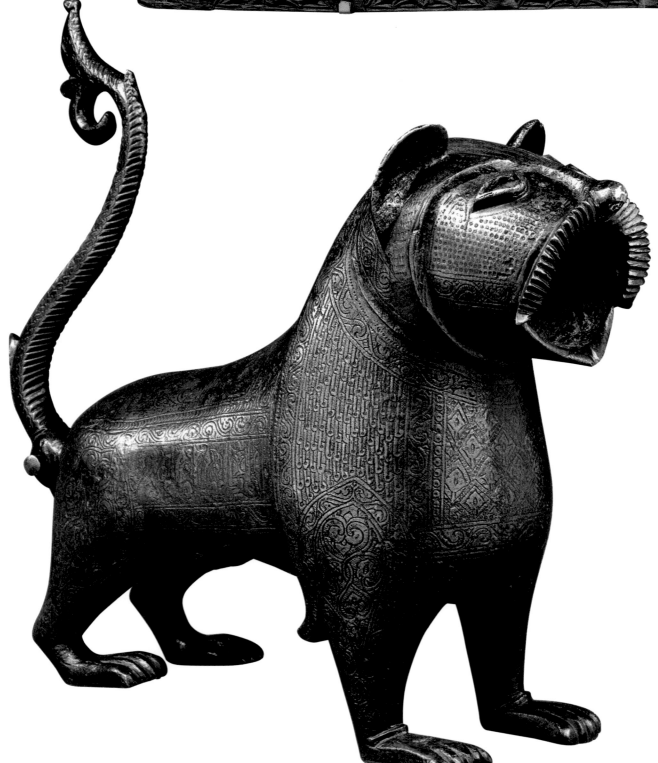

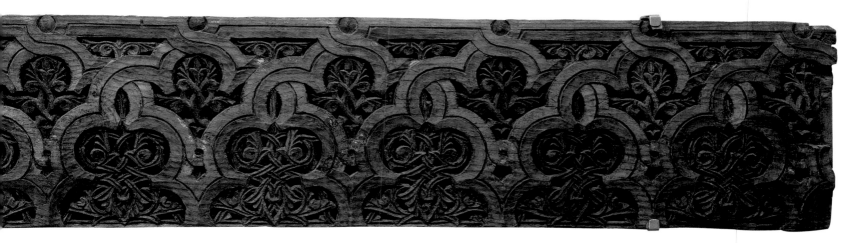

ever designed to be tilted. Their purpose was therefore decorative, enhanced by the sumptuous designs of figural images (such as gazelles), arabesques and inscriptions containing good wishes painted on them in gold and cobalt blue on a white ground.

ART OF THE MUDEJARS

The completion of the Christian reconquest was not the end of the story of Islamic art in Iberia, for Muslims living under Christian rule (the Mudejars) continued to create fine works. Among the most famous are the lusterwares of Manises near Valencia, produced from the early fourteenth century to 1600 (see illustrations, previous pages). The earliest references to this pottery type call it "Malaga ware," presumably because the ateliers were set up by potters coming from Malaga, the center of the Nasrid pottery industry, where the Alhambra vases and other lusterware was produced. Manises potters specialized in large plates and bowls, although vases are also known. Among the latter are *albarello*s, waisted jars for storing pharmacists' preparations, although the word comes from the Arabic *al-barrada*, a drinking vessel. Because of the change in clientele any inscriptions on these pieces are either in Latin characters or in pseudo-Kufic. The vegetal and geometric patterns found on the Alhambra vases are retained, but a new feature is the heraldic shields of the prominent families who commissioned the wares. Emblems of Italian families have also been found, showing the high esteem in which this pottery was held.

After the fall of the Nasrids, religious intolerance increased in Spain. The remaining Muslims were forced to convert to Christianity and in Granada in 1567 another decree forbade these "Moriscos" (crypto-Muslims) to dress differently or even to speak Arabic. Their revolt against such laws was quickly put down, and further decrees (1609–14) resulted in their expulsion from Spain. Most resettled in Morocco or Ottoman Turkey.

OPPOSITE
The Court of the Lions at the Alhambra has a basin supported by 12 lions, from the mouths of which water streams into shallow basins (see page 78). The original site of this incised copper-alloy lion is unknown, but its wide mouth and a hole in its stomach show that it was designed for the same purpose. From Spain, Almohad period, 12th–13th century.

THE ALHAMBRA

LAST BASTION OF MUSLIM SPAIN

Because of its Iberian location, the Alhambra palace was one of the first Islamic monuments to be investigated by European scholars. In the nineteenth century large folio publications of its glories became available in many languages. Hence it quickly became a byword for luxury, and in the twentieth century the Alhambra rivaled the Ritz or the Odeon as a name for movie theaters. This reputation is deserved, as it epitomizes the culmination of Islamic architecture in the West—nothing that was produced in later centuries matches the inventiveness and exuberance of its decoration, the area in which western Islamic architecture excelled.

The name is from the Arabic Madinat al-Hamra, the Red City, and indeed the clifftop enclosure overlooking Granada was much more a palatine city than the fortress comprising its outer walls. However, only two palaces out of an original six remain, and these are partially overshadowed by a Renaissance palace begun in 1526 by Emperor Charles V. The subsequent demolition and rebuilding in the vicinity of the older palaces means that their original urban context is unlikely ever to be recovered.

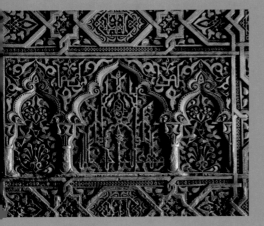

ABOVE
A detail of the stucco decoration (1333–54) in the Hall of the Ambassadors, part of the Palace of the Myrtles in the Alhambra. The hall was the showcase of Nasrid power, where the sultan Yusuf I placed his throne to receive guests.

THE PALACE OF THE MYRTLES

Rather than being two courtyards of one palace, it is probable that the Court of the Myrtles and the Court of the Lions, as they are now known, were two independent palaces, with separate entrances: the existing opening between the two was made only in the nineteenth century. The Palace of the Myrtles (named for the myrtle bushes surrounding the pool in its central courtyard) was probably used mainly for state business. It does have residential rooms along its courtyard, but these would

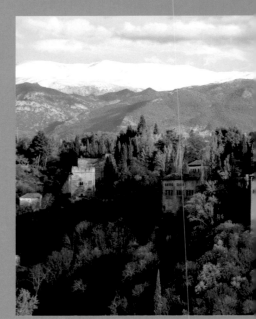

RIGHT

A plan of the Alhambra complex, showing the Palace (now Court) of the Myrtles (1) on the left with the Comares Tower and the Hall of the Ambassadors (2) at the top. The Palace (now Court) of the Lions (3) is on the right, connecting to the Hall of Two Sisters (4).

have fitted uneasily with the processions of ambassadors to its main reception hall, so the sultan's main residence was likely elsewhere, either in the Palace of the Lions or in one of its now destroyed neighbors.

One of the most interesting aspects of the Alhambra is the poetry that graces its walls and throws light on the interpretation of its constituent parts. The arcade preceding the reception hall in the Palace of the Myrtles has a poem in praise of the Nasrid sultan Muhammad V (ruled 1354–9 and 1362–91) and his military victory at Algeciras near Gibraltar in 1369. An inscription on a niche leading to the Hall of the Ambassadors begins: "I am a bride in her nuptial attire, endowed with beauty and perfection." This conceit of the building as speaker continues within the hall in the central alcove opposite the entrance: "My lord, the favorite of God, Yusuf, has decorated me with clothes of splendor and glory and he has chosen me as the throne of his rule," establishing that

BELOW

Fortress, palace, and town. This panorama of the Alhambra gives an idea of its vast extent. The large tower at the left of the picture houses the Hall of the Ambassadors, commanding a magnificent view over the ravine towards the town of Granada.

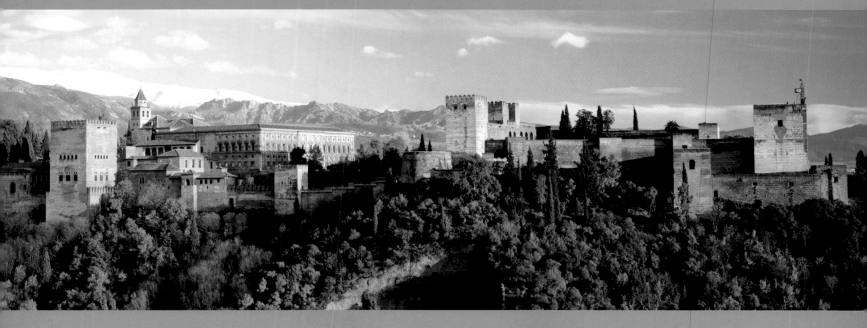

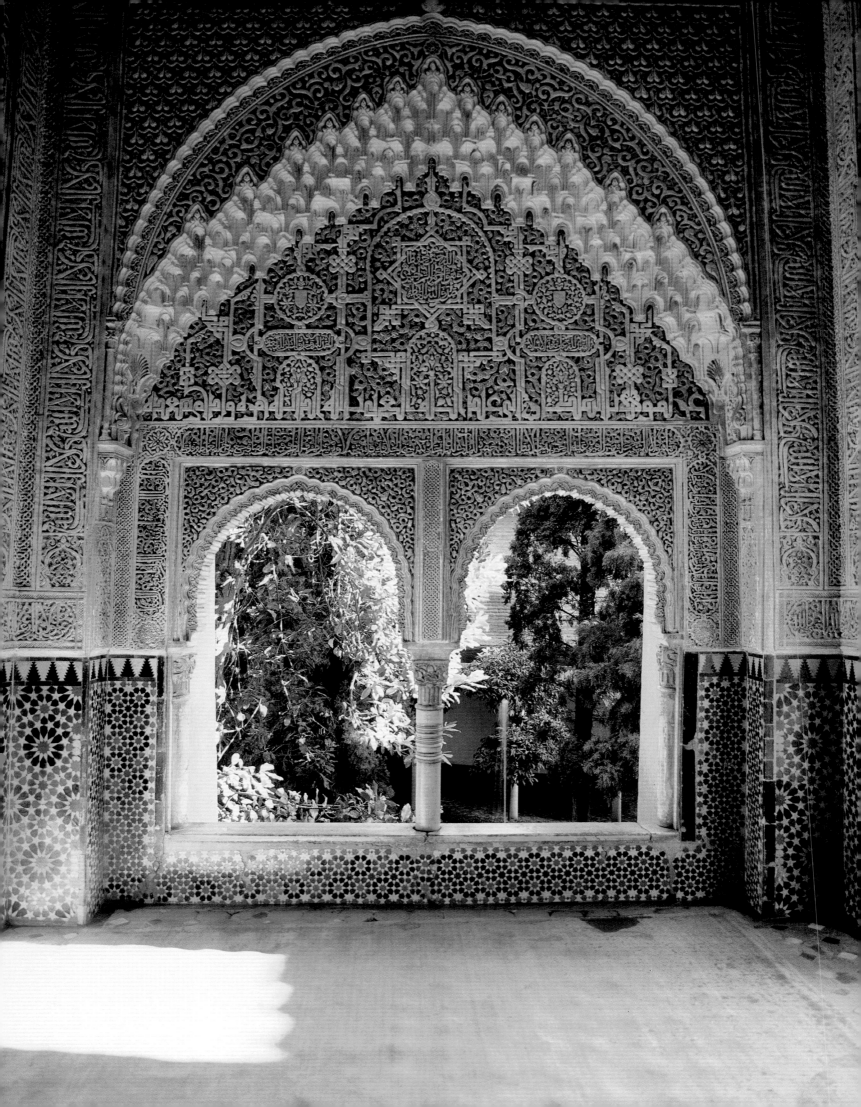

Yusuf I (ruled 1333–54) sat in majesty on a throne that would have been placed within the alcove. Even the Quranic inscriptions and the decoration were carefully selected to match: the verse at the base of the ceiling refers to the Creator of the seven heavens, and above in the inlaid wooden ceiling are seven levels of stars.

THE PALACE OF THE LIONS

The layout of the Palace of the Lions is very different from that of the Palace of the Myrtles, with an arcaded courtyard in which water channels arranged in a cross form four parterres. The channels, fed by a basin supported by the lions that give the palace its name (see illustration, page 78), lead on the long axis to small pavilions, and on the sides to two rooms each of which is capped with the most spectacular *muqarnas* domes ever built. The many windows at the base of the domes enable the myriad facets of the *muqarnas* dome to reflect the changing light as it revolves during the course of the day.

A short distance from the main palace lies the Generalife gardens, in fact the remains of a more informal summer palace built by Isma'il I (ruled 1314–25). Its main courtyard, like the Court of the Lions, has a quadripartite garden with sunken beds. An Italian traveller of the early 1500s saw myrtle beds and orange trees there, now replaced by more colorful plants. The water jets that line the central canal are also modern, but the same traveller reported a nearby fountain that shot 33ft (10m) into the air. The play of water in these gardens is seen in the steep stairway descending the hill above them; its handrails are channels in which the water was controlled by sluices from above, enabling a gentle flow or splashing waterfalls that provoked amusement by soaking the guests.

OPPOSITE
"In this garden I am an eye," begins the poem in the Lindaraja *mirador* (belvedere) in the Palace of the Lions, emphasizing its view looking on to the garden, and, when it was originally built, beyond to Granada below.

BELOW
Now isolated, the pool and pavilions beyond it were originally part of the Partal palace, most of which has long gone. It was built in the reign of Muhammad III (ruled 1302–09).

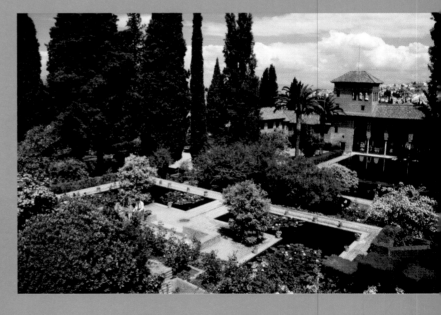

MUD MOSQUES OF THE DESERT

SUB-SAHARAN AFRICA

The Arabs were great seafarers and quickly spread Islam along the African coasts. In addition Islam was carried overland by Berber tribes into sub-Saharan Africa, with substantial populations emerging along the major trade routes, such as at Timbuktu. This was an important city within the successive medieval empires of Ghana and Mali, prospering from trade in gold, slaves, and salt. In the fourteenth century the Sankore mosque in Timbuktu was transformed into a madrasa and its fame as a center of learning quickly grew as it was joined by other madrasas.

One of the most original styles of mosque design is exemplified by the Great Mosque (Friday mosque) of Djenné, also in Mali, 220 miles (354km) southwest of Timbuktu. The town is at the juncture of savannah and desert, and the building is similarly a merging of architectural styles. A mosque existed in this spot as early as the 1200s; the present one dates from 1907, but sketches of the earlier mosque by a French visitor of 1896 show many of the same characteristics, including the large covered prayer hall and massive buttressed walls. Its monumentality is enhanced by the plinth on which it stands, designed to protect it from the city's annual floods.

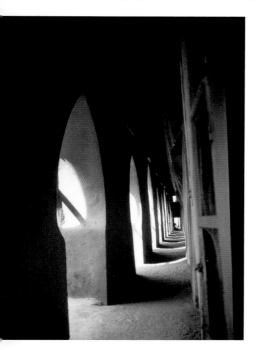

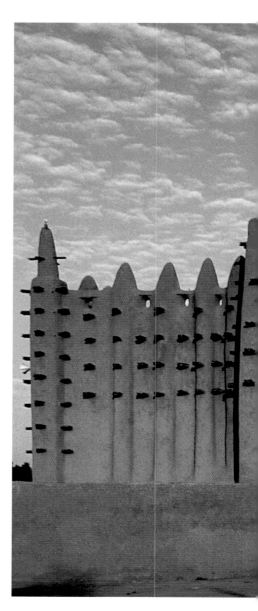

Three colossal towers on the *qibla* side dominate the façade. Its ranks of projecting palm beams, crenellations, and pilasters create the impression of a fortress. Because mud brick is used as a building material throughout, the interior of the prayer hall is remarkable for the massiveness of its ninety closely spaced piers, supporting low pointed arches. This has the disadvantage of leading to an almost claustrophobic space with limited sight lines and little light; however, the materials make a wonderful insulator, keeping the interior cool all year round.

OPPOSITE, BELOW
The mud brick building materials of the Great Mosque of Djenné, Mali, are packed together densely to ensure that they can support the great height of the building, which produces an almost claustrophobic interior space.

BELOW
The vertical accents of the towers of the *qibla* wall of Djenné's Great Mosque are vigorously counterpointed by the horizontality of the projecting wooden scaffolding beams embedded in the façade. However, the scaffolding is not merely decorative; it also serves the structural purpose of keeping the mosque upright. Each year the community celebrates with a festival when people help to apply a new mud coating to repair damage done both by rains and dehydration.

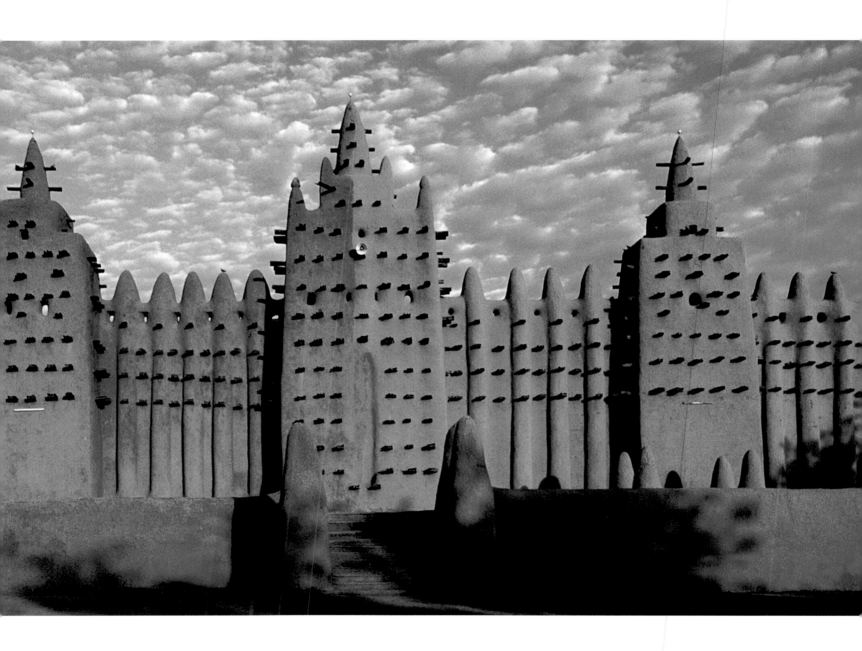

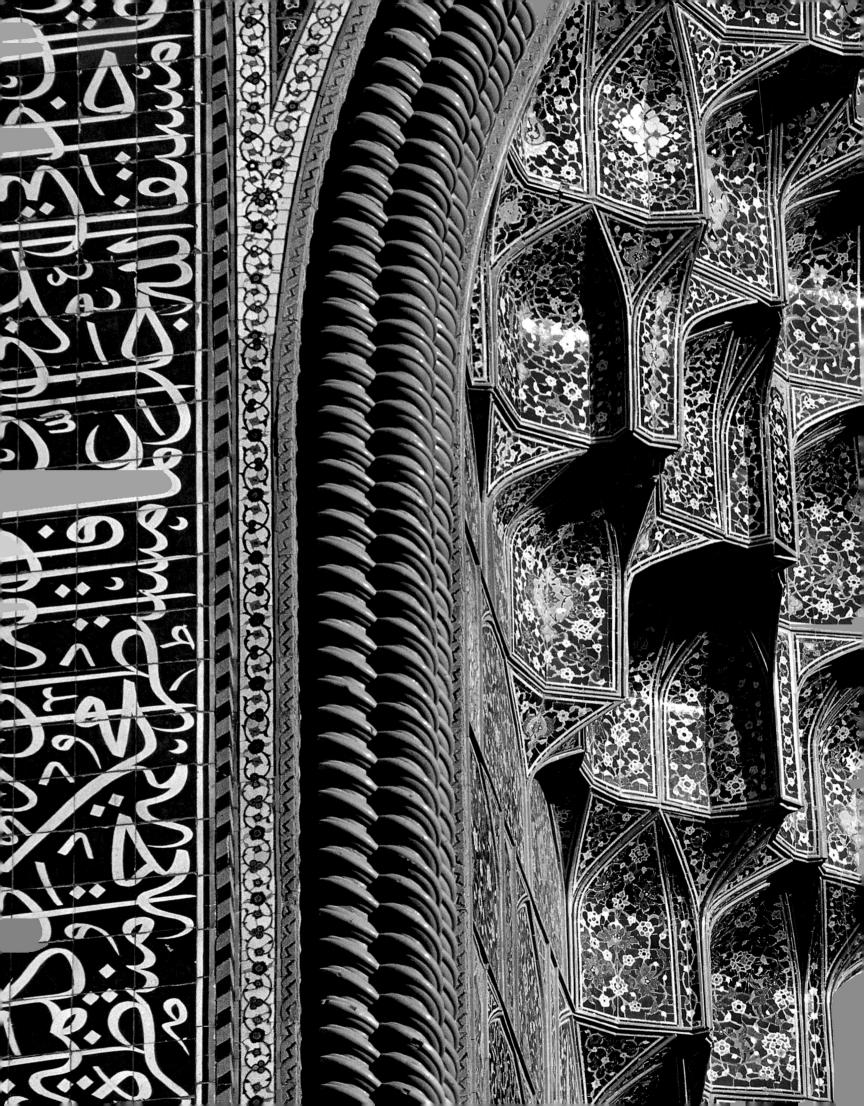

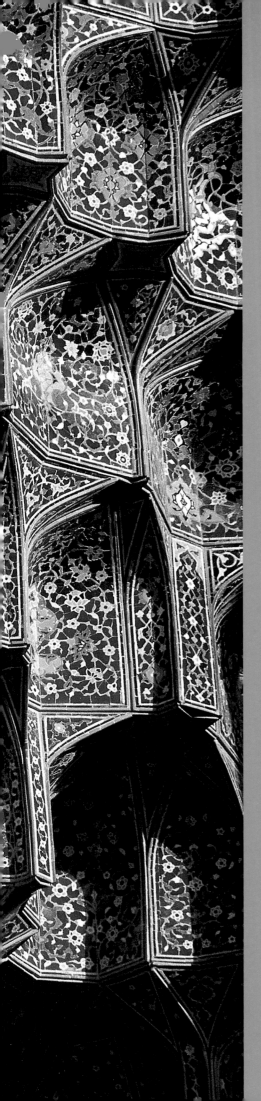

chapter 5

SULTAN
AND SHAH

IRAN AND CENTRAL ASIA

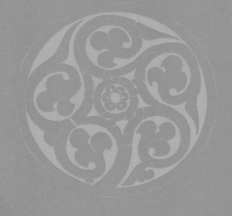

IRAN FOR THE IRANIANS

THE SAMANIDS AND BUYIDS

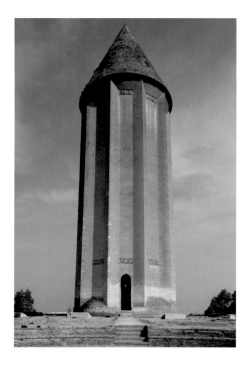

ABOVE

Immortality in death. Like the greatest funerary monuments, this both celebrates and defies death. Its concentration on form at the expense of decoration gives it a very modern aesthetic. Tomb tower of Qabus (dated 1007), Gunbad-i Qabus, Iran.

The centrifugal tendencies that led to the break-up of the 'Abbasid empire (see page 47) were apparent at an early date in Iran. Although it would be simplistic to think of this in terms of Persian nationalism, the Samanids, one of the earliest independent dynasties (819–1005), were among the first to patronize Persian poets. The most famous of them was Firdausi, the author of the *Book of Kings* (*Shahnama*), the Iranian national epic, which in 60,000 couplets traces the history of Iran from its mythological beginnings to the end of the Sasanian period in the seventh century. When book painting became popular in the thirteenth century, the *Book of Kings* was one of the first texts to which paintings were added.

The territory ruled by the Samanids spanned the area from the heart of Iran to the borders of Islamic dominion in Central Asia. Across these borders were the pagan Turks, a fruitful source of slave-soldiers who had earlier filled the armies of the 'Abbasids in Baghdad and who also rose to positions of responsibility in the Samanid army. Having converted to Islam, many achieved martyrdom fighting the Central Asian pagans, and the desire to commemorate these warriors who died for the faith may explain why this area has an unusually large number of mausoleums, a building type that was sometimes viewed with suspicion by the religious orthodoxy.

Under the Samanids a new style of ceramics arose, one in which writing played a major role. Plates and bowls are provided with epigraphs, or inscriptions, usually consisting of pious phrases or maxims such as "generosity is a quality of the people of paradise," arranged in a circular format. The black letters are sometimes the only decoration on the white base, providing a stark contrast whose minimalist aesthetic has great appeal to modern sensibilities. Other examples decorate the lettering with knotting or floral terminals, or balance it with vegetal elements.

BELOW

Pre-Islamic survivals. The main motif at the center of this octagonal silver plate is the hippogriff, a Sasanian mythical hybrid creature of auspicious import, somewhat resembling the griffin of Western tradition. However, the lack of relief contrasts with Sasanian silver plates (see page 14), suggesting that this is instead an early Islamic example.

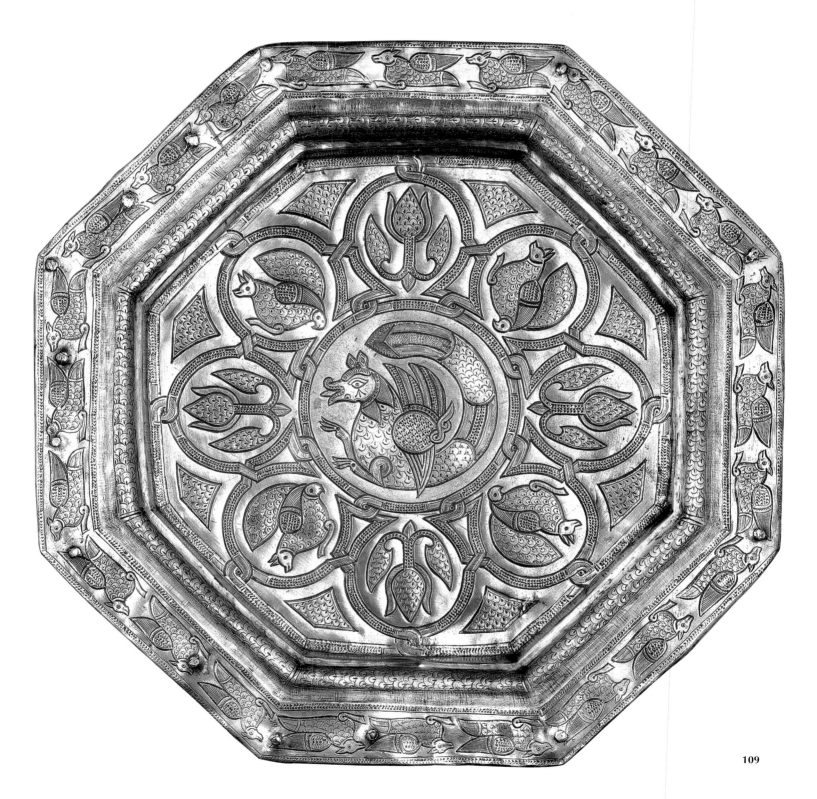

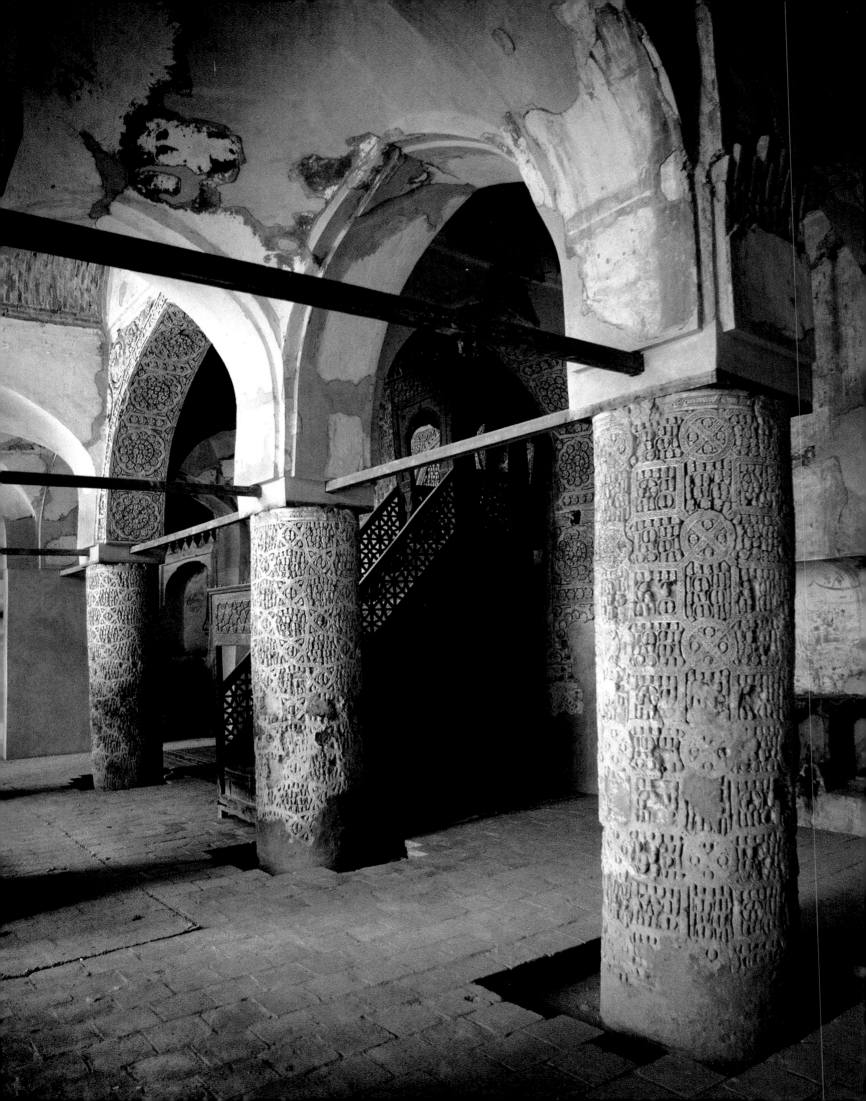

Vineyard in the desert. God's
bounty in providing products
of the earth is a frequent theme
in the Quran, here matched
visually by the grape-draped
piers of the Friday Mosque of
Nayin, Iran (ca. 960).

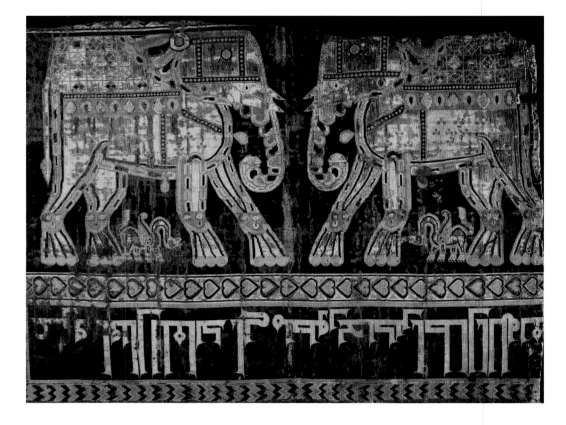

SHI'ISM IN THE ASCENDANT: THE BUYIDS

In the meantime in central Iran another dynasty, the Buyids (932–1062), gained power after expanding from their base in the mountainous region that lies to the south of the Caspian Sea. They are distinguished from their contemporaries by being the first important Shi'ite dynasty to rule a substantial territory, one that even included Baghdad, the seat of the 'Abbasid caliphate. Like the Samanids, the Buyids also attempted to link themselves with the Iranian past by concocting a fictitious genealogy that connected them with their Sasanian predecessors.

Little architecture remains from this time, but one of the most charming buildings in Iran, the Friday Mosque of Nayin (built ca. 960), has stucco in the bay in front of the *mihrab* that shows us the riches that have been lost from other buildings. The undulating borders framing the vines on the circular piers can be read as a combination of octagons and quatrefoils, but the borders also deconstruct themselves by weaving over and under their neighbors in parallel directions so that from any one viewpoint their extremities are invisible—a wonderful example of the visual ambiguity that characterizes much of the finest Islamic decoration.

ABOVE

The inscription says that this silk was made for the Turkish commander of the Samanid army, Abu Mansur Bukhtagin (executed in 961). It displays richly caparisoned elephants which, imported from India, were part of the Samanid army. They appear here for the first time in Islamic art.

IRAN FOR THE TURKS

THE GHAZNAVIDS AND SELJUKS

OPPOSITE

The rounded forms of the letters here are the first monumental example of *naskhi* script known in the Islamic world. Its ease of legibility soon made it commonplace. Detail of cenotaph from the mausoleum of the early Ghaznavid sultan Mahmud (died 1030), Ghazna, Afghanistan. The cenotaph is also notable for its fine ornamental carving.

Toward the end of the tenth century the Turkish governors who ruled the remote outpost of Ghazna in eastern Afghanistan on behalf on the Samanids became powerful enough to assert their independence. The empire of the Ghaznavid dynasty (977–1186) quickly expanded to become one of the largest of its time, at its peak in the mid-eleventh century stretching from central Iran to northern India. India was raided for booty and slaves, and its elephants were also a coveted addition to Muslim armies.

Among the few Ghaznavid buildings still to be seen at Ghazna are the remains of two spectacular minarets with unusual star-shaped bases. Old drawings show them with circular upper tiers; even though these disappeared over a century ago, what is left displays some of the finest terracotta ornamentation known. In this technique small ornamental pieces are molded or cut and added as a surface facing (revetment). The panels at the top of the earlier minaret proclaim the name of Sultan Mas'ud III (ruled 1099–1115). The second minaret is plainer than the first—surprisingly, since it is the work of Mas'ud's son, Bahramshah (ruled 1117–50, 1152–57). Sultans generally strove to outdo their predecessors, but Bahramshah's empire was partially overrun by another dynasty, the Ghurids (1100–1215), from mountainous central Afghanistan, so he may have lacked the funds for a work to compete with that of his father.

The Ghurids themselves produced (1175) one of the most spectacular minarets ever built at their capital, Jam, Afghanistan, in an area now difficult to access (see illustration, page 114). The Ghurids also ruled Herat at a time when a relatively new way to decorate metalwork was being exploited, using silver and copper inlay to create color contrasts, and incising the silver to add detail to a wide range of figural decoration.

THE TRIUMPH OF ORTHODOXY: THE SELJUKS

Partly coterminal with the Ghurids, the Seljuks were a Turkish tribe living in the Central Asian steppes who had converted to Islam at the end of the tenth century. The struggles of the Samanids, Buyids, and Ghaznavids left a power vacuum that the Seljuks were eager

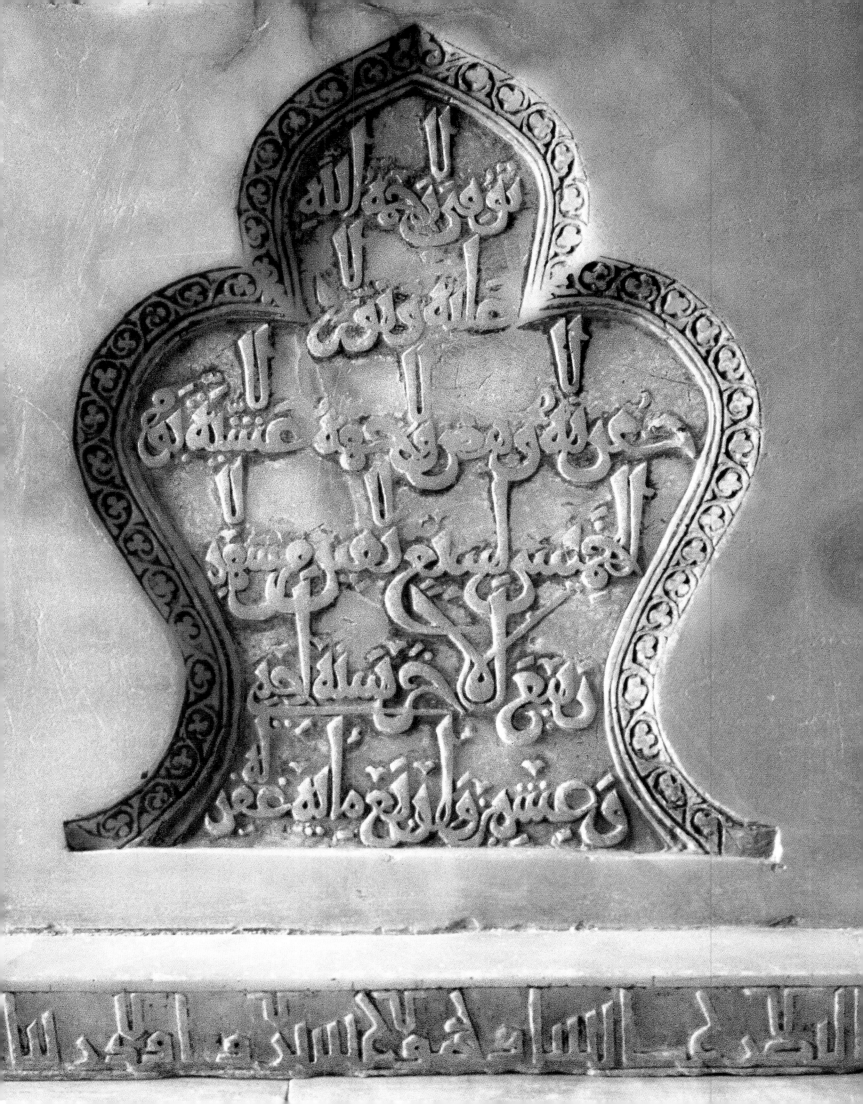

LEFT, BELOW

Victory tower or minaret? The isolation of this stunning brick tower (213ft/65m in height, dated 1175) has led to different interpretations of its purpose. However, the recent excavation of an adjacent large courtyard building suggests that the conventional explanation—that the tower is the minaret of the Friday Mosque of Jam, the Ghurid capital in the center of Afghanistan—is the most likely one.

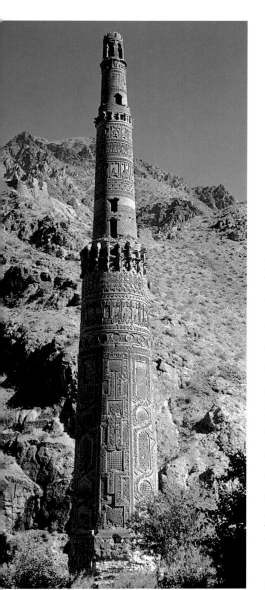

to fill. In under two decades they moved from Central Asia to Baghdad, arriving there in 1055 as the champions of orthodoxy, freeing the caliphate from the Shi'i Buyids.

One means by which the Seljuk dynasty (1040–1194) tried to counter Shi'i propaganda was the madrasa, a school where orthodox religious sciences were taught, but which also furnished many government bureaucrats. Nizam al-Mulk, an important vizier of the time, reputedly sponsored a madrasa in every major town in the realm. It went on to become one of the most important building types in Islamic architecture.

ARCHITECTURAL INNOVATIONS

The Friday Mosque in the Seljuk capital, Isfahan, was probably the first place to see one of the period's most lasting innovations: the addition to the Arab hypostyle mosque plan of first a dome chamber (sponsored by Nizam al-Mulk) on the *qibla* side, followed by the insertion of four *iwans* (vaulted halls open on one side) around the courtyard. This combination of elements remained typical of Iranian mosques for centuries. Some earlier mosques had dome chambers in the bay in front of the *mihrab*, but the Isfahan one took up the space of sixteen bays, creating what was then the largest masonry dome chamber in the Islamic world. The patron, Malikshah, visited the Great Mosque of Damascus in 1086 and may have been inspired by its dome to build an even more magnificent one in his capital. Exceptionally, the mosque also has another Seljuk dome chamber on the north side, built in 1088 by Taj al-Mulk, a rival of Nizam al-Mulk. This one is smaller, but more elegantly proportioned; it is particularly successful in the design of the vaulting, starting with the dome with its unique five-pointed star pattern. This dome chamber originally stood outside the mosque; the Quranic quotations relating to justice on its walls perhaps suggest that it was used for the presentation of petitions to the vizier, deputizing for the sultan.

As primarily spaces for prayer, it makes sense that mosques should be as unimpeded as possible to allow the faithful to line up in rows for prayer and be able to see the *imam* (prayer

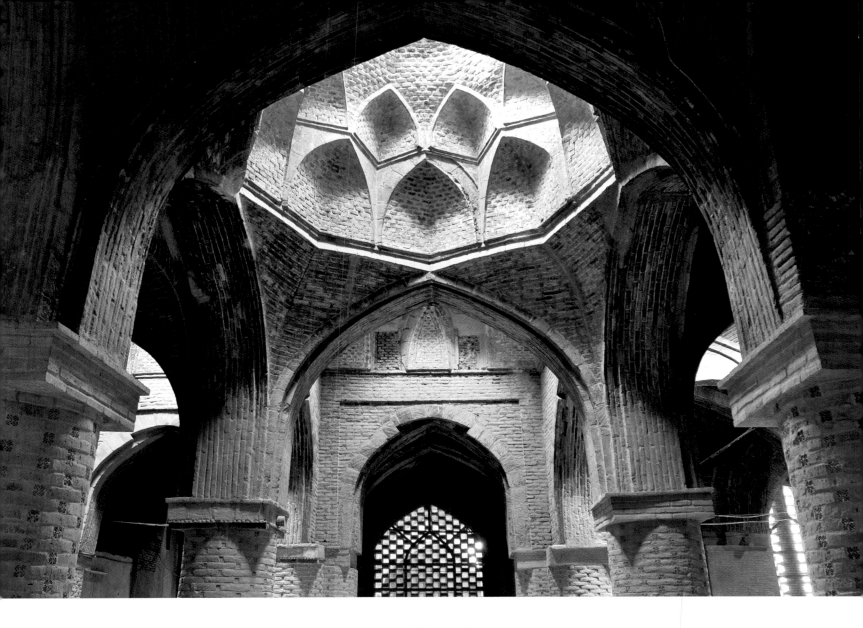

leader). The *iwans*, perhaps added after a fire in 1121, nullify both objectives, so there must have been strong reasons for their introduction, such as the need for a more defined space for teaching. Another, purely aesthetic, reason might have been to break up the repetitive hypostyle courtyard façade, while also emphasizing the axes of the *iwans* across from each other.

The same concern for monumentality seen in Nizam al-Mulk's domed chamber is found in the even larger mausoleum of the Seljuk sultan Sanjar (ruled 1118–57) in Merv, Turkmenistan. Of course smaller mausoleums continued to be built, among the most attractive being two tomb towers at Kharraqan (1067 and 1093), which display some seventy types of brickwork patterns. The interior of one has painted plaster decorated with images including peacocks, lamps, and stars, all possibly related to paradise. The death of Sultan Sanjar in 1157 was followed by a political fragmentation that greatly facilitated the conquest of Iran by the Mongols in the next century.

ABOVE

Under the Seljuks the Friday Mosque of Isfahan changed from a traditional hypostyle plan to the classical Iranian one with four *iwans* and a *qibla* dome chamber. In the 12th century some of the mosque's hypostyle areas were also rebuilt with more spacious bays and innovative vaults, as here.

SELJUK CERAMICS AND METALWORK

RICHES OF THE EARTH

In any museum with a comprehensive collection of Islamic art, objects from the Seljuk period, especially pottery and metalwork, are likely to be in among the most numerous. Despite the uneasy truce which held between the Fatimids and the Seljuks, trade seems to have thrived in this period, and increasing prosperity may have been one of the reasons why so many works of art of this kind were produced. Most of them are dedicated to anonymous patrons rather than rulers, making it more likely that a new urban middle class was in a position to buy and commission more works of art than in previous centuries. Surprisingly, most of the material from this period dates to the late twelfth and early thirteenth centuries, when the Seljuk state had broken up into a number of smaller kingdoms.

The Fatimids were the first to employ stonepaste for their pottery, which involved a switch from a clay-based body to a quartz-based body, enabling it to be both stronger and whiter. The Seljuks capitalized on this new technology, producing bodies with a previously unparalleled delicacy and translucence. The spur may well have been pottery from China; although the kaolin clay used to make the porcelain body of Chinese wares was not available in Persia, the use of stonepaste enabled the production of ceramics that were a close visual substitute.

Some of the monochrome-glazed wares have shapes with scalloped edges directly derived from Chinese prototypes. Previous potters in the Islamic world could not refrain from adding decoration to a plain surface, but it is in some of the Seljuk examples that the appreciation of the object purely for its form is first seen in Islamic ceramics.

Underglaze-painted wares benefited greatly from the stonepaste body, as the glaze bonded more closely with the body and permitted the underlying colors to reflect the light

RIGHT

"Jealous of the splendor of your face, the full moon of the 14th night expresses astonishment," reads a verse on this early 13th-century luster-painted Seljuk bowl made in Kashan, Iran. The gazelle is a poetic metaphor for a beautiful girl, so the presence of love poetry is not so surprising.

BELOW

Seljuk imitation of Chinese wares was not limited to the thin translucent body made possible by the new stonepaste, but is also found in some patterns, such as the underglaze water-weed motif on both the interior and exterior of this early 13th-century bowl.

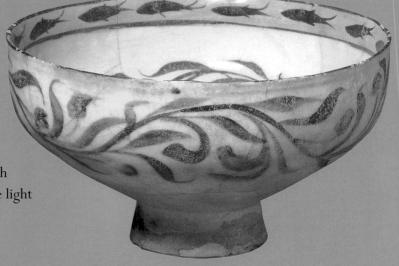

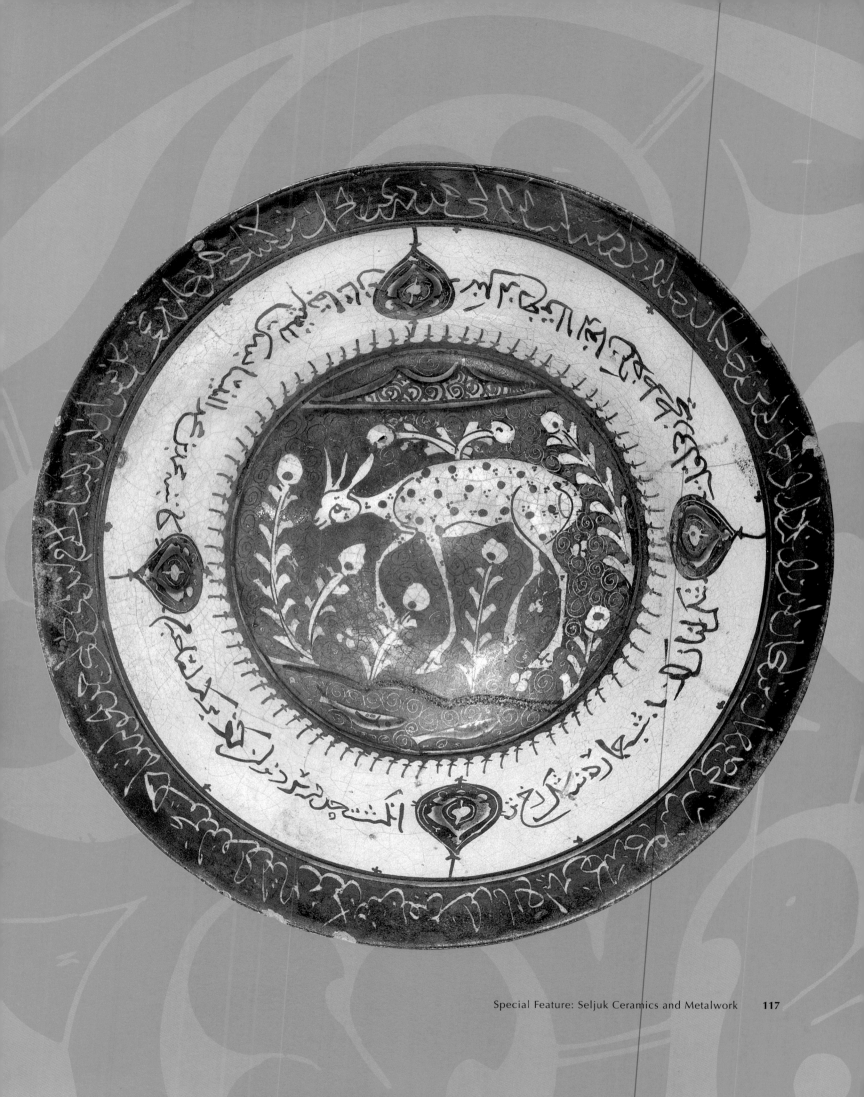

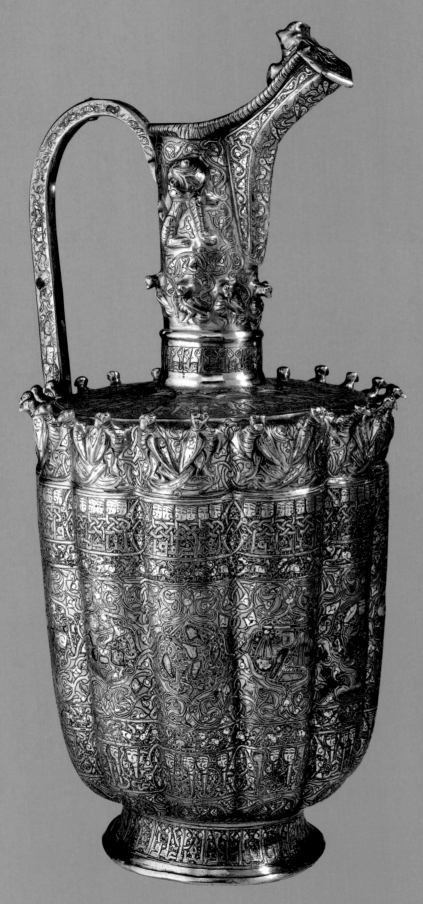

LEFT
The 12 sides of this sumptuous
ewer display medallions with
astrological signs of the planets.
Even more impressive are the
birds and lions, raised from
the sheet metal by hammering
out from behind. Copper alloy,
incised and inlaid with silver,
Herat, Afghanistan, ca. 1200.

with a greater intensity. These continued the main color
scheme of blue and white used in 'Abbasid pottery, but
radial designs were now more popular.

DOUBLE-FIRED CERAMICS

One of the innovations of the Seljuks was the production
of overglaze-enamel wares, usually called by the Persian
word for enamel, *minai*. These wares were fired twice,
once for the white glazed base and a second time for the
enamels. The second firing had to be at a low enough
temperature to stop the enamels from running on the
surface, and had the disadvantage of resulting in a matt
appearance. But this was more than offset by the ability
to paint in a variety of brilliant colors on the surface,
including illustrations from the *Book of Kings* as well as
enthronements and other court scenes.

The most prestigious Seljuk pottery was luster, a
technique that also required two firings, the second in a
smoke-filled kiln in order to withdraw oxygen from the
silver or copper oxide used in the glaze. The kiln had to be
at just the right temperature for just the right amount of
time, and the difficulties in getting the technique exactly
right would have contributed to its expense, but the end
product justified the cost, having a brilliant surface sheen,
imperceptible to the touch, of highly reflective metal.
Painterly effects were also possible with this technique,
with scenes often accommodating a multitude of figures.

INLAID METALWORK

Although the technique of inlaying metalwork had been known in earlier centuries, it was not fully exploited until the Seljuk period. In addition to the color contrasts of the silver and copper inlay against the brass ground, it was possible to incise the silver to produce fine detail, as on a spectacular ewer made in Herat in what is now Afghanistan and dated to ca. 1200 (see illustration, opposite). This wine vessel has twelve sides, each featuring medallions containing astrological images, as well as raised images of birds and lions achieved by beating the metal from behind. It is also adorned with benedictory inscriptions in a variety of ornamental scripts.

On another remarkable example, a bucket (used for washing in bathhouses) dated 1163, two bands contain images, including figures drinking, playing backgammon, and fighting on horseback. The bucket illustrates another recent innovation: the use of animated inscriptions, whose uprights end in human heads and with animal heads among the lower parts of the letters. The novelty and value of such vessels is seen in a poem inscribed on a ewer in the Tiflis Museum, Georgia, of which this is an extract:

> "My beautiful ewer, pleasant and elegant,
> In the world of today who can find the like?
> Everyone who sees it says 'It is very beautiful' ....
> Glance at the ewer, a spirit comes to life out of it,
> And this is living water that flows from it."

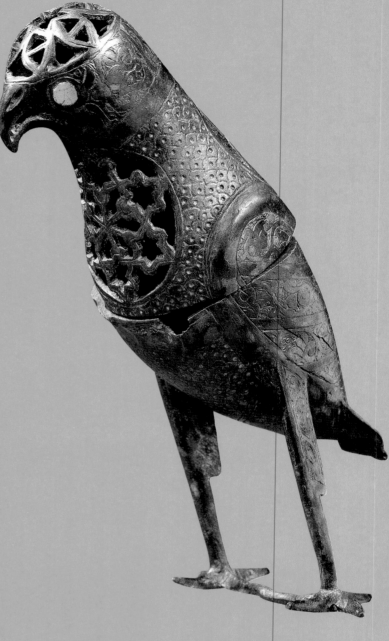

ABOVE
Seljuk craftsmen are known to have produced a series of metal zoomorphic incense burners, of which this may be one of the last examples. The eyes of inlaid turquoise glass paste are an unusual touch. Cast copper alloy, incised, possibly from Herat, Afghanistan, ca. 1200.

HEIRS OF CHINGHIS KHAN

THE COMING OF THE MONGOLS

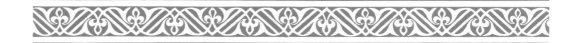

Early 14th-century luster-painted tiles from Kashan, Iran. The tile opposite depicts a peacock, "Sultan of the Good and Righteous," as one medieval author described it. Its many connotations included a dweller in paradise, a symbol of royal gardens, and, from its lustrous fanned tail, the sun. The tiles below include part of a Quranic inscription, "There is no God but He, the Mighty." The uprights of the letters are extended and knotted to provide a frame for the finely drawn floral scroll.

The Mongol invasions were initially a catastrophe for the Islamic world. When Chingis Khan's ambassadors were murdered in northern Iran in 1218, he retaliated by sending his sons at the head of armies of an unprecedented size. Any city that refused to capitulate was sacked and its inhabitants slaughtered. The caliph himself was murdered when Baghdad was taken by Hulagu in a second campaign in 1258.

The Mongol khans that ruled Iran from 1256 to 1336 are known as the Ilkhanids. It took only four decades for the conquerors to be assimilated to Perseo-Islamic urban culture, and in 1292 Ghazan Khan (ruled 1294–1304) converted to Islam and ordered a mosque to be built in every town. The greatest of Ilkhanid mausoleums was the twelve-sided tomb tower that Ghazan Khan built for himself in a vast complex next to Tabriz. It was around 69ft (21m) in diameter and almost 180ft (55m) in height, but like most medieval buildings in Tabriz, it has disappeared—the city is at the center of an active earthquake zone.

Some idea of its magnificence can be gained from the mausoleum of Ghazan Khan's brother and successor, Uljaytu (ruled 1304–16), in the new capital of Sultaniyya. It remains the largest mausoleum in the Islamic world,

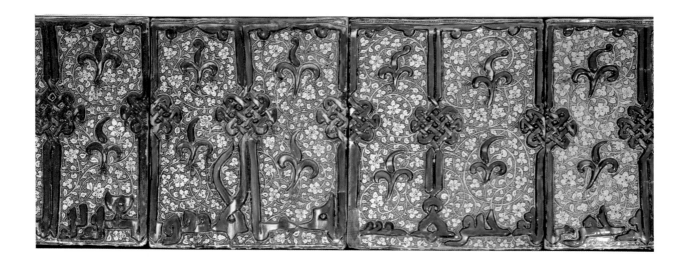

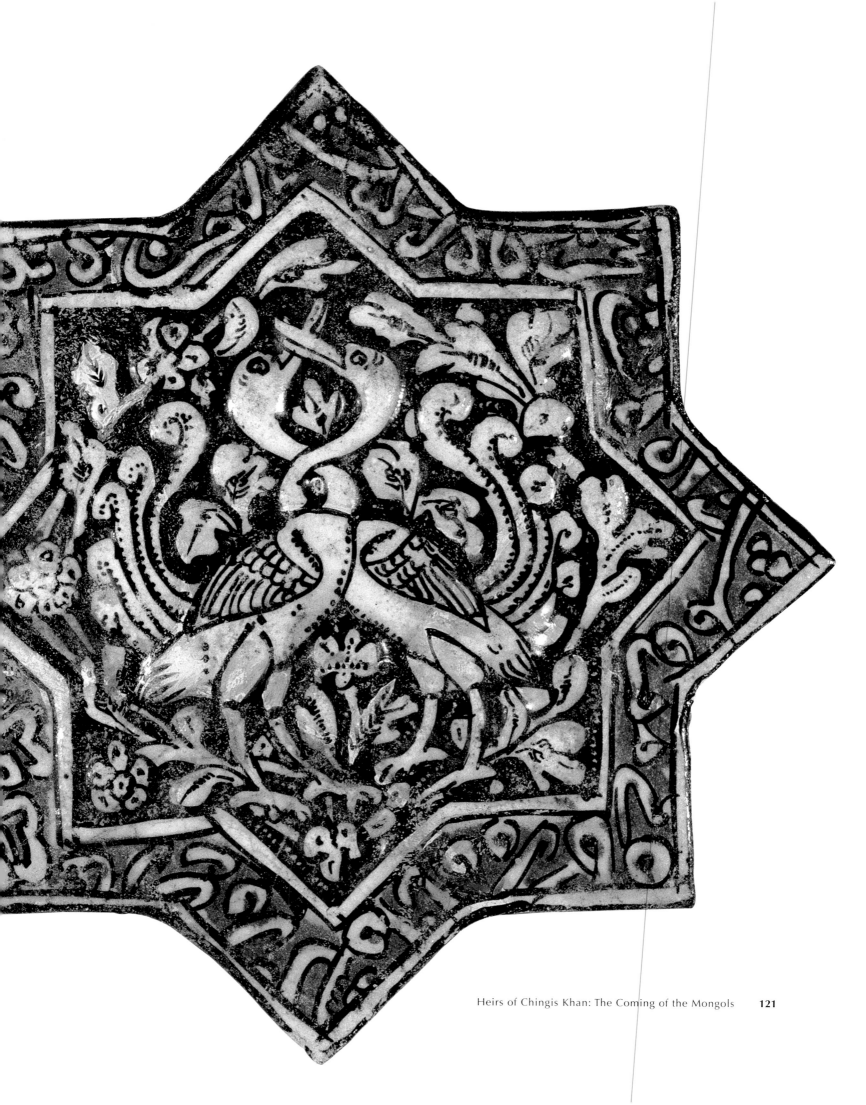

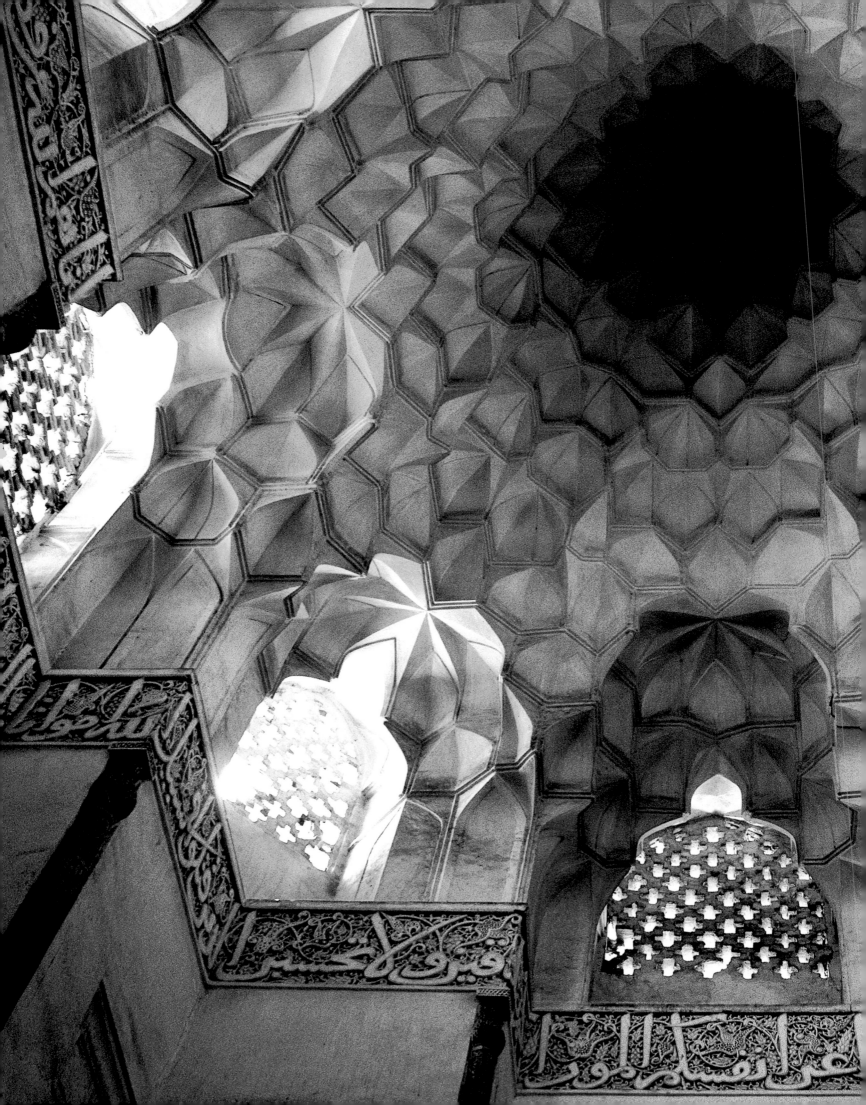

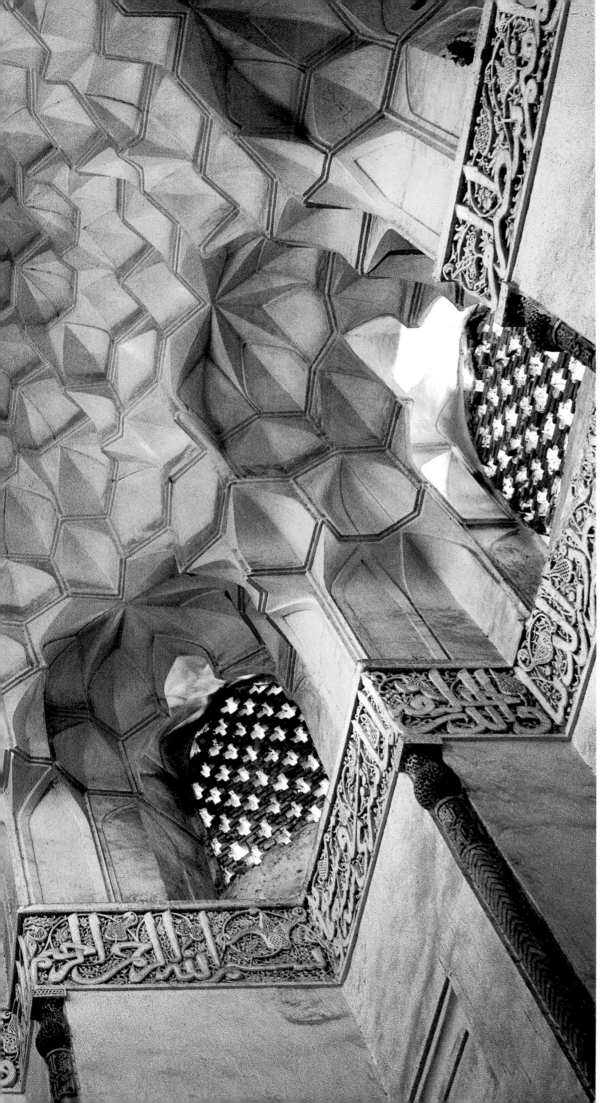

LEFT

This mausoleum at Natanz, Iran, was built for 'Abd al-Samad, a Sufi of the Suhrawardiyya order. One of his eminent forebears in the order, 'Umar al-Suhrawardi, is buried in Baghdad under a shrine with an elaborate *muqarnas* dome. The choice of the intricate *muqarnas* dome here, at Natanz, may have been inspired by the earlier example. Ilkhanid period, 1308.

RIGHT

The trickster tricked. The householder managed to convince a thief to attempt to slide down a moonbeam—onto his waiting cudgel. The painter conveys an almost tactile feel for the textures of the woven bedspread, tiled dado, stucco window grille, and Chinese blossoms in the margin. Nasr Allah, *Kalila and Dimna*, a painting cut from a manuscript and mounted as an album page. Jalayirid, ca. 1370–74.

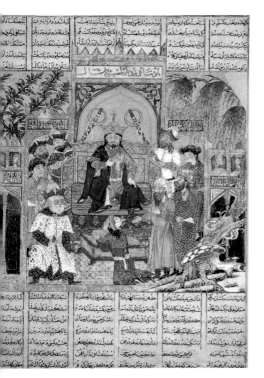

ABOVE

"The reign of Zav son of Tahmasp was five years," says the caption at the top of this illustration to Firdausi's *Book of Kings*. The blue rocks and red fungus in the landscape are symbols of fortune borrowed from Chinese painting. Tabriz, Iran, ca. 1330–35.

82ft (25m) wide and 164ft (50m) high. Its upper galleries, decorated with superb stucco, prefigure those that appear three centuries later on the Taj Mahal (see pages 200–203). A unique feature was the eight minarets crowning the corners of the exterior.

The decoration of the interior was also outstanding, with innovative tilework, mainly of geometric design, covering most of the wall surfaces. Shortly before Uljaytu died, this tilework was hidden beneath a painted plaster coating with Quranic inscriptions related to Mecca and Madina. It used to be thought that Uljaytu, having converted to Shi'ism, originally planned the monument as a tomb and shrine for Shi'i martyrs, but then renounced his conversion and redesigned the mausoleum for himself. However, there is no evidence of his renunciation of Shi'ism from contemporary sources. It is more likely that he wished to update the inscriptions because of his aspirations to control the holy cities of Mecca and Madina: just before he died, Uljaytu launched an army to support rebels there who were favorable to him.

THE SHRINE BENEATH THE PLANE TREE

The team of tileworkers that built the mausoleum of Uljaytu may also have been responsible for the earlier shrine of 'Abd al-Samad (early fourteenth century; see previous pages) at Natanz, one of the loveliest of Iranian villages. Shaded by a venerable plane tree are the remains of the entrance to the *khanaqah*, a building that housed Sufis and only one of many such *khanaqah*s that were built in this period. These institutions frequently provided funds for distribution to the poor, and visiting Sufis from other lands could usually stay for free within them for at least three days, as recorded in the fourteenth century in the account of the greatest Muslim traveller, Ibn Battuta. The white walls of the tomb would have provided a strong contrast with the colorful luster tiles of the dado, now sadly dispersed in numerous museum collections around the world. Light is filtered from above through eight grilled windows and also percolates upward, where it slowly diffuses into the penumbra at the top of the *muqarnas* (faceted) dome.

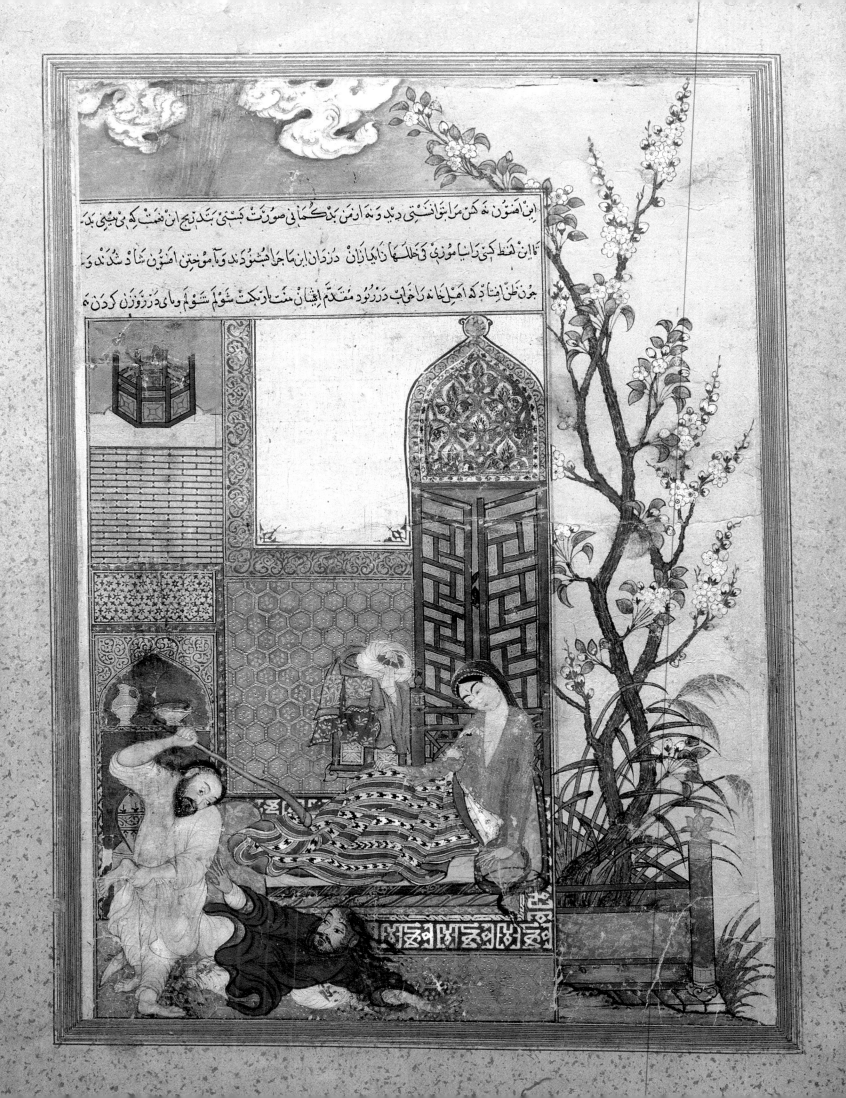

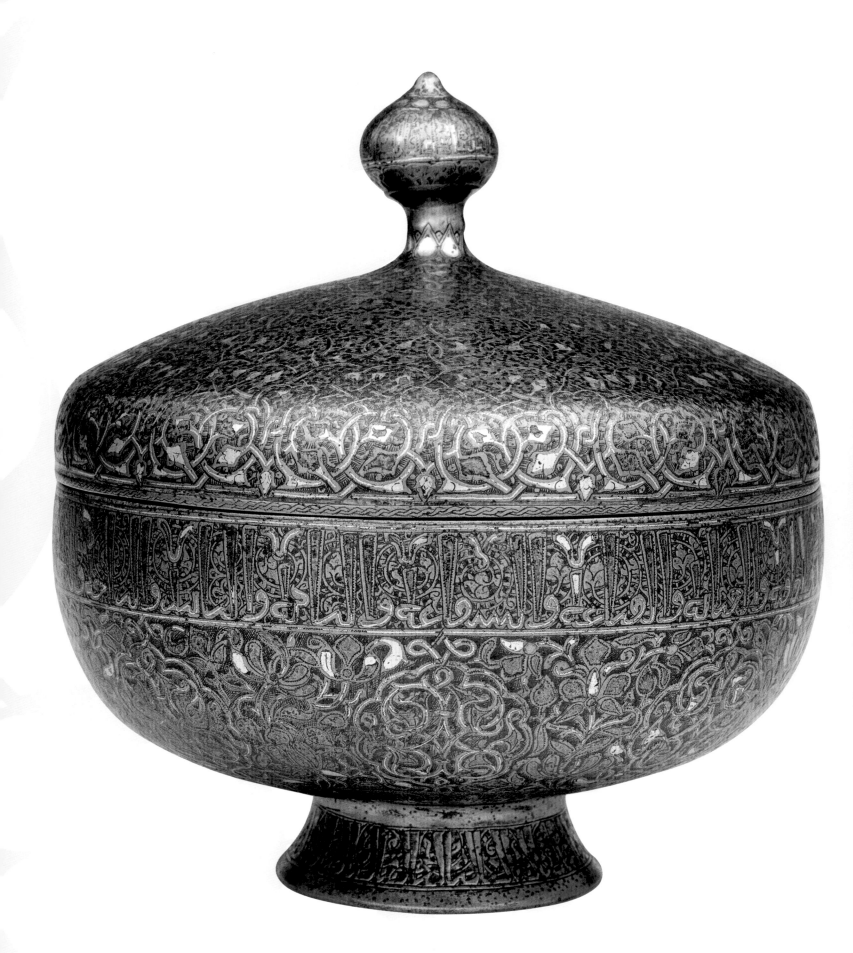

LEFT
Most lidded cups of this type
date from Seljuk times, but the
stylized Chinese lotuses that
adorn the base argue for the
Ilkhanid period. Copper alloy,
incised, engraved, and inlaid
with silver, copper, and niello.
Herat (?), Afghanistan, ca. 1265.

The trend toward monumentality is seen in the mosque that the vizier 'Alishah erected in Tabriz ca.1320. Only a fragment of one vault remains, but it was designed to be wider and taller than the largest similar vault (and still the world's largest standing brick vault)—that of the Sasanian palace at Ctesiphon (see page 16). Its sheer size may have been its undoing, for the Tabriz vault fell not long after its completion. 'Alishah's mosque was also remarkable on account of its courtyard with a large pool, at the center of which was an octagonal dome with fountains in the form of lions. There were even four boats within the pool, providing a leisure activity more indicative of a palace than a mosque.

Like many previous dynasties, the Ilkhanids patronized the makers of large Quran manuscripts, but they also revolutionized the production of illustrated books. In earlier manuscripts any paintings had occupied a small fraction of the page. Now both the number and size of paintings within manuscripts increased, as best exemplified by the *Book of Kings* produced in the reign of Abu Sa'id (1316–35). Some sixty paintings survive out of as many as 200 originally. The page size is already much greater than in most previous manuscripts, but even so most of the paintings take up half of the page or more. There are many enthronement scenes, and also an unusual number of images from the story of Alexander the Great, the foreign conqueror and ruler of Iran whose history the Mongol patron may have seen as a parallel to his own.

The Ilkhanid dynasty collapsed with surprising speed upon the death of Abu Sa'id. Among the smaller dynasties that sprang up in its wake, the Jalayirids managed to retain control of two of the key cities in Ilkhanid territory, Tabriz and Baghdad, and probably inherited the Ilkhanid painting atelier. The Jalayridis are particularly renowned for their own patronage of painting, as we shall see in the next section.

ABOVE
Shadow of God on earth. This unique silk roundel depicts a ruler on a throne flanked by viziers representing the different spheres of government, men of the pen on the right and men of the sword on the left. The textile itself could have functioned as the lining of a royal parasol, like that seen above the throne. Ilkhanid Iran, early 14th century.

SIYAH QALAM

THE MASTER OF THE BLACK PEN

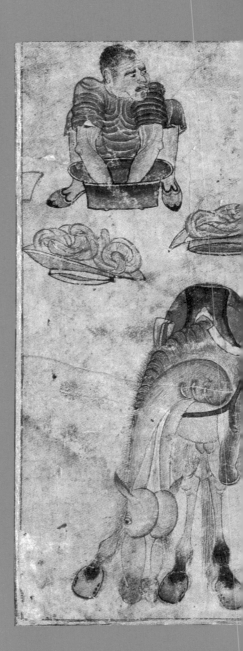

The name Siyah Qalam means "black pen" in Persian, and it is found, not as a signature, but as an attribution on many paintings in albums now in the former library of the Ottoman sultans, probably captured from the Safavids (see pages 138–143) in the early sixteenth century. These are among the most exciting and enigmatic examples of Islamic art, the product of an artist who incorporated elements from Western, Persian, and Chinese painting and transformed them into images of amazing power and originality.

The style and subject matter of these works immediately set them apart from mainstream Persian painting. They depict demons, nomads, and black people, drawn with a startling realism (if such a term can be appropriate for demons). Unlike the great majority of other paintings sponsored by Islamic patrons, they have no associated text. Equally unusual is the almost complete lack of setting for the figures portrayed.

Associated with the Siyah Qalam group are other large-scale paintings that have a little more in common with mainstream manuscript illustration. Many of these have features derived from Chinese paintings—a number of Chinese originals were also found in the albums. This second group contains pen and ink drawings as well as polychrome paintings. The diversity of these groups makes it likely that they were the work of several artists. Initial publications of this material posited a Central Asian origin; later research suggested fifteenth-century Iran, but the most recent study proposes an earlier date, at the court of the Jalayirid sultan Uvays (1356–74), a ruler of Mongol nomadic stock, whose main court was at Baghdad. One factor that has made dating the material so difficult is that up to four versions of some paintings are found in the albums, suggesting that they were templates used for practice by later generations of court artists.

It seems likely that the representation of nomads in the collection was the work of a city-dweller—no barefooted nomads, as depicted in the albums, are likely to have existed in medieval Iran or elsewhere. And indeed parts of the paintings, such as the princess in *Demons Carrying a Palanquin*, are in a style extremely close to book painting patronized by the Jalayirid court. The artist also made use of Western themes, such as

The Encampment. Although at first resembling an encampment depicting figures kneading dough, baking bread, attending to their saddles, and grazing horses, it is not clear if these are individual studies or were meant to be viewed as a coherent scene. Tabriz or Baghdad, Jalayirid period, ca. 1350–70.

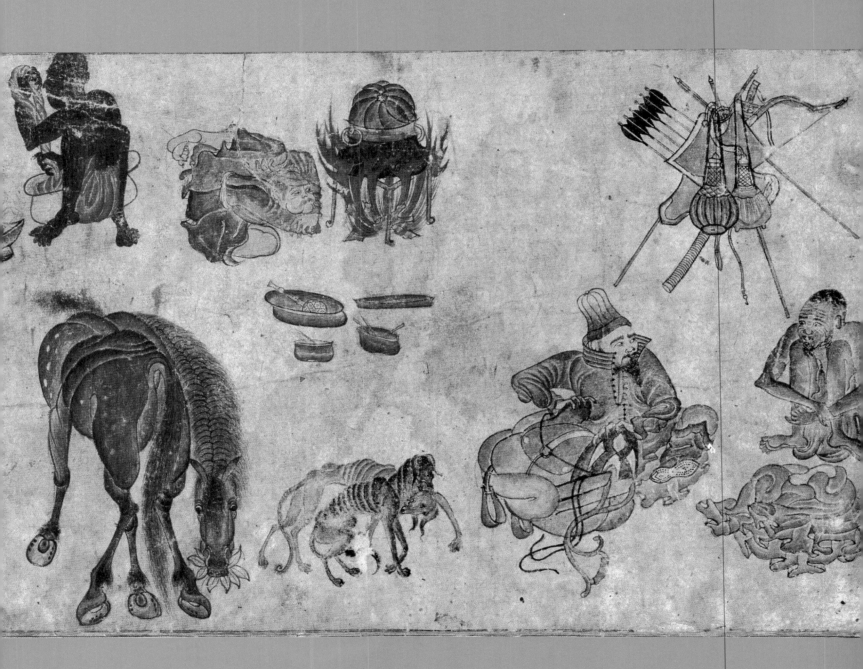

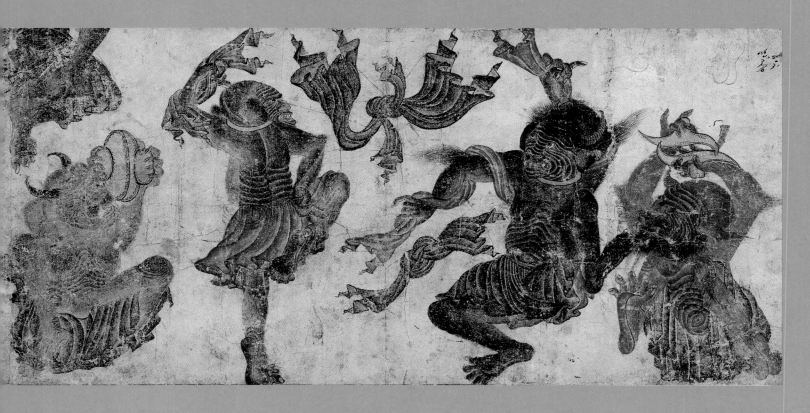

the figure of the lion-rider, similar to European representations of Samson strangling the lion, an image that could have been obtained from Italian merchants who were active in Baghdad and Tabriz in the first half of the thirteenth century, both under the Mongols and their successors, the Jalayirids.

A STORYTELLER'S ALBUM?

Who these paintings were created for is not an easy question to answer. Some, such as *Demons Carrying a Palanquin*, are painted on silk and are cut down, suggesting that their format was that of a scroll painting, one which could have been viewed only by a limited few, presumably at court. Others are on paper, such as *The Encampment*, although their size makes it unlikely that they were ever planned as illustrations for books. Many paintings seem to have a strong narrative content, although in most cases the stories represented are not known. A few can be identified as illustrations from Firdausi's *Book of Kings*. Others might be associated with the Quranic accounts of Sulayman (King Solomon),

Demons Carrying a Palanquin.
As they are unaccompanied
by texts, any identification of
the iconography of the Siyah
Qalam group of paintings must
be a guess. The Quran mentions
Solomon's army of demons,
so he and the Queen of Sheba
are possible candidates for the
figures in the palanquin. Painted
on silk, Tabriz or Baghdad,
Jalayirid period, ca. 1350–75.

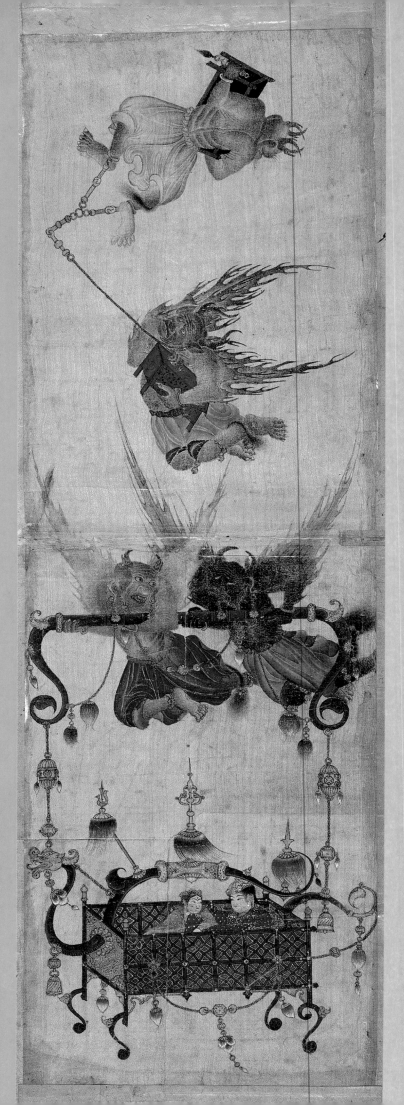

who was able to make demons (*djinn*) do his bidding. It
is not impossible that children of courtiers were one of
the intended audiences; but whether for children or their
parents, the frequently large size of the pictures could have
enhanced storytelling sessions to a select court audience.

It may be wondered why this material remained
such a great secret—why Siyah Qalam had so little impact
on later book painting in Iran. Firstly, perhaps, because the
images were unrelated to any one text and therefore not
designed for a book. Second, because some of them were
painted in a different format (scroll rather than bound
book), and third, because carefully mounted paintings
in albums were not yet the norm, as happened later in
the fifteenth century. By the time the vogue for albums
became more widespread the Siyah Qalam paintings were
perhaps seen by royal patrons as too outlandish for their
taste to be worth compiling in any systematic fashion.

Fortunately for us the Siyah Qalam paintings were
so far ahead of their time as to be unappreciated when they
were painted, and remained within the court workshops.
Had they been made into books they might, like so many
others, have been scattered or lost. But the atelier albums
formed part of the treasuries of successive dynasties —
Mongols, Jalayirids, Timurids and Aqqoyunlu—until their
capture by the Ottomans ensured that they remained
intact until their rediscovery in the twentieth century.

LORDS OF SAMARQAND

TIMUR AND HIS SUCCESSORS

The deep relief carving of the Chinese lotus and surrounding flowers prevents the turquoise and cobalt glazes from running into one another. Terracotta panel, mausoleum of Shad-i Malik, 1372, Shah-i Zinda necropolis, Samarqand.

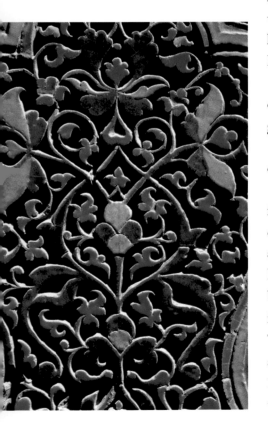

Using ruthless tactics borrowed from earlier rivals, Timur (or Tamerlane, ruled 1370–1405) quickly rose from being a petty Turco-Mongolian tribal chieftain based in Samarqand (in present-day Uzbekistan) to lead forces that conquered most of the territory between Syria and India. His sweep through Iran at the end of the fourteenth century eliminated the Jalayirids and other smaller dynasties.

Timur was particularly interested in monumental architecture. On two occasions he is known to have ordered his own buildings to be rebuilt, at least in part, on a grander scale. Mausoleums, such as those of the Shah-i Zinda necropolis outside Samarqand, were initially small-scaled, but the tomb Timur erected for his grandson, in which Timur himself was eventually buried, is one of those that he ordered to be rebuilt—its drum looks disproportionately tall as a result.

After Timur's death his son Shah Rukh ruled (1405–47) a much reduced area, consisting of Iran, Afghanistan, and Transoxiana, from Herat, of which he had been governor. Civil war broke out after his death in 1447, with stability only being won in 1470 with the accession of Husain Bayqara (1470–1506), but at the cost of the loss of central and western Iran to Turkman tribes.

Nevertheless, under the later Timurids architecture, painting, and literature flowered. Shah Rukh's son Baysunghur, governor of Herat in his father's absences, competed with his brother Ibrahim Sultan, ruler of Shiraz, for the finest poets and artists, but the best ones inevitably ended up in the capital, where there was more lucrative employment. Baysunghur was the patron of many illustrated manuscripts before his death in 1433, aged only thirty-five, of excessive alcohol consumption. Alcohol inevitably accompanied any social gathering, so it is no surprise that the most common Timurid metalwork object is the wine jug. The paintings in Baysunghur's manuscripts are magnificently executed but perhaps a little cold and stylized. In the reign of Sultan Husain Bayqara at the end of the fifteenth century a more realistic style became popular, with Bihzad its most famous practitioner.

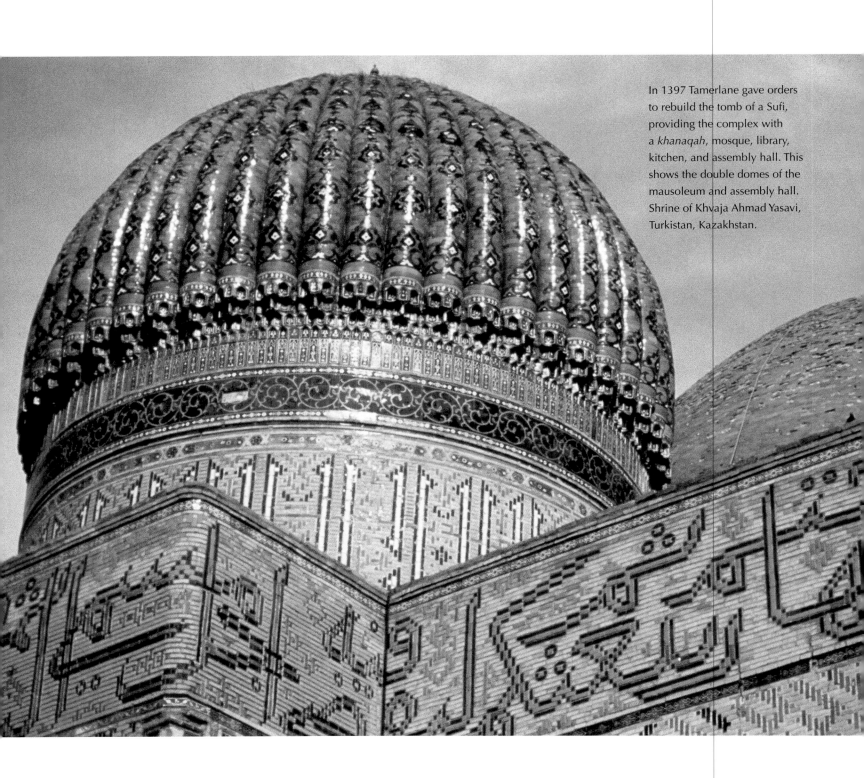

In 1397 Tamerlane gave orders to rebuild the tomb of a Sufi, providing the complex with a *khanaqah*, mosque, library, kitchen, and assembly hall. This shows the double domes of the mausoleum and assembly hall. Shrine of Khvaja Ahmad Yasavi, Turkistan, Kazakhstan.

PERSIAN MANUSCRIPT PAINTING

THE ART OF THE BOOK

The urge to produce beautiful Qurans led to a thriving industry of calligraphy and illumination (see pages 60–63). The production of books in the Islamic world soon embraced other texts, including religious works, histories, literature, and works of science. Many scientific manuscripts were translated from Greek at the 'Abbasid court, and some of the earliest 'Abbasid book paintings of the twelfth century were versions of the explanatory illustrations found in the originals. Arab and Iranian painters soon started to illustrate literary texts, the *Book of Kings* (*Shahnama*) being one the most popular early Persian subjects; examples of which survive from the beginning of the fourteenth

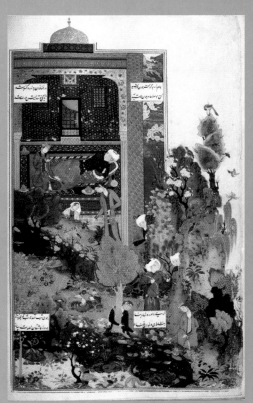

century. The *Khamsa* (*Quintet*) of Nizami, a masterpiece of lyric poetry, eclipsed the *Book of Kings* in popularity in the fourteenth century and remained a perennial favorite.

The format and style of painting changed dramatically in Iran between the earliest known examples from the second half of the thirteenth century and its fusion into a more uniform style at the end of the fourteenth. The paintings began by taking up a relatively small proportion of the page. Their size gradually expanded until they spilled out over the ruled margins that delimited the text space, at times taking over the whole page.

CHINESE INFLUENCES

What set Persian painting apart from its Arab predecessor was the integration of Chinese styles, aided by the import of

LEFT
Poetic allegory. The hero's visits to the seven pavilions represent steps on his path to spiritual enlightenment. This was painted at the court of the Aq Quyunlu, Turkman rulers of western Iran less famous than their contemporaries the Timurids, but who could obviously command equally fine painters. "Bahram Gur at the Yellow Pavilion," from the *Khamsa* of Nizami, Tabriz, Iran, ca. 1480.

RIGHT
The sultan reprimanded. On hearing that the old woman had been robbed by a soldier, the sultan replied that he had more important things to think about. "What's the use of conquering foreign armies if you can't make your own behave," she retorted. Nizami, *Khamsa*, Safavid, Tabriz, Iran, ca. 1540.

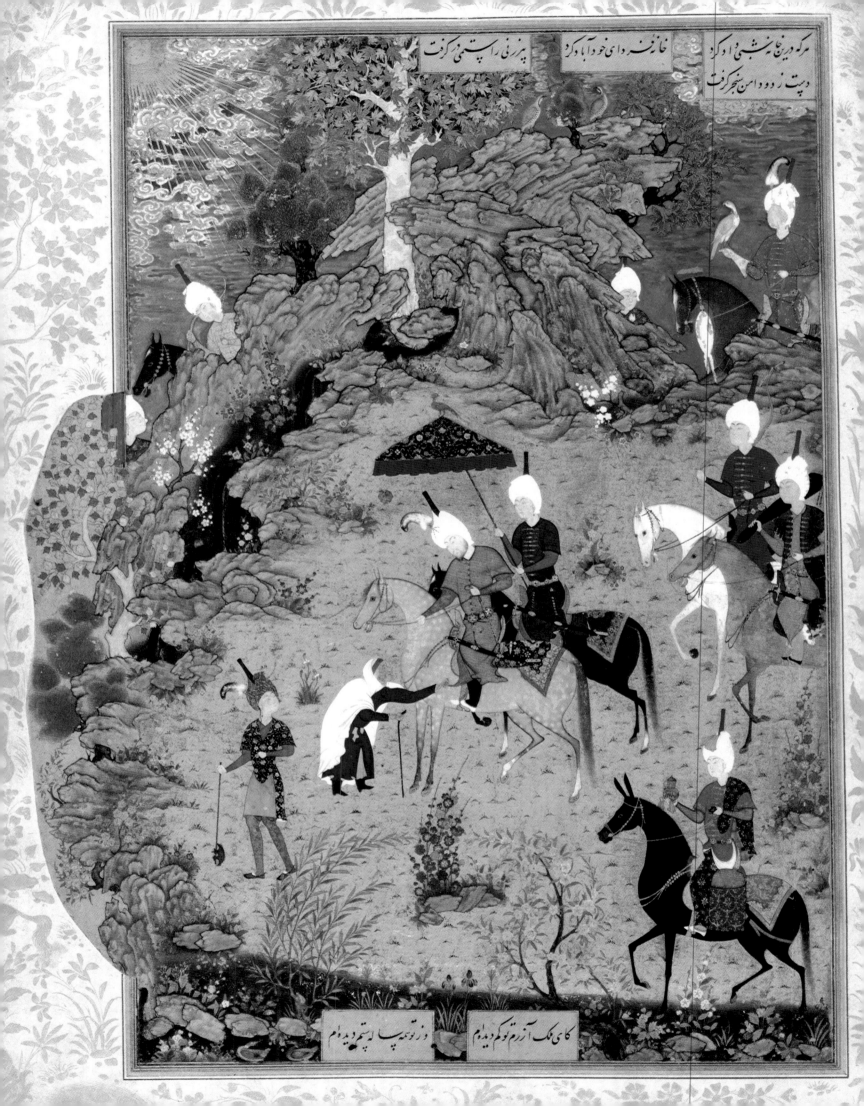

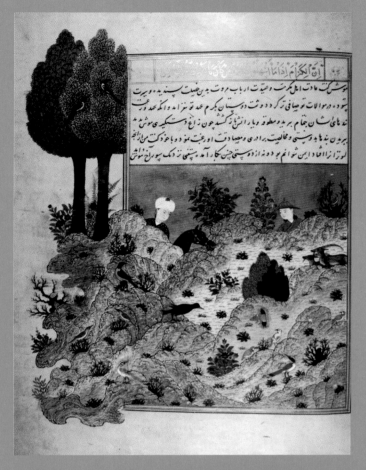

Chinese originals under the Mongol Ilkhanids (1256–1336). Of great importance was the idea of the frame as a window through which to view another world, which could be cut off arbitrarily at the edges. Other borrowed motifs included distant views of tree-studded mountains, gnarled tree trunks, and Chinese forms of mythic animals such as the dragon and phoenix.

The use of Chinese perspective became an unwavering feature of Persian painting. This is very different from the vanishing-point perspective used in Western painting from the Renaissance; instead, a high viewpoint is used which, at least on a small scale, permits clarity in spatial arrangements. Instead of Western atmospheric perspective (using paler or darker shades to suggest depth or distance), colors are applied undiluted. The lack of shading and shadows also gives the colors a purity that makes them leap off the page; bright yellows, reds, blues, and greens combine with an ease unmatched in other schools. The setting makes the most of color: landscapes are bathed in perpetual spring and interiors swathed with textiles and tilework. The fairytale atmosphere is perhaps most successful in the lyrical scenes which abound in Persian literature; the frequent battles seem less suited to the idyllic setting.

ARTISTS AND PATRONS

Patronage of painters was very much a court activity. Although the dynasties that sponsored the greatest Persian book painting were non-Iranian (Mongol Ilkhanids and Jalayirids; Turkish Timurids and Safavids), the patronage of Persian literature and the attendant arts of the book were an essential component of the courtly ethos of the time. Kings had the greatest resources and usually were the most active patrons, although occasionally, as in the case of Baysunghur, son of Shah Rukh (see page 132), it was a prince rather

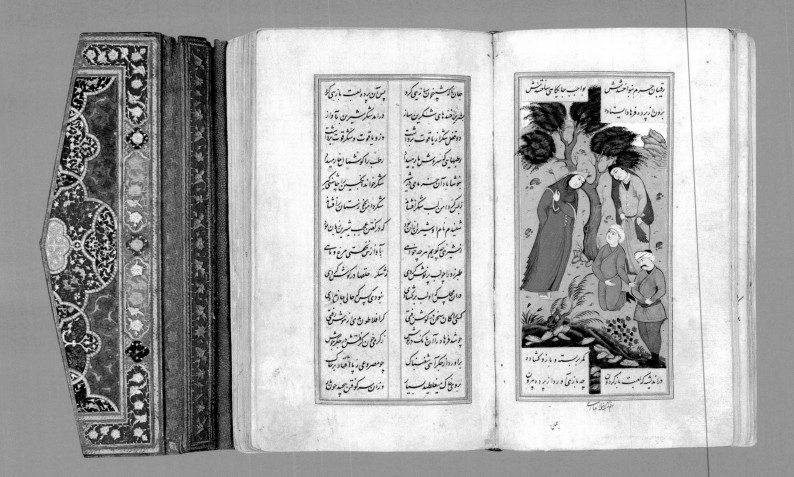

than the ruler who most actively pursued his literary interests. Only in Shiraz, in the late fifteenth and sixteenth centuries, did commercial ateliers emerge, producing manuscripts in greater quantity but with lesser quality paintings than court schools.

The development of a commercial school shows that demand was widespread, yet for most court-sponsored manuscripts the audience must have been limited to the royal family and a number of court officials. That the value of painted manuscripts was fully appreciated is shown by their frequent inclusion in ambassadorial gifts.

Arguably the greatest team of Persian painters was assembled by the Safavid ruler Shah Tahmasp (ruled 1524–76) to illustrate his *Book of Kings*. The paintings were carefully chosen to emphasize Iranian victories over the Turanians (the inhabitants of Central Asia), mirroring Shah Tahmasp's attempts to repel the Uzbeks on his northeast frontier. On its completion the book contained 258 large-scale paintings, many of them great masterpieces. After his sight deteriorated, Shah Tahmasp lost interest in book painting and sent the manuscript as a gift to the Ottomans—ensuring its survival to the present.

THE SHAHS OF ISFAHAN

THE GLORIES OF SAFAVID IRAN

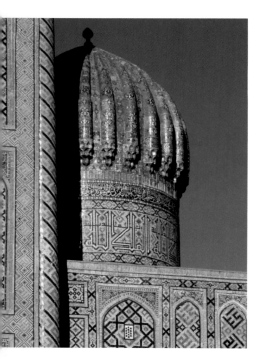

The Safavids (1501–1722) were in origin a tribe of warrior Sufis from northwest Iran. Like the Aqqoyunlu, who dominated the area before the rise to power of the Safavids, they were Turkish speakers. Their initial successes came from the fanatical loyalty given to their leader, Shah Isma'il, only fourteen years old when he ascended the throne in 1501. Within ten years he had gained control of the whole of Iran. His supporters were called the Qizilbash (Redheads) on account of the red twelve-sided baton they wore in their turban, representing the twelve Imams and the branch of Islam, Shi'ism, which they and their leader espoused. Shi'ism always had many followers in Iran, but the Safavid emphasis on promulgating it as a state religion was new and led to heightened political rivalries between the Safavids and their neighbors, the Ottomans to the west and the Uzbeks to the northeast. It also changed the religious map of Iran, which has remained staunchly Shi'i to the present.

Isma'il's prestige suffered a major blow when he was defeated by the Ottomans in eastern Anatolia in 1514. Although it was regained temporarily under Shah Tahmasp (ruled 1524–76), control of northwest Iran passed regularly between Safavid and Ottoman hands until the great Shah Abbas I (ruled 1588–1629) cemented the border at the beginning of the seventeenth century.

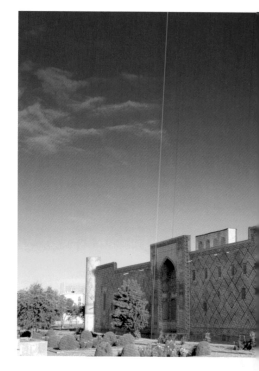

THE UZBEKS OF SAMARQAND

Just as the early Safavids faced the Ottomans in the west and northwest, they faced the rising power of the Uzbeks in the northeast. At the beginning of the sixteenth century the Uzbeks gained control of the territory in Central Asia that had formerly been under Timurid rule. They occupied Herat and other towns in Khurasan several

The Timurid madrasa (1418) of Ulugh Beg, on the left, was met with first by the Uzbek Shirdar madrasa (1619–36) of Yalangtush Bahadur, opposite, and further, from the same patron, by the Tila Kari madrasa (1646–60) in the center. Registan Square, Samarqand, Uzbekistan.

times in the 1500s, each time being forced to retreat by the Safavids, until Shah Abbas, after a decisive victory in 1597, confined them to Transoxiana. Their rule there was less centralized, with different areas sometimes being distributed among various family members. However, the Registan, the central square of Samarqand, became a showcase for their architectural patronage. The Shirdar madrasa (1619–36) was built opposite the madrasa of Ulugh Beg (1418), Timur's grandson, and mirrored its façade of pairs of minarets and dome chambers flanking a huge central arch. The new monument was clearly designed to outdo its predecessor, and certainly achieves this in size, even if the quality of Uzbek tilework never matched that of the Timurids.

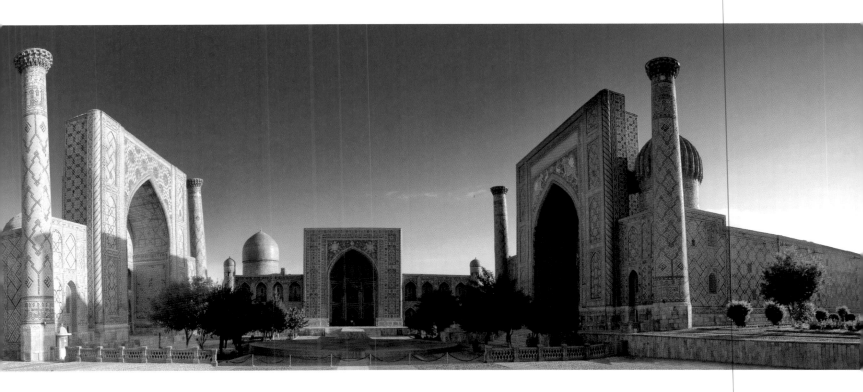

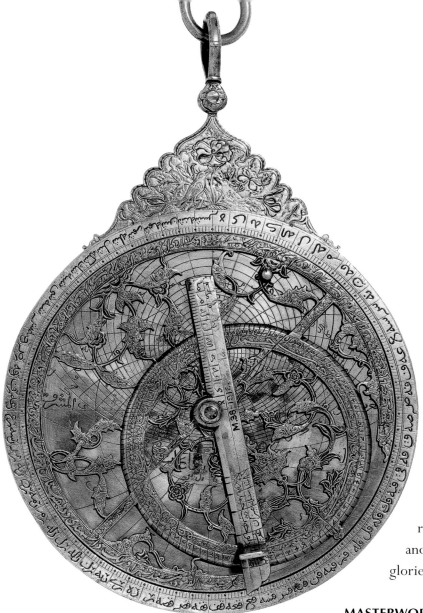

The builder of the Shirdar madrasa, the governor Yalangtush, later built another madrasa, the Tilakari (1646–59) that closed off a third side of the square. Although it too is almost slavishly based on Timurid prototypes, the ensemble certainly creates a public space of impressive monumentality.

In the Safavid domains, in contrast, little architecture seems to have been sponsored during the reign of Shah Tahmasp, who was more interested in books (see page 137). Shah Abbas, however, relocated the Safavid capital from Qazvin to Isfahan and transformed it into an architectural showcase for the glories of the dynasty (see pages 144–147).

MASTERWORKS IN FABRIC

Textiles and ceramics were two other areas in which Safavid artists excelled. Because of their fragility, few early Persian carpets have survived, although from book paintings we can get an idea of how much they and other textiles were used to enhance both interiors and even exteriors. It is from examples of the Safavid period onward that Persian carpets have acquired their inestimable reputation. Looking at the Ardabil Carpet (pages 142–143), it is not difficult to see why. Ardabil was the dynastic shrine of the Safavids, and even though no secure documentary evidence links the carpet with the shrine, its floral design, absent of figures, is in keeping with a religious setting, and its size and date (1539–40) are such that it is likely to have been a royal commission of the shah himself. Its design, combining varying levels of intricacy, with a central polylobed sunburst medallion placed on a background of floral arabesques, is typical of the finest Safavid carpets, as are its vivid colors and fine weave.

ABOVE

Astrolabes in the Islamic world served many useful purposes: for determining latitude for navigation; for telling the time (important for muezzins giving the call to prayer); and for determining the direction of the *qibla*. Copper alloy, incised and engraved, Isfahan, Iran, Safavid period, 1666.

FOLLOWING PAGES

In addition to the inscription that names the weaver, Maqsud of Kashan, and gives the date (1539), a cartouche at the top of the Ardabil Carpet contains two lines by the 14th-century poet Hafiz: "Other than your threshold I have no place in the world. My head has no resting place other than this doorway." This alludes to the room destined for the original pair of Ardabil carpets, which was probably conceived as the tomb of the current Safavid ruler, Shah Tahmasp.

It is easy to forget how important silk production was to the Iranian economy before disease devastated the silkworms in the 1860s. The most profitable export of Safavid Iran was silk, and the industry employed more workers than any other craft. Most production was monopolized by the Safavid court, and its luxuriousness may be estimated from the custom of burning the royal wardrobe every seven years to recover the gold and silver woven in the form of metallic threads into the garments. Many of the finest silks included human and animal figures amidst a landscape setting in a style identical to that of contemporary painting in books and on walls within the royal pavilions of Isfahan.

Similar figural scenes are also found on underglaze pottery of the type known as Kubachi, after the town in the Caucasus where many examples were found. However, recent analysis of the body of this pottery has suggested Isfahan as a more likely place of manufacture. The most popular kind of Safavid wares were imitation Chinese blue and white, produced mainly in Kirman and Mashhad, and of such high quality (including potter's marks) that they were able to pass for originals in European markets.

The demise of the Safavids, like that of the Ilkhanids, was surprisingly sudden, caused by Afghan invasions in 1722. Only with the coming of the Qajars (1779–1925) was a dynasty once more able to reunite all of Iran under a single ruler. The increasing importance of European styles under the Qajars affected their painting in particular, which now included large easel paintings as well as book painting. In architecture they were for the most part content with repeating previous styles, and they even occasionally resurrected rock-cut sculpture, the first dynasty to do so since the Sasanians.

BELOW

The dancers that decorate this monochrome-glazed flask could have come straight from the page of contemporary Safavid illustrated manuscripts (see page 137). Isfahan, Iran, 17th century.

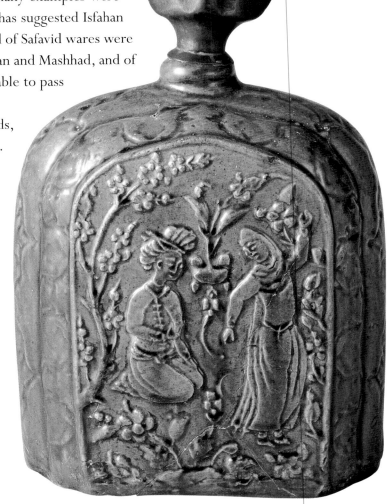

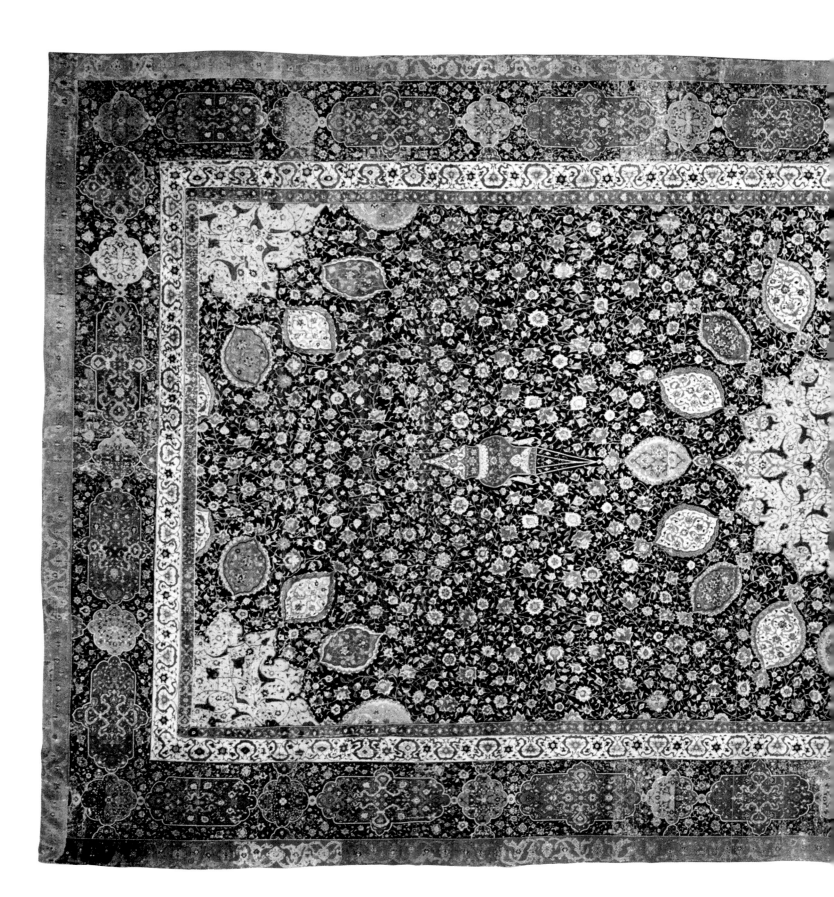

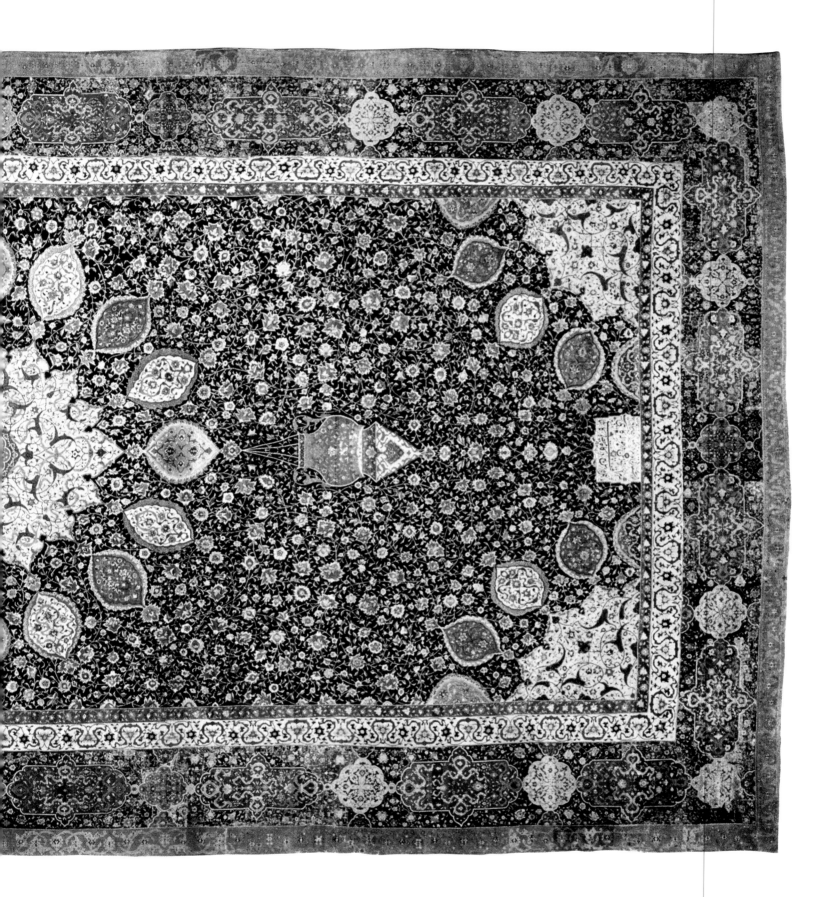

ISFAHAN

THE SPLENDOR OF "HALF THE WORLD"

Although Isfahan had always been an important town, its present glory derives from the transformation of the city by the Safavid ruler Shah Abbas I (see pages 138–139). In 1590, realizing the vulnerability of the previous capital, Qazvin, to Ottoman attack, he moved the seat of government to Isfahan. At first he concentrated on revitalizing the old town center near the Friday Mosque and its adjacent bazaar, but suspicion of the merchants caused him to plan a much more radical scheme of urban renewal. The result was a capital city which one contemporary, marveling at its architectural wonders and cosmopolitan population, dubbed *nisf-i jahan* – "half the world."

In 1602 work began south of the old city on the Maidan-i Naqsh-i Jahan (World-Imitating Square), a colossal rectangle 1,312ft by 476ft (400m by 145m), lined with two-storey shops on all sides. On the west side was the entrance to the previously existing palace grounds, now marked by the erection of the 'Ali Qapu (Lofty Gateway). Facing this Shah Abbas built a mosque, originally known as the Domed Mosque, but one in which Shaikh Lutf Allah, an important cleric who hailed from Lebanon, was given living quarters and which hence became known as the Shaikh Lutf Allah Mosque.

On the north side Shah Abbas ordered a monumental portal which led to an extension of the old bazaar, and decorated it with paintings showing his recent victory over the Uzbeks. On the south is the ensemble's crowning glory, the new Friday Mosque, known subsequently as the Masjid-i Shah (Royal Mosque).

The palace gateway (the 'Ali Qapu) has a high viewing platform with a *talar*, a roof supported by thin columns. From here the shah and his entourage could watch the polo games, military reviews, and fireworks that were frequently staged in the square. The interior was decorated with exquisite paintings of chinoiserie landscapes inhabited by birds.

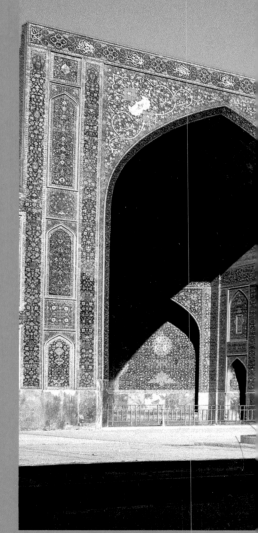

Plan of the Maidan-i Naqsh-i Jahan (World-Imitating Square), Isfahan. Located south of the old city, the square (1) links to it by a monumental portal, the Gate of the Qaysariyeh (2). At the opposite end, Shah Abbas's new Royal Mosque (below) was built, known today as the Mosque of the Imam (3). In the center, to the west, is the 'Ali Qapu (4) palace gateway, opposite the Shaikh Lutf Allah Mosque (5).

BELOW
To divert patrons from the old Friday Mosque, the new one built (1612–38) by Shah Abbas needed to be as attractive as possible. He achieved this effect by marrying the classical simplicity of the Iranian four-*iwan* courtyard plan with all-over tile decoration. Representing the crowning glory of the square's ensemble, the new mosque was called the Masjid-i Shah (Royal Mosque).

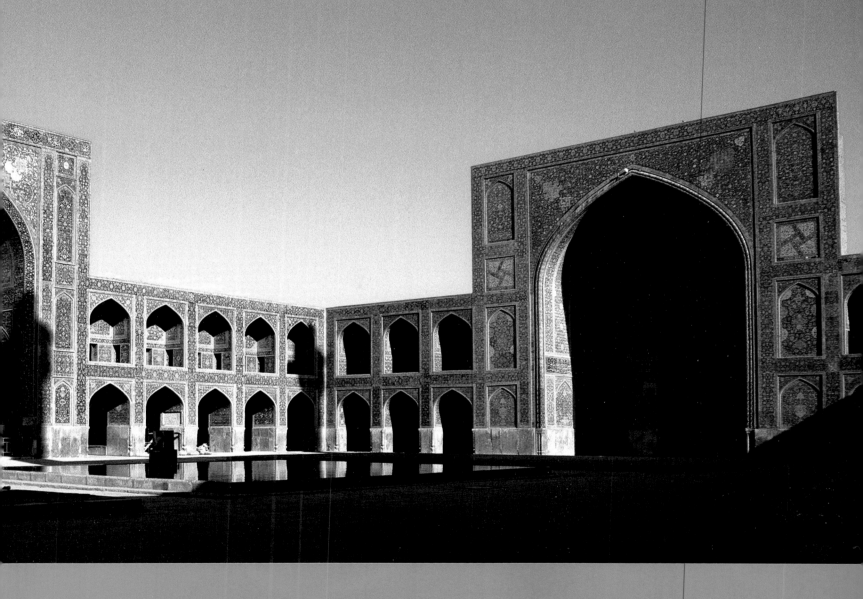

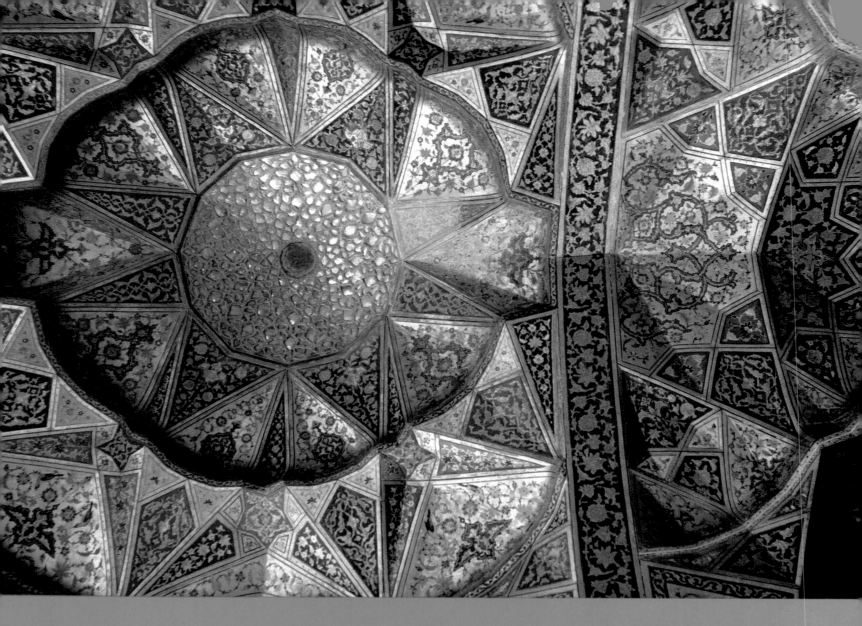

The gateway led to a loose arrangement of state pavilions and smaller informal buildings. Two of the most important pavilions survive, although they are from the reign of later shahs. The Chehel Sutun was originally built in 1646, but burnt down in 1706 and was immediately rebuilt as close as possible to the style of the original. Its entrance is also in the form of a *talar*, leading into a grand hall with large murals of former Safavid kings. The Hasht Behesht (Eight Paradises) dates from 1670 and is octagonal, as its name suggests. From its central domed hall four large *iwan*s open to the exterior, bringing a view of its garden to those within the pavilion. The central fountain and water channels mirror those of the outside, emphasizing the interpenetration of the pavilion with its verdant surroundings. The spandrels of its outer arches are decorated with lively tile panels encompassing a large range of figural imagery from single animals, both real and imaginary, to hunting scenes with dragons and lions. Beyond these pavilions was the Khiyaban, an avenue extending for a mile (2km) down to Isfahan's river, the Zayanda Rud, on each side of which Shah Abbas's *amir*s were encouraged to build *chahar bagh*s, partitioned gardens with pavilions.

To encourage the use of the riverbank as a promenade, several bridges were built of which the most magnificent was the Pul-i Khvaju (1651). Within its lower tiers of arches, teashops and coffee merchants plied their trades.

DOMED MASTERPIECES

Seen from the square, the dome of the Lutf Allah Mosque is not, as one might expect, directly behind the entrance *iwan*, but off to one side. This is perhaps because the axis of the square and that of the mosque's *qibla* wall are at a 45-degree angle to one another: it would have been possible to align the two, but the difference may have been a way to remind passers-by of the building's function. The entrance leads to a narrow passageway that bends first left and then right so that by the time one enters the chamber opposite the *mihrab* one has forgotten the difference in orientation. The interior is perhaps the culmination of Persian dome design: a perfect combination of masterful form and stunning decoration. Eight turquoise arches support the dome base, but their turquoise cable moldings enable the square base to blend into the squinches of the zone of transition. The dome's medallions culminate in a splendid sunburst radiating from the apex.

The difference in orientation of the Royal Mosque could not be disguised so easily, but here too the transition from exterior to interior is masterful. One wall of the *iwan* opposite the *qibla* is angled and cut away so as to be visible to anyone entering the mosque, but a waist-high barrier channels the worshiper either to the ablutions area or to the courtyard. Within the courtyard the reflections of the large pool double the vision of the surrounding arcades. Behind the side *iwan*s are domed chambers, meant to be seen only from the interior, but on the *qibla* side the towering arabesque-clad dome could be seen many miles away, from the Shiraz road south of the town.

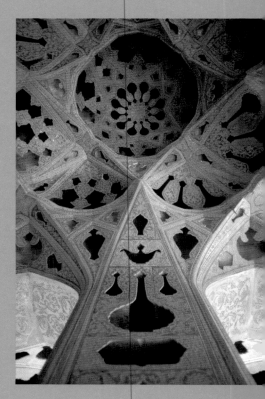

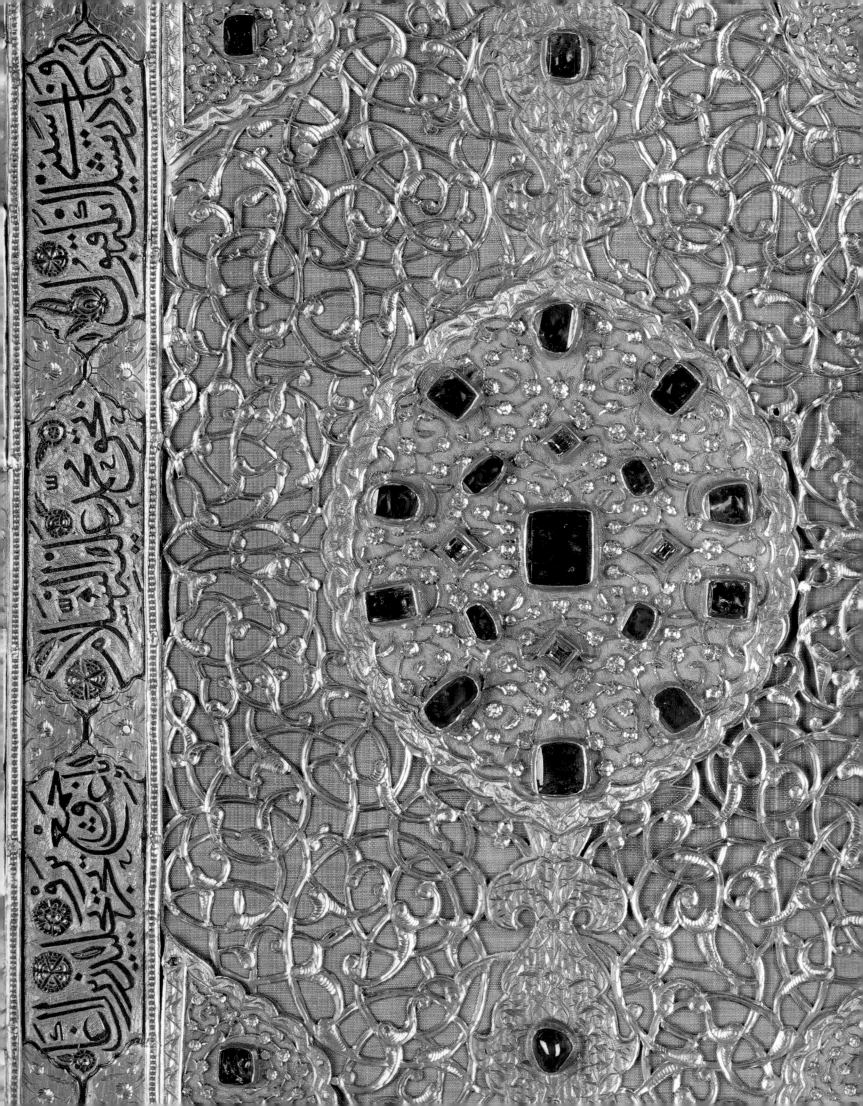

chapter 6

PRINCIPALITY TO EMPIRE

ISLAM IN ANATOLIA

SULTANS OF RUM

THE SELJUKS IN ANATOLIA

BELOW

Trompe l'oeil. The play of light on the hexagonal bosses and geometric interlacing on the inner edge of the *iwan* at the Karatay madrasa (1251) at Konya gives the impression of many more hues than the two colors of glaze actually used.

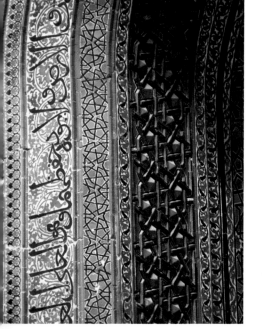

In 1071 at Malazgirt (Manzikert) the Seljuk Turks inflicted a major defeat on the Byzantine army, opening up Anatolia for the invasion and settlement of many Turkish tribes. In the second half of the twelfth century Anatolia slipped from the control of the Seljuks in Iran (see pages 112–115) with the rise of the Atabegs, army commanders who had been appointed as tutors to young Seljuk princes, but who frequently abrogated power for themselves. The most successful of the many principalities jockeying for power in what is now Turkey were the Anatolian Seljuks, so called to distinguish them from the Seljuks of Iran. They are also called the Seljuks of Rum ("Rome"), this being the Muslim name for their oldest foe, the Byzantine empire.

The Seljuk capital was Konya (ancient Iconium), in west-central Anatolia, from where they gradually expanded to rule most of the Anatolian plateau by the early thirteenth century. After their defeat at the hands of the Mongols in 1243 the Seljuks were permitted to remain as nominal rulers subject to payment of an annual tribute to the Ilkhanids in Iran (see pages 120–127). This eroded Seljuk prestige, and when the Ilkhanid state itself collapsed in the fourteenth century, Anatolia reverted to a series of petty principalities.

Anatolia's wealth of tufa, a volcanic stone that makes excellent building material, means that a great many medieval buildings remain from Seljuk Anatolia, including, for example, around one hundred caravanserais, versus a mere half a dozen from the same period in Iran. Anatolia also has more rainfall than most of its Near Eastern neighbors, with the result that wood from trees was readily available for building and decoration.

MASTERPIECES OF TILE AND STONE

The Karatay Madrasa (1251) has one of the finest tiled interiors of its time. An earlier madrasa in Konya, the Sirçali (1242), has the signature in tile of an artisan from Tus in eastern Iran. Like many others, he probably fled from the invading Mongols, or left in search of worthy patrons. In any case, just when tilework stagnates in Iran, it prospers in

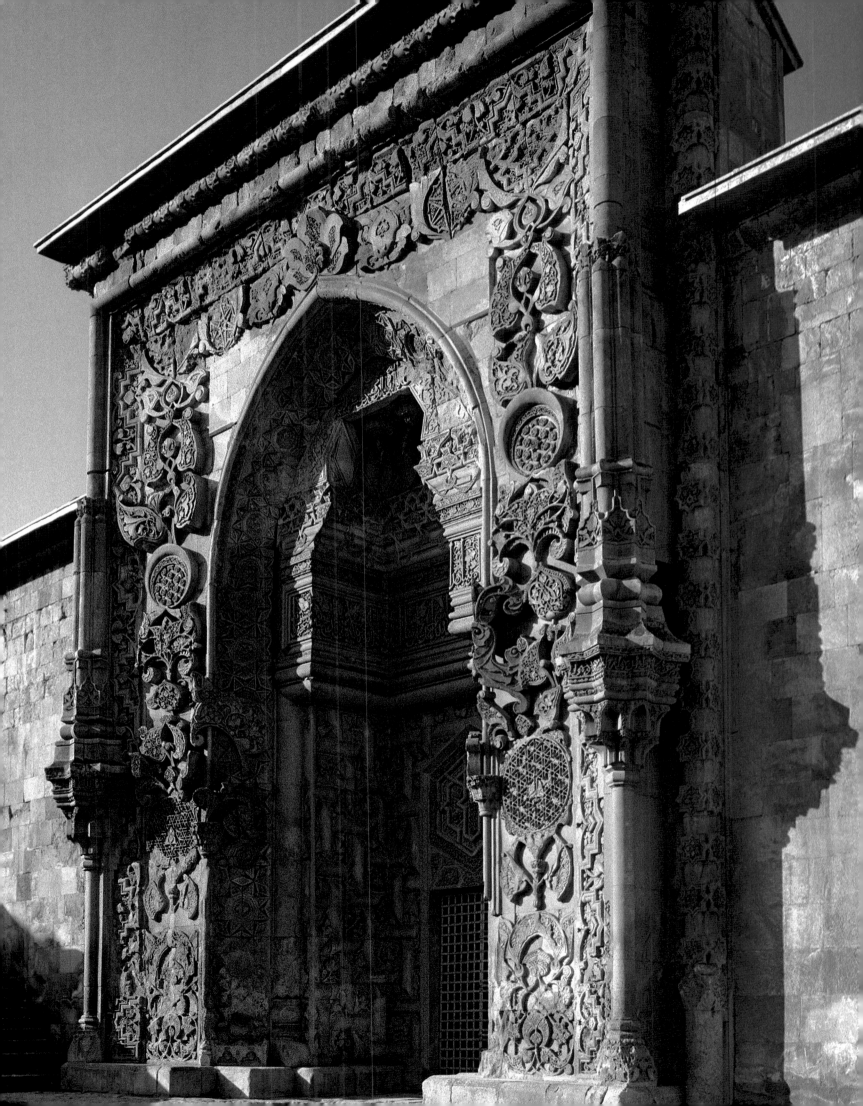

PREVIOUS PAGE
High relief arabesques are scattered on the façade of the Great Mosque of Divrigi (1228) without, at first sight, regard to logic, but bilateral symmetry imposes visual order.

BELOW
The normal method of reading the Quran was to sit cross-legged on the floor in front of a folding wooden stand like this one, which has an inscription praising the sultan Key Ka'us (probably II, ruled 1246–57).

Anatolia, as exemplified by the Karatay. The madrasa uses only three colors, black, light blue, and dark blue, but with the white stucco ground there seems to be a much greater variety of hues. This is partly obtained by the three-dimensional relief of one of the geometric patterns, whose faceting reflects the light at different angles (see page 150).

The Seljuks were equally adept at building in stone. The most breathtaking example of this is the north portal of the mosque at Divrigi (see illustration, page 151) in eastern Anatolia (1228, actually built by a minor dynastic neighbor of the Seljuks). It juxtaposes elements in a way that at first seems bizarre. The engaged circular column framing the composition starts in the usual manner by rising from a large base, but one third of the way up suddenly expands through *muqarnas* into a much larger eight-sided column, then mutates into a cluster of engaged columns only to change abruptly into a smaller one again. Within this frame are fragments of giant arabesques in high relief, in one case even leaping across an inner molding and attaching itself to the adjacent frieze. These fragments are carved in many layers of vegetal ornament, adding depth and intricacy to the composition. A deconstructionist masterpiece before its time, this is one of those rare works of art that flouts every rule and gets away with it.

TRAVELLER'S REST: THE CARAVANSERAI

Next to mosques, caravanserais are the most numerous surviving building type of medieval Anatolia, an impressive testimony to the civic responsibility of the Seljuk state.

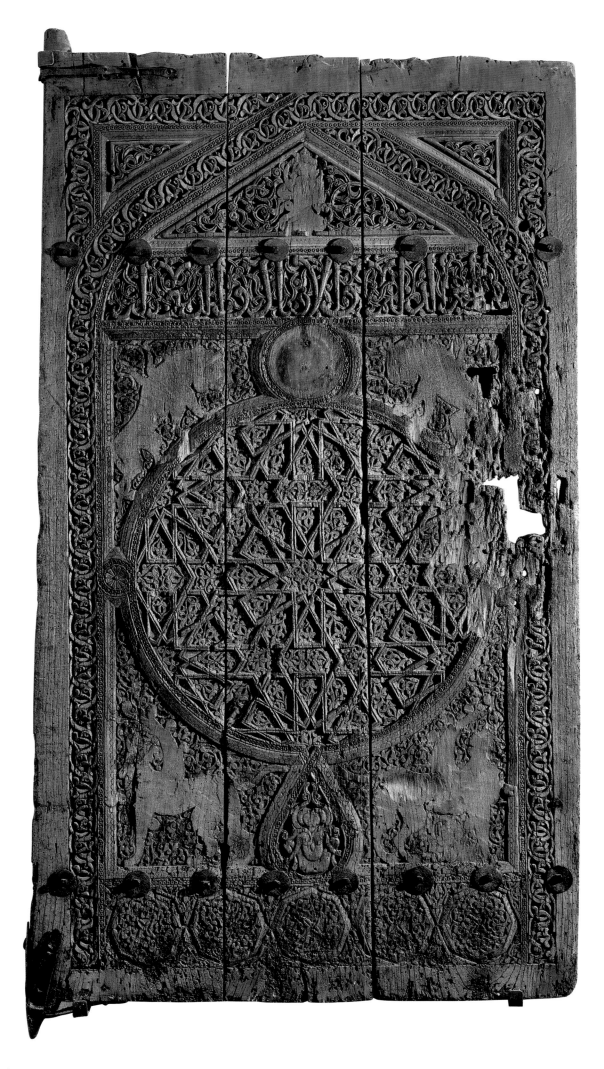

LEFT
Figural decoration, even in
a religious context, was more
common in Seljuk Anatolia than
anywhere in the Islamic world.
This shutter, from the Ibrahim
Bey *imaret* (a type of almshouse),
Konya (1433), is a rare example
with griffins and lions from
the later Karamanid dynasty.
Sadly, someone objected to
the images—originally in high
relief—and they were planed
down.

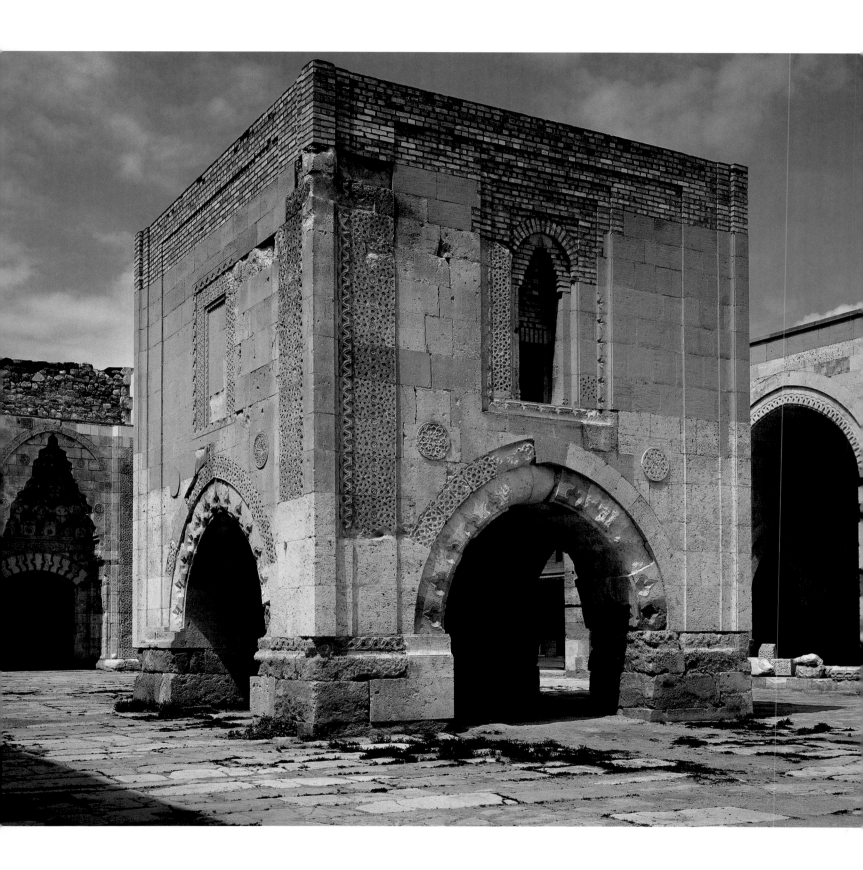

LEFT

Religion and commerce. The much-restored mosque in the center of the outer courtyard of the Sultan Khan (caravanserai) on the Konya-Aksaray road (1229) was raised above ground level to prevent defilement by wandering animals. In the background on the left is the entrance to the covered hall. The Sultan Khan was one of a number of caravanserais built by the Seljuk sultan 'Ala al-Din Key Qubad (ruled 1220–37).

They were erected between towns at a distance of a day's march, providing security for the traveller and for merchants' goods. This explains their semifortified appearance. Anatolian caravanserais, or *khans* (modern Turkish *hans*), have a great variety of designs, but the finest are unusual in consisting of two parts, a covered hall and a preceding courtyard building. The hall was the first part to be built, so that in case of delays or financial shortfall it could be used on its own. This may explain the often majestic proportions of such structures, taking the form of a basilica with a lofty central dome. The courtyard could have many associated functions, combining stables, latrines, rooms for wealthier or more prestigious guests, a bath, and sometimes a mosque.

Some of the finest caravanserais were built by Sultan 'Ala al-Din Key Qubad (ruled 1220–37), in particular two on the Konya-Kayseri and Konya-Aksaray roads. Exceptionally, both have a small mosque in the center of the courtyard, raised on four arches to prevent the interior from being soiled by animals. One contemporary historian also credits 'Ala al-Din with immense ability in architecture, and crafts including knife-forging, sculpting, painting, and saddlery, as well as being a connoisseur of jewels. Even allowing for courtly license, this is an impressive list.

MASTERS OF INNOVATION: SELJUK ARTS

The art of the Anatolian Seljuks was no mere provincial offshoot of the Iranian Seljuks. Using the vocabulary of forms inherited from a variety of sources, including those of pre-Islamic Anatolia and the Crusaders as well as previous Islamic dynasties, they were trailblazers whose original artistic syntheses paved the way for later innovations.

Among the most precious carved wooden objects from the Seljuk period are folding Quran stands. These are of a low height to permit the reader to sit cross-legged in front of them. One was made for the mausoleum of Jalal al-Din Rumi in 1279, possibly to hold a manuscript of Rumi's *Masnavi* commissioned by the same patron. Not only were its outer surfaces carved with inscriptions and arabesques, its inner surfaces

BELOW

The inscription on this tomb (1335) at Gevash near Lake Van names the buried woman as Halime Khatun. The craftsman was Asad, son of Pahlavan Khavand of Ahlat (north of the lake), whose work is known from earlier tombstones (1317–17).

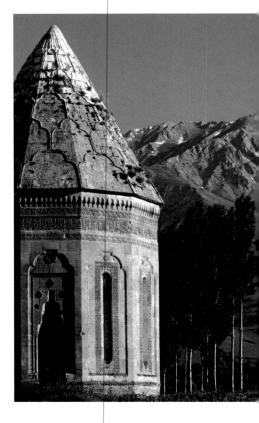

BELOW

Purveyors of light. Four
dragons with scaly necks,
red-painted teeth, pointed ears,
and horned heads rear up to
snap at this candlestick shaft.
The association of dragons
with eclipses also led to their
connection with light. Copper
alloy, 14th–15th century,
southeast Anatolia.

were lacquered with a medallion incorporating a double-headed eagle surrounded by seven pairs of lions. Another (see illustration, page 152) that was found in the dynastic mausoleum of the Seljuks in Konya has an inscription in the name of the sultan (probably Key Ka'us II, ruled 1246–57). The outer part of the stand is decorated with carved arabesques whose tendrils end in small circles, a characteristic Anatolian approach to scrollwork which was imitated even in metalwork.

DRAGON DECORATION

Quran stands illustrate one of the most unusual features of Seljuk art and architecture: the extent to which animal figures were employed as decoration. Seljuk artists expanded both the repertory of subjects and the types of buildings on which they were found to include not just secular structures such as fortifications, bridges, and caravanserais, but also religious buildings including mosques, minarets, and madrasas. Dragons were among the most popular subjects, perhaps because they had a multiplicity of meanings. The simplest was that of protection, with one pilgrimage guide of 1215 stating that at Mayyafariqin in southeast Anatolia there was a talisman against dragons in the form of a snake with two heads. Although dragons in pre-Islamic times represented destruction and death, it was thought that those who had mastered the power of magic could make them beneficent. The dragon was also related to darkness or light through its connection with the heavenly bodies. On the one hand, a dragon was believed to devour the sun or moon during eclipses; on the other, pairs of dragons could also have the opposite meaning: the dragon as provider of light, after the belief that two dragons or a double-

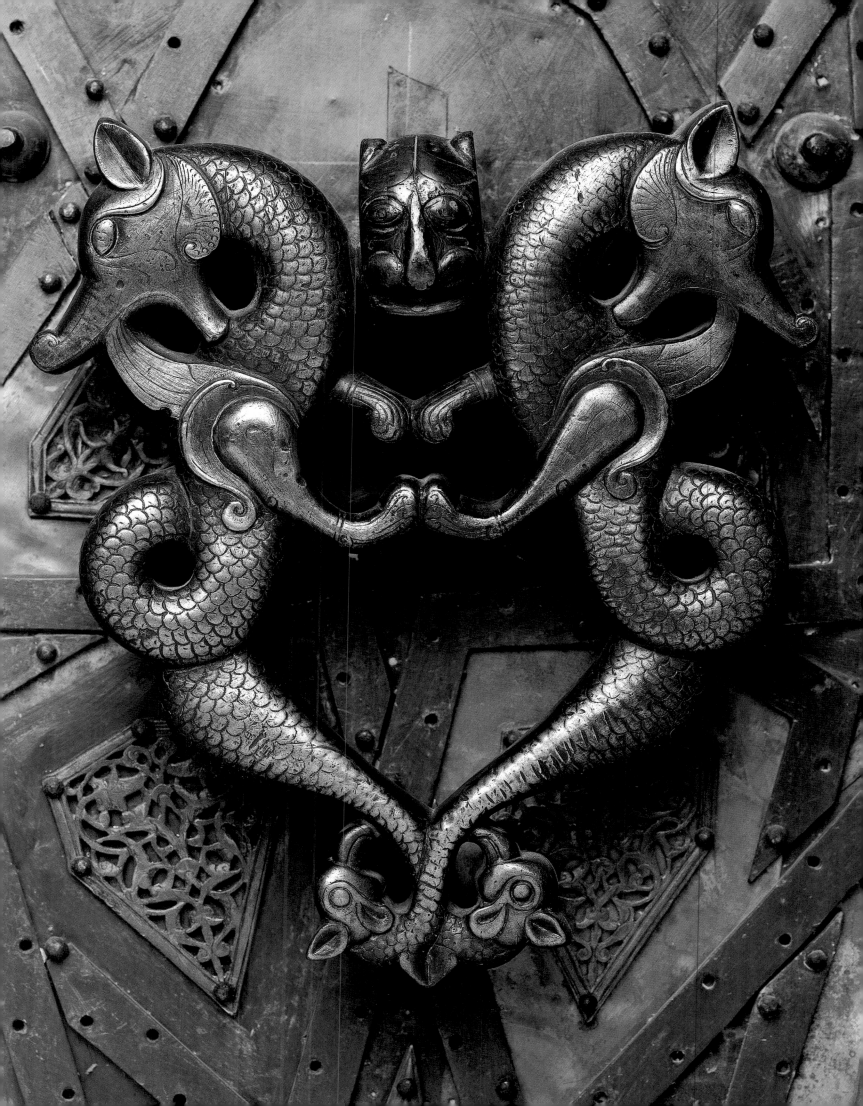

بعند قرع می کند از ماه مشک

همی گفت فریاد از این تیره بخت

بجران برآتش فکند این شم

بوادی سوی آسمان کرد سر

تو دانی که ت صبر و طاقتم

کفت آن سهی سرو را در کنا

می افکند آن سرو بر خاک خشک

کی اوفکند برجان من بند سخت

ندانم چه خواهد همی زین در

همی گفت ای داور دادگر

نوده سیّدی زین بر زاحم

ببوسید رخساران نو بهار

ورقه گلشه

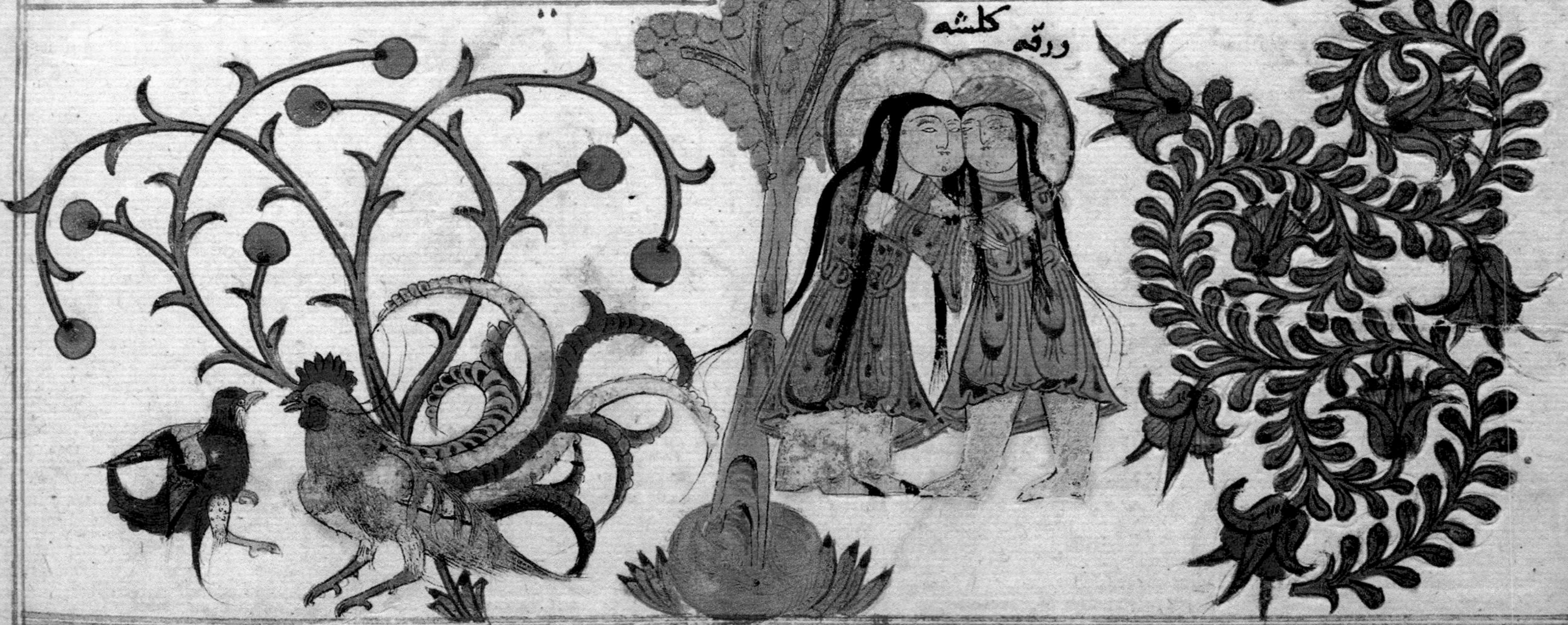

headed dragon was responsible for the cycle of day and night. Hence the frequent use of dragons on candlesticks (see illustration, page 156) and their suitability as the door-knocker of the mosque at Jizre (see illustration, page 157). An earlier manuscript copy of a work on automata (*Compendium of Science and Useful Practice in the Making of Mechanical Devices*) by al-Jazari, an author at the court of the Artuqids in Diyarbakir in eastern Anatolia, has an illustration showing a palace door with almost identical knockers.

Figural decoration combines with epigraphic, vegetal, and geometric motifs on a window shutter (see illustration, page 153) made for a complex erected by the successors of the Seljuks in Konya, the Karamanids (ruled 1256–1483), who for a time rivaled the Ottomans as the main power in Anatolia. Surrounding the central medallion with its impressive twelve-pointed star are pairs of winged lions and griffins, animals with royal connotations that were still not seen as out of place in a religious building.

ANATOLIAN CULTURAL RICHES

Medieval Anatolia was an interesting admixture of Turkish, Persian and Arabic cultural traits. The importance of Persian there may be gauged from the names adopted by several of the sultans, such as Key Khusraw, Key Ka'us, and Key Qubad, all drawn from the Iranian heroes of Firdausi's *Book of Kings* (*Shahnama*; see page 108). Persian was the literary language of the Seljuk court, and the now-destroyed walls of Konya and nearby Sivas had verses from the *Book of Kings* prominently displayed on them. The eponymous founder of the Karatay Madrasa was a patron of Jalal al-Din Rumi, the author of the *Masnavi*, the most celebrated mystical poem written in Persian. Rumi in turn was the founder of the Mevlevi order of Sufis, famous in the West as the Whirling Dervishes.

It is almost certainly to an Anatolian workshop that we owe the earliest surviving illustrated Persian manuscript. This is the romance of *Varqa and Gulshah*, whose scribe was known to be working in the Karatay Madrasa in Konya in 1253. The paintings in the manuscript are simple in style, similar to those in earlier Arab manuscripts. But they

OPPOSITE

"She took that lofty cypress apart and covered the cheeks of that man, beautiful as a Buddhist temple, with kisses," runs the verse above the painting in Ayyuqi's *Varqa and Gulshah*, the oldest surviving illustrated manuscript in Persian. The verse expresses the tenderness of the lovers before their indefinite separation. The artist has heightened the tension of their final embrace by adding a setting replete with symbolism. Even the striking vegetation might have symbolic meaning, representing the convoluted twists of the lovers lives before they are reunited (the plant on the right), together with the mix of pleasure and pain that is in store (the thorny fruit tree on the left). Konya, ca. 1253.

LEFT, BELOW, AND OPPOSITE

The rivals. At almost the same time, in 1271, madrasas were built in Sivas in eastern Anatolia by two rival viziers. Juvaini, the Ilkhanid vizier, founded the Çifte Minare (Twin Minaret) madrasa (on the left), but was trumped by the carved marble façade (opposite) that forms part of the Gök madrasa erected by his competitor, the Seljuk vizier Fakhr al-Din 'Ali. Both display the mastery of stone carving for which Seljuk architecture in Anatolia is renowned.

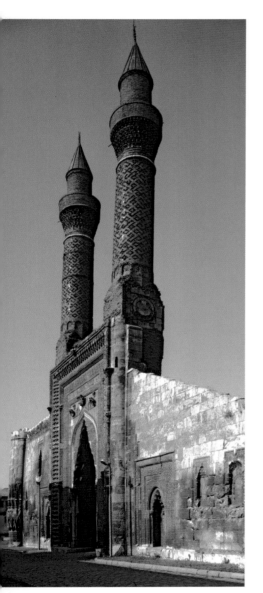

have one unusual feature, the use of animals to underline the human action. In one scene of the lovers' embrace before fate separates them (see illustration, page 158), a cock and hen are the only other creatures in the painting. The cock symbolizes several themes in medieval Arabic and Persian literature, including magical powers, piety (owing to its crowing the hours of prayer), beauty, and fortitude. The hen symbolizes the values of domesticity, so together they reflect the virtues of the unfortunate couple.

RIVAL WORKS OF GLORY

One of the major commercial entrepots of eastern Anatolia was Sivas, a town through which Turkish slaves from the area west of the Caspian Sea were exported to other Muslim lands; the future Mamluk sultan Baybars, for instance, was sold there in 1242. It was the scene in 1271 for an unusual contest between rival patrons. The first was the Ilkhanid chief vizier, Shams al-Din Juvaini, who founded the Çifte Minare madrasa, the second the most important vizier of the Anatolian Seljuks, Fakhr al-Din 'Ali, founder of the Gök madrasa. The Çifte Minare madrasa was Shams al-Din's major foundation. The name of his madrasa means "Twin Minarets," a common feature in mosque and madrasa portals in Anatolia, and one that enables us to imagine how the portal of the Sultan Hasan complex in Cairo (see page 74) was originally designed to look. The façade is of carved stone with high-relief ornamentation like the Divrigi portal, but the minarets are of lighter brick decorated with tile.

The Seljuk vizier Fakhr al-Din 'Ali was also exceptionally powerful; although the foundation on the portal of his Gök madrasa names the Seljuk ruler, another in the interior *iwan* gives only Fakhr al-Din's name and titles. Instead of the usual tufa, the main entrance portal is built in marble, a material much harder to carve and therefore more expensive. But it is also longer lasting, and the finely chiseled details of its many geometric and arabesque friezes still retain their crispness, reinforcing Fakhr al-Din 'Ali's victory over his Ilkhanid rival in the prestige of their architectural patronage.

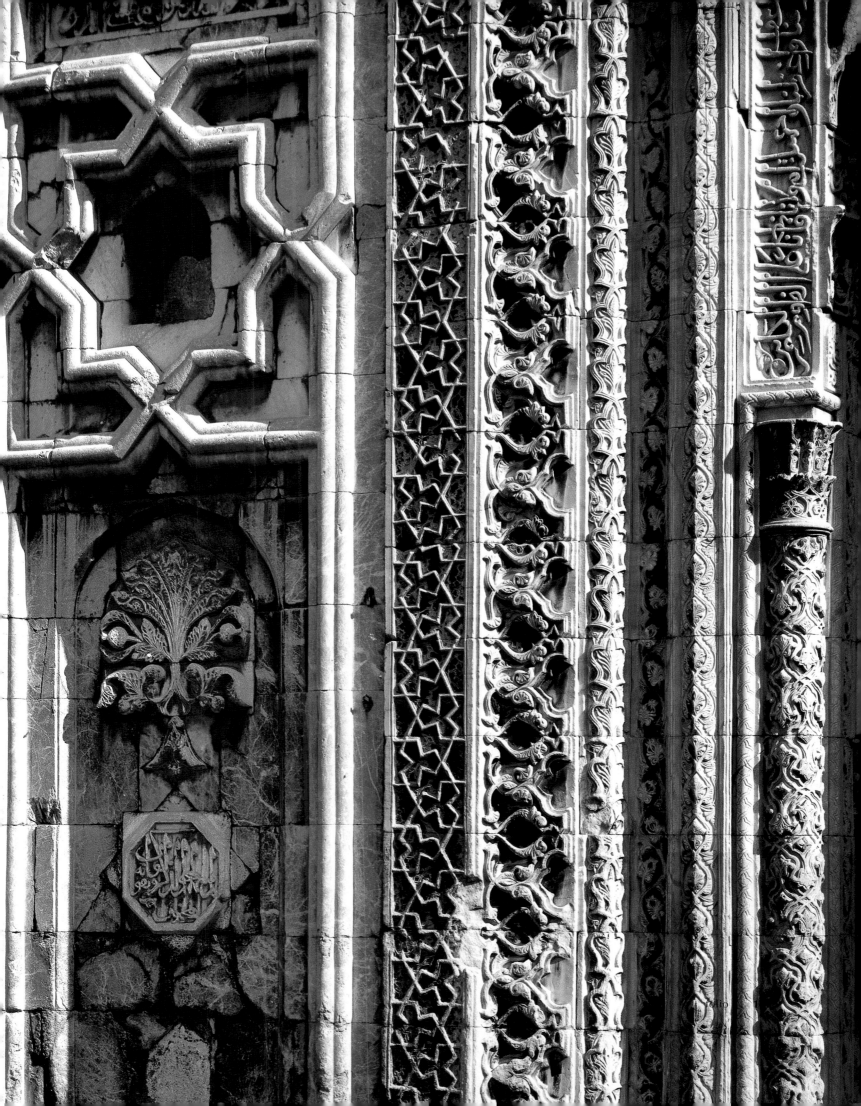

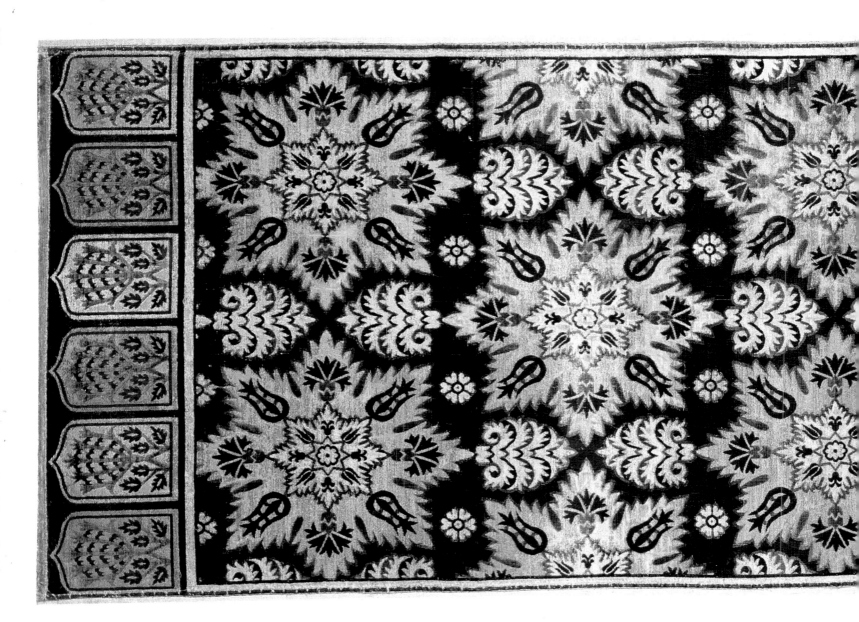

IMPERIAL SPLENDOR

THE GLORIES OF THE OTTOMANS

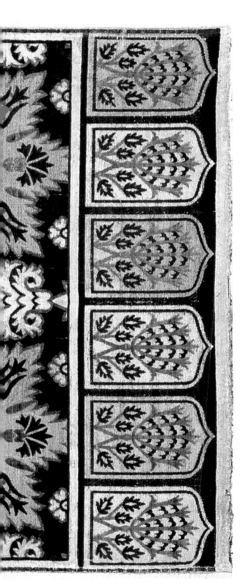

At its height, the Ottoman empire stretched from central Europe and the Maghreb to the Iranian frontier. However, at the beginning of the fourteenth century the Ottomans were just one of around ten Turkish principalities competing for power in Anatolia. Along with factors such as good government, a relatively close adherence to primogeniture, and long reigns of successive sultans, one cause in particular may have contributed to their rapid expansion: being based in northwest Anatolia, they were a frontier state engaged in fighting non-Muslims. *Gazis*, warriors for the faith, swelled the Ottoman armies.

EAST MEETS WEST: OTTOMAN EXPANSION

Initially invited as mercenaries in an internal Byzantine quarrel, the Ottomans crossed the Dardanelles Strait into Europe in 1346. The second half of the fourteenth century saw the occupation of Bulgaria and the Balkans, followed quickly by further expansion in Anatolia. The Ottoman commitment to European territories was shown by moving the capital from Bursa in northwest Anatolia to Edirne (Adrianople). They established a policy of resettling Christians in Anatolia and Turks in Europe in order to lessen local ties and supplant them with loyalty to the state. The *devshirme* system was started at the same time; this was the forced levy of Christian boys who were raised as Muslims and trained for the military and civil service. They formed the janissary corps, the crack troops of the Ottomans and those most loyal to the sultan. The janissaries became a significant power, managing to have the *devshirme* banned in the seventeenth century so that their own heirs would be eligible for recruitment into the corps.

Sultan Beyazid died in the captivity of Timur in 1402, but the re-establishment of the Ottoman empire within a few decades showed its solid foundations. In 1453 Mehmed II (1444–46, 1451–81) finally captured Constantinople, which as Istanbul became the Ottoman capital. The remainder of the fifteenth century saw the consolidation of Ottoman control of Anatolia, but it was Selim I (1515–20) who made the most significant

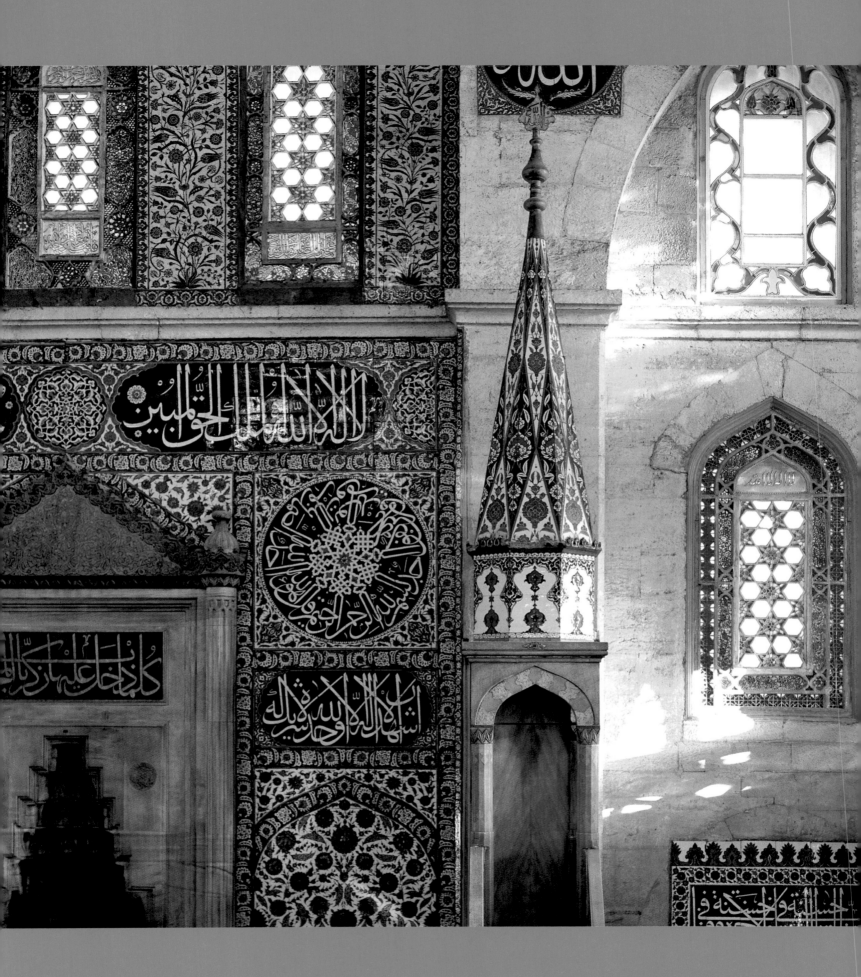

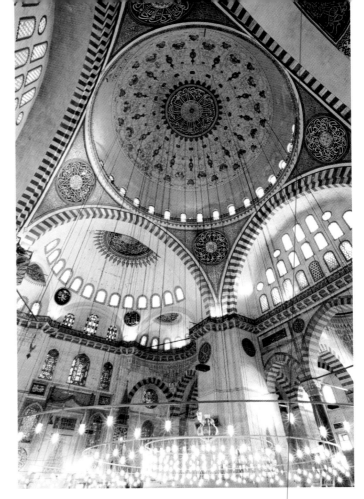

Ottoman gains. After a decisive victory over the Safavids of Iran in 1514, Selim defeated the Mamluks outside Aleppo in 1517, leading to the Ottoman occupation of the Arab Near East until shortly after the First World War.

OTTOMAN ZENITH AND DECLINE

Suleyman the Magnificent (1520–66), came to the throne with unequaled wealth and power. His splendid court promoted superb examples of all the decorative arts, and architecture unrivaled in both quantity and quality. His armies reached as far as Vienna, where his siege was foiled only by months of bad weather. At his death the empire was at its greatest extent, stretching from Hungary to the Caucasus and from Iraq to Algeria. In this multiethnic state the *millet* system enshrined the autonomy of non-Muslim religious communities, such as Balkan Christians, the Jews, and Armenians. Such was the Ottoman reputation for tolerance that most Jews fleeing persecution in Spain settled in Istanbul.

The Ottoman state was highly centralized, with appointments to both orthodox and Sufi-based religious institutions—free of state control in other Muslim states—supervised by the government. However, the vast increase in the government apparatus, the expense of maintaining the court, and annual campaigns in Europe and Asia all placed strains on the economy. The slow decline of the empire after Suleyman's death was masked by the disunity of the European powers, and in 1683 the Ottomans again besieged Vienna, only to be narrowly repulsed. Eventually the Habsburgs pushed back the Ottoman frontier, while the Russians at the same time moved southward towards the Black Sea. On the eve of the First World War, Turkish territories in Europe had been reduced to their present area of eastern Thrace. The entrance of the Ottomans into the war on the side of the Central Powers led to the loss of their Arab possessions.

ABOVE
The architecture of radiance. The brilliance of the glow from the lamps in the huge chandelier is matched by the lights that floods in from the numerous windows, one of the architect Sinan's great accomplishments. Mosque, Suleymaniye complex, Istanbul (1550–57).

OPPOSITE
The full panoply of floral motifs from Iznik tilework was chosen to complement the inscriptions on the *qibla* wall of the mosque. Unusually, even the conical top of the *minbar* has been tiled. Mosque, Sokullu Mehmed Pasha complex, Istanbul (1571–72).

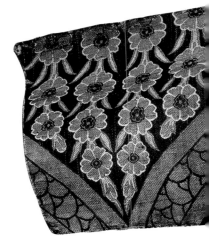

GENIUS IN STONE: OTTOMAN ARCHITECTURE

Architecture is the most visible manifestation of Ottoman artistic genius; its legacy transformed not only Turkey but also major Arab cities under Ottoman occupation such as Aleppo, Damascus, and Cairo.

Two tendencies characterize Ottoman architecture. One is the use of complexes, multifunctional sets of buildings, usually with a congregational mosque at their center. Although found earlier in Seljuk Anatolia and Ilkhanid Iran, the Ottomans varied and increased the components of complexes and marshaled them within urban settings with greater unity than ever before. The second tendency is the use of the dome as the main unit of construction. The earliest examples are modest single-domed buildings, but from the Uç Sherefeli (1437–47) at Edirne onward, the prayer hall of major mosques is dominated by a dome of greatly increased size, preceded by an arcaded courtyard.

In the late fourteenth and early fifteenth centuries at the former capital, Bursa, mosques on a T-shaped plan were created by stringing together dome chambers. These also had small chambers at the sides which were used as hospices (*tabhane*s) in which dervishes or pilgrims resided. *Tabhane*s remained standard in Ottoman mosques until the early sixteenth century, an echo of them being found in the wings of Beyazid II's mosque in Istanbul (1505). The finest of the Bursa mosques was erected by Mehmed I (ruled 1403–21); it is known as the Yeshil Jami (the Green Mosque) from the color of its tiled dadoes, the work of an atelier from Tabriz in northwest Iran. The superb overglaze-painted tiles that it also displays were first used extensively in Timur's Samarqand, but since nothing from central Iran has survived from this period the mosque is invaluable in filling a gap in our knowledge of the development of tile decoration.

The Uç Sherefeli mosque (1437–47), in addition to its massive dome (79ft/24m in diameter), is of interest for its use of painted plaster, another common Ottoman decorative technique. The domes around the arcaded courtyard display surprisingly well-preserved variations on arabesques and inscriptions (see illustration, page 170).

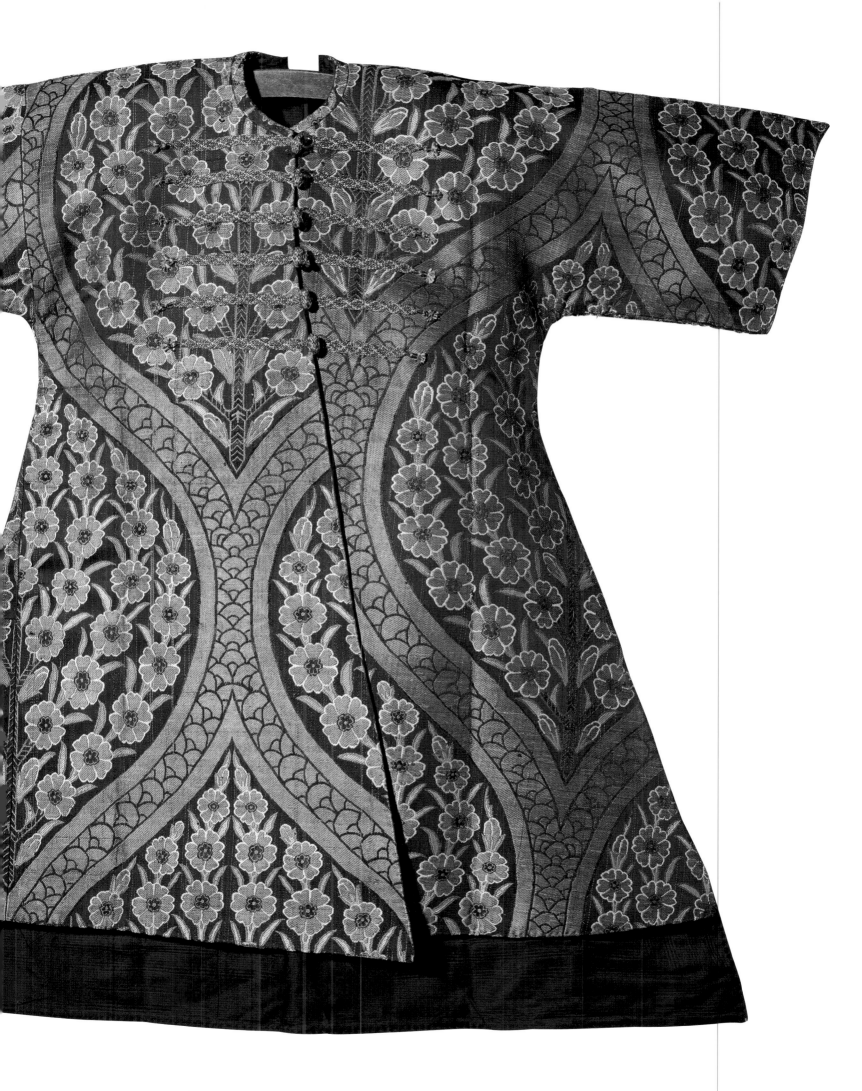

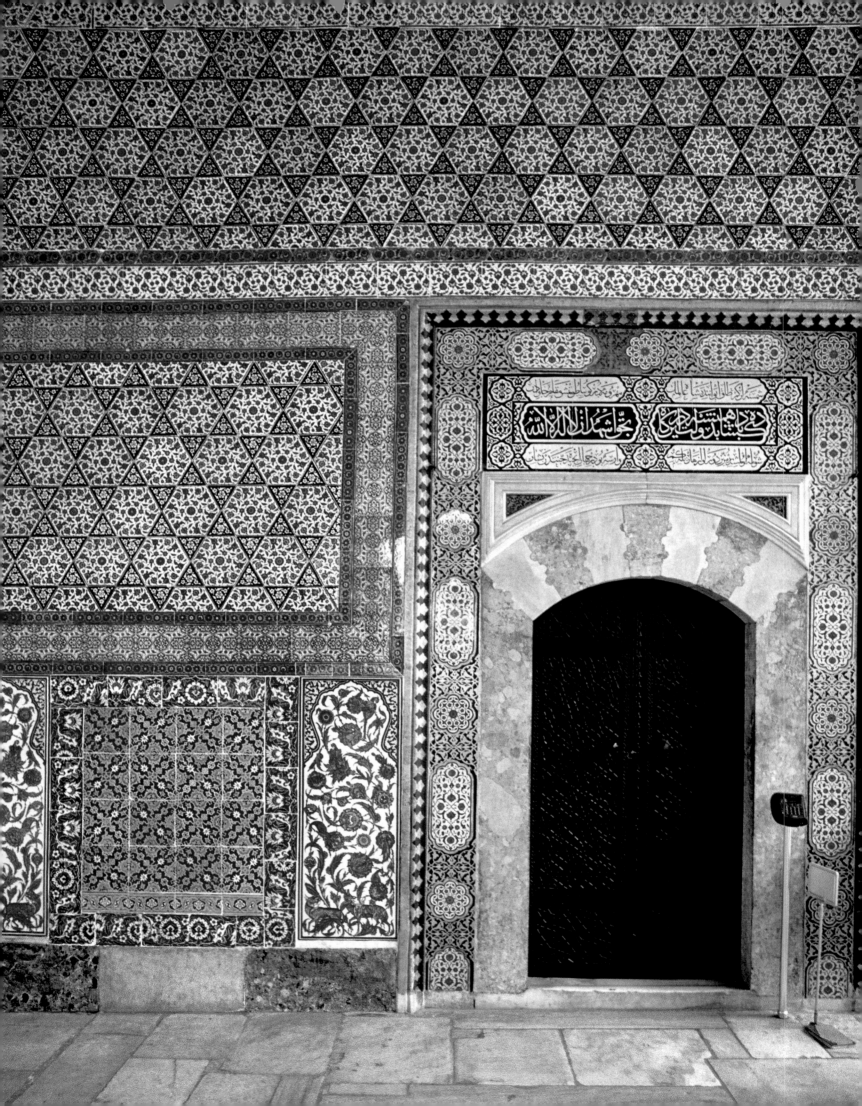

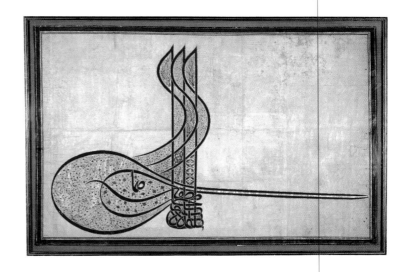

The recent removal of whitewash revealed that the interior was similarly decorated, although sadly the naturalistic trees—glimpses of the paradise awaiting the believer—on the walls below the smaller side domes were obliterated in the subsequent restoration.

SINAN THE MASTER

After the capture of Constantinople in 1453, the Haghia Sophia cathedral became a mosque and its huge dome presented itself as a challenge to Ottoman architects. The gauntlet was taken up by Suleyman the Magnificent's chief architect, Sinan (1491–1588), whose genius was expressed in buildings both great and small. He began his professional career as a janissary, recruited in the *devirshme* under Selim I (1515–20). From 1522 to his appointment as chief architect in 1538, Sinan travelled with the army on campaigns from Hungary to Iraq, which enabled him to acquaint himself with a wide range of building styles. His three largest complexes—the Shehzade, Suleymaniye, and Selimiye—each represent a significant step in his maturity.

The death of Sultan Suleyman's son Mehmed in 1543 gave Sinan his first major commission, the Shehzade (literally "prince") complex at Istanbul (1543–48). Its plan of a central dome surrounded by four semidomes can be seen as the first of his variations on the Haghia Sophia plan, which has a dome flanked by two semidomes. At the Shehzade the supporting walls were thickened with buttresses at regular intervals to open up the intervening spaces and thus allow many more windows than normal. Another novelty was the roofline. Sinan enlarged the height and diameter of the turrets supporting the main dome, and obtained a pyramidal effect by raising the height of the four corner domes to be in line with the diagonal axis created by the central dome and the turrets.

Sinan's Suleymaniye in Istanbul (1550–57) was the single most ambitious Ottoman project, with some fourteen buildings of various functions accommodated ingeniously on the sloping site around the mosque. Set on a hill overlooking the harbor, the mosque still dominates the city's skyline. Sinan reproduced the Haghia Sophia vaulting scheme

ABOVE

From the mid 14th century, Ottoman sultans used *toghra*s (monograms) as identification marks or signatures on official documents. This unusually large example (5.2ft by 8ft/1.6m by 2.4m) of Sultan Suleyman (ca. 1540s) might have been designed to hang in a council chamber. The gracefulness of the letters is complemented by the exquisite infilling of illumination.

OPPOSITE

The Sunnet Odasi (Circumcision Room) in the Topkapi Palace was renovated by Ibrahim I in 1642, but incorporated superb tilework from an earlier building on the same site probably built by Sultan Suleyman in the late 1520s. Circumcison of imperial children was celebrated with great pomp; for instance, for that of his son in 1582, Sultan Murad III inaugurated a festival that lasted more than 50 days.

BELOW

Islamic art is famous for abstract patterns, but few match this one for dynamism. A central star and whirling leaf forms create a vortex of energy. Uç Sherefeli mosque, Edirne (1437–47).

RIGHT

The design and colors of this wool carpet are typical of those produced in Ushak in northwest Anatolia in the 16th century. The motif of a central medallion with four quarter medallions in the corners is also found in such varied media as doors and book bindings, and most likely indicates the involvement of the Royal Design Workshop in the Ottoman capital, Istanbul.

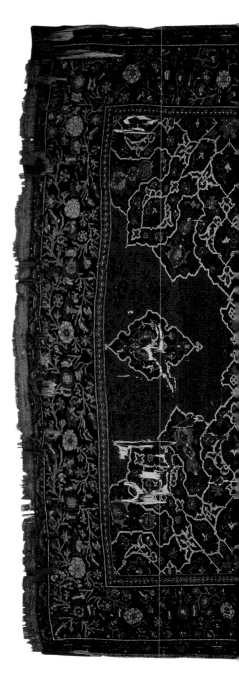

of two axial flanking domes. At ground level, however, the vast interior is adjusted to the requirements of Islamic ritual by having the maximum uninterrupted space, to enable the faithful to pray in rows. Light floods into the interior through the twenty-three windows of the side tympana (see illustration, page 165); this is made possible by the massive flanking buttresses whose bulk is made less apparent by changes in level. Like the Shehzade, an arcade links these buttresses on the sides of the exterior, although its function here is partly to provide overhanging eaves for the ablution facilities underneath.

The Selimiye (see pages 176–180) represents the culmination of Sinan's career, but he took just as much care with many of his smaller projects. The complex of Rustem Pasha, the imperial grand vizier (chief minister), at Istanbul was finished not long after the vizier's death in 1561. Its mosque is of interest for being raised on a vaulted substructure that enables it to dominate its commercial neighborhood. The mosque has relatively simple architectural lines, with a dome on an octagonal base, and is famed chiefly for

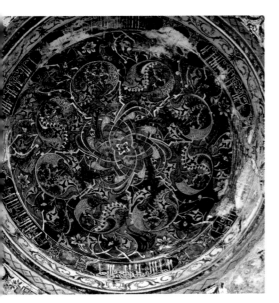

its lavish revetment of Iznik tiles. Following a recent restoration, these once again provide an effective contrast to the plain walls of the upper structure.

The complex of the grand vizier Sokullu Mehmed Pasha at Istanbul (1571–72) was expertly fitted into an awkward sloping site downhill from the ancient hippodrome. Here it is the interior (see page 164) that is of greatest interest. The dome is seamlessly incorporated within the rectangular prayer hall, without using columns, by means of a hexagonal base. The balance of decoration is appropriately weighed: the central arched panel on the *qibla* wall is revetted to its full height near the base of the dome with Iznik tiles patterned with large-scale blossoms.

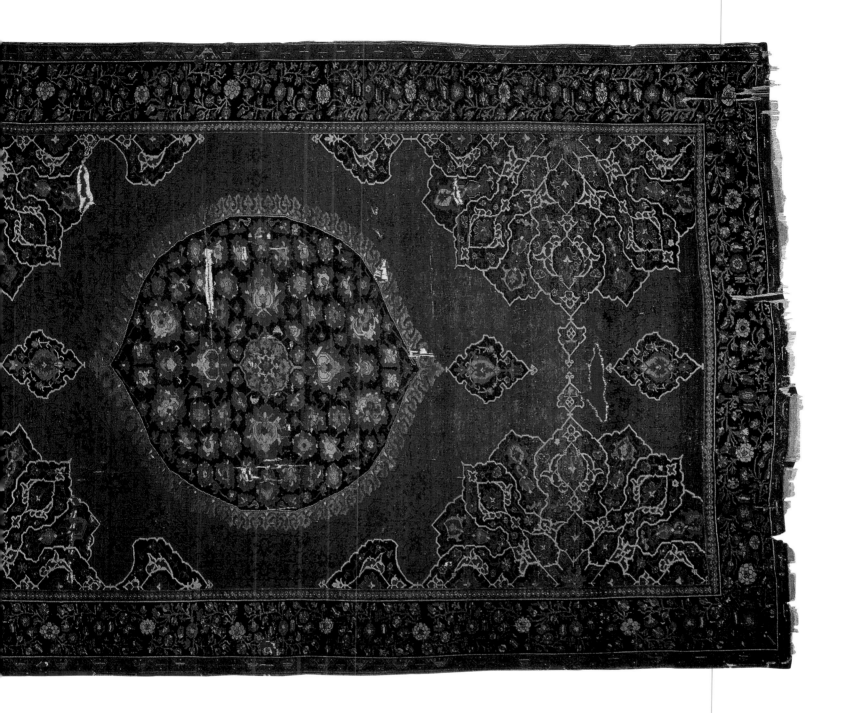

WONDERS OF IZNIK

The Iznik tiles that decorate these mosques are the product of kilns that made some of the world's finest pottery. Iznik, in northwest Anatolia, was producing underglaze-painted blue and white wares at the end of the fifteenth century. This was a favorite color scheme of potters in other parts of the Islamic world, but the technical genius of the Iznik potters lay firstly in their ability to prevent the colors running under the glaze, and second in their

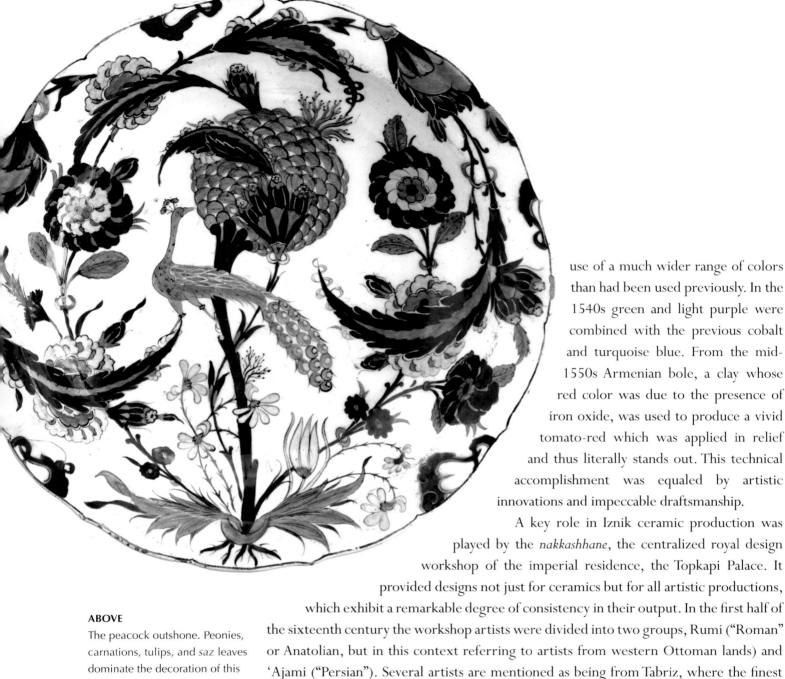

ABOVE

The peacock outshone. Peonies, carnations, tulips, and *saz* leaves dominate the decoration of this Iznik plate (ca. 1550), leaving the diminutive peacock at its center forlorn at its eclipse.

use of a much wider range of colors than had been used previously. In the 1540s green and light purple were combined with the previous cobalt and turquoise blue. From the mid-1550s Armenian bole, a clay whose red color was due to the presence of iron oxide, was used to produce a vivid tomato-red which was applied in relief and thus literally stands out. This technical accomplishment was equaled by artistic innovations and impeccable draftsmanship.

A key role in Iznik ceramic production was played by the *nakkashhane*, the centralized royal design workshop of the imperial residence, the Topkapi Palace. It provided designs not just for ceramics but for all artistic productions, which exhibit a remarkable degree of consistency in their output. In the first half of the sixteenth century the workshop artists were divided into two groups, Rumi ("Roman" or Anatolian, but in this context referring to artists from western Ottoman lands) and 'Ajami ("Persian"). Several artists are mentioned as being from Tabriz, where the finest Iranian painters had trained under the Safavids. One, Shah Kulu (head of the workshop from 1526 to 1545) was a master painter in the *saz* and *hatayi* styles. *Saz* refers to feathery leaves with serrated edges; *hatayi* means from Cathay, referring to chinoiserie decoration. These styles could be combined in Iznik pottery with more traditional arabesques, although in many later examples of Iznik ceramics carnations, tulips, or other naturalistic flowers are masterfully contrasted with the lustrous white ground.

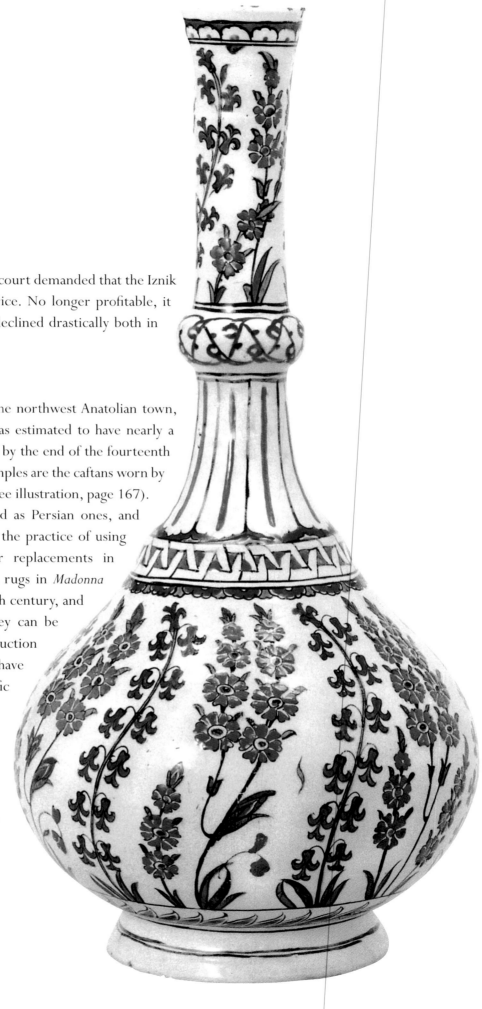

RIGHT

By the 1560s the Iznik potters
had acquired the ability to add
tomato-red to the blue, green,
and black palette of previous
decades. The freehand drawing
of the prunus blossoms on this
water bottle provides an effective
contrast with the deep blue of the
hyacinths.

Unfortunately, in the early 1600s the court demanded that the Iznik potters work only for it, and at a fixed price. No longer profitable, it is hardly surprising that Iznik wares then declined drastically both in number and quality.

RICHES IN SILK AND VELVET

Textiles were also mainly a monopoly of one northwest Anatolian town, in this case Bursa, the former capital. It was estimated to have nearly a thousand looms for weaving silk and velvets by the end of the fourteenth century. The most spectacular surviving examples are the caftans worn by the court and given as presents to officials (see illustration, page 167).

Turkish carpets are just as renowned as Persian ones, and survive from even earlier times, thanks to the practice of using them as padding underneath their later replacements in mosques. European artists showed Turkish rugs in *Madonna and Child* paintings as early as the fourteenth century, and as the paintings are frequently datable they can be used as a *terminus ante quem* for the introduction of particular motifs. The earliest examples have mainly geometric fields, with pseudo-Kufic being used for the borders.

As with textiles and ceramics (see page 171), another northwest Anatolian town, Ushak, was selected as the main supplier of carpets to the court. These are on a much grander scale than previous examples and

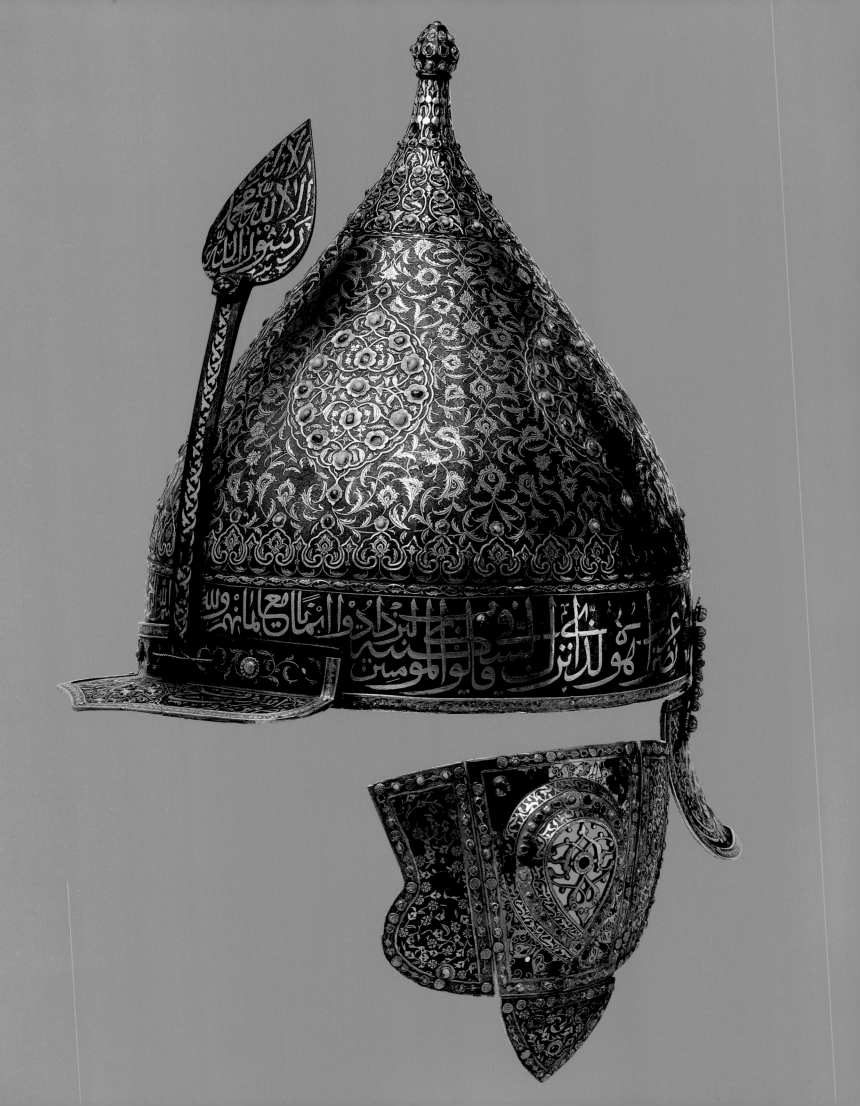

are organized more like contemporary Persian carpets (perhaps owing to the influence of the royal design workshop), some with large central medallions containing stylized flowers, some with stars in the central field.

PLACES AND PATRONS: OTTOMAN PAINTING

Early Ottoman book painting was also heavily indebted to Persian styles. Later examples use Persian perspective but often shun spontaneity in favor of serried ranks of courtiers. The originality of Ottoman painting lay particularly in topographical scenes and portraits. Matrakchi's *Descriptions of the Halting Stations of Suleyman's Campaign in the Two Iraqs* (1537) has paintings that remain valuable sources for the urban history of many towns including Istanbul. Two further manuscripts with views of Hungarian and Mediterranean cities combine Matrakchi's original perspective with that obtained from European prints.

This penchant for realism is partly echoed in the portraits that also appear around the mid-1500s, perhaps encouraged by Mehmed II's relations with the Italian artists Costanzo de Ferrara and Gentile Bellini, both of whom visited Istanbul in the 1470s and struck portrait medallions of the sultan. From the later eighteenth century the sultans began having their portraits painted in oil on canvas, although again the first example is Bellini's painting of Mehmed II. As a result we have an almost unbroken pictorial record of Ottoman rulers from the sixteenth century until the end of the dynasty in 1922.

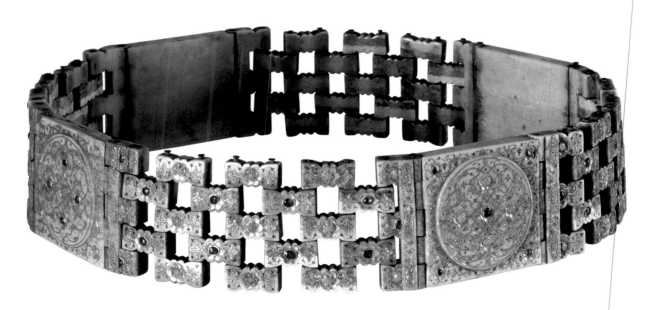

SELIMIYE MOSQUE
SINAN'S ARCHITECTURAL PARADISE

OPPOSITE

The crowning glory of Ottoman architecture. The four soaring, pencil-thin minarets of the Selimiye mosque surround its lofty central dome, 105ft (32m) wide. The honey-colored sandstone contrasts with the black lead of the roof and the turrets which surmount the eight buttresses supporting the dome. Edirne, 1568–74.

BELOW

Plan of the Selimiye complex, showing the mosque (3) and equal-sized inner courtyard (4) within the outer courtyard (5), with the two madrasas (1) and the covered bazaar (2).

The Selimiye (1568–74) is arguably the culmination of Ottoman architecture, its vast dome crowning the city of Edirne and the legacy of its great architect, Sinan. The mosque's founder, Sultan Selim II (1566–74), was lieutenant-governor of the city in 1548–50, and this, as well as a lack of a space in the capital, may explain his reason for siting it in Edirne. It also differs from many other Ottoman complexes in the relatively small number of other buildings. This may be partly because Selim died just before its completion, and partly because he was buried beside the Haghia Sophia in Istanbul (so the Selimiye contains no mausoleums). In his autobiography Sinan wrote that "the architects of the infidels" had claimed that Muslims could never surpass the Haghia Sophia dome. He therefore set out to better it, and indeed succeeded in building one of greater diameter.

The decision to place the soaring minarets at the corners of the mosque instead of the courtyard (as at the Sulemaniye), and the pointed caps of the turrets that add weight to the building's eight piers, reinforce the crown-like appearance of the exterior. Instead of the cool gray masonry of the Sulemaniye, a much warmer sandstone is used here, further enlivened by polychrome masonry around many of the arches and windows.

The courtyard's axial entrance is low, but this prevents it from obstructing the view of the dome. In contrast, the arcade on the entrance façade of the mosque within the courtyard is necessarily much taller, but visually lightened by interspersing its three large arches with two smaller ones. Unfortunately this means the much lower arcade at the sides of the courtyard spring from halfway up the columns supporting the end of the north façade, but this was a dilemma never satisfactorily solved in Ottoman architecture.

A WORLD OF LIGHT

The surprise of the interior is not so much the impressive dome as the astonishing influx of light from every level through a great number of

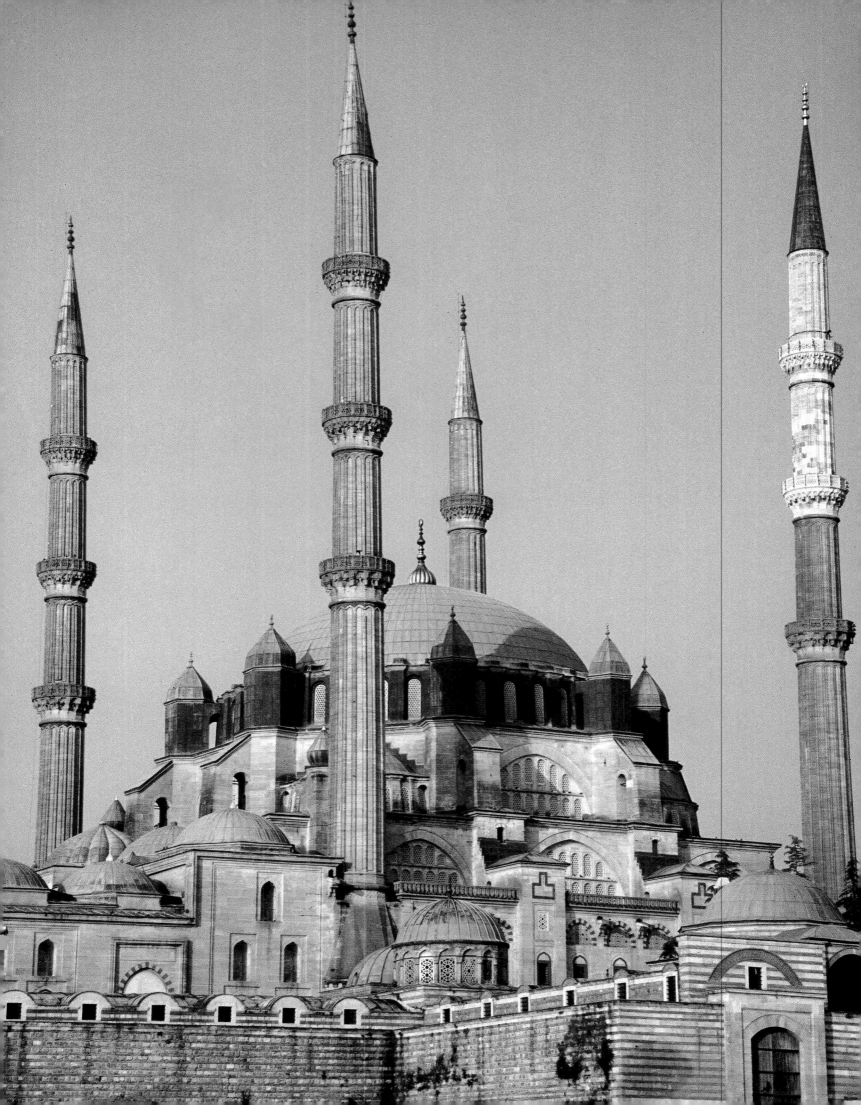

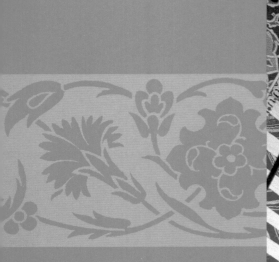

RIGHT

By connecting the supporting
buttresses to the outer walls,
the architect Sinan was able
to minimize their obtrusion in
the central dome chamber and,
to an even greater extent than
in the Suleymaniye at Istanbul
(see illustration, page 165), to
incorporate as many windows as
possible into the design. Every
tympanum, four on each side,
contains 12 or 14 windows,
each of the four squinches nine
windows, and the base of the
dome itself 32. And this count
does not include the larger
windows in the two storeys of
the lower walls.

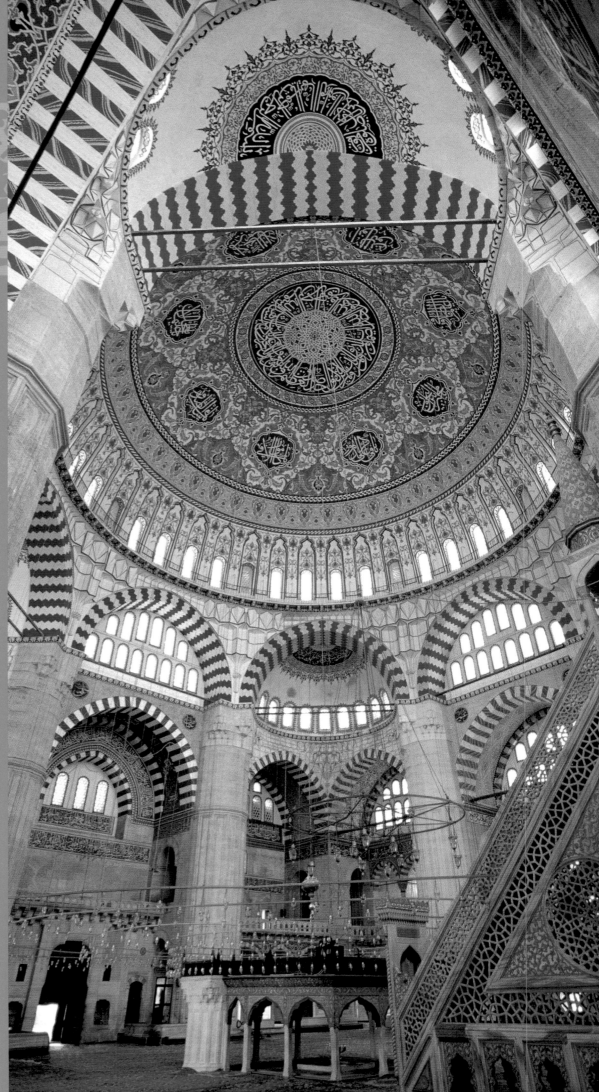

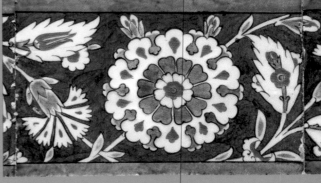

windows. How was Sinan thus able to pierce the fabric of the building but still support the huge dome? The dome is borne by eight piers whose massiveness is skillfully disguised. On the *qibla* side, the *mihrab*'s projecting walls align with the piers; the top half of the lateral piers is hidden by the arches that join them, and the bottom half lightened by connecting them with a narrow arch to the concealed buttresses leading to the outer walls.

Earlier Ottoman imperial mosques had joined the muezzin's gallery to one of the side piers, but here it is in the middle, emphasizing the centripetal tendencies of the plan. It serves a dual function, revealing a pool with drinking water on the lower level, a reminder of the indoor ablutions areas of earlier Seljuk and Ottoman mosques.

The only flaw in the design of the interior may be the *mihrab* which, recessed in its niche, is much darker than the surrounding spaces. But this may have been alleviated by the light from the pairs of massive candles that furnished most Ottoman mosques.

The exterior also departs from the design of traditional mosques. The lateral façades are taller, efficiently disguising the bulk of the two buttresses that descend from the weighty turrets above the piers. But the massiveness of these façades is also cleverly disguised by breaking them up into three storeys with arches of varied size in each, and by the balustrades on the lowest arcade and the roofline. The rear façade displays none of the buttresses seen on Sinan's previous mosques, since they are contained within the *mihrab* recess. The only discordant note here is the arcade at ground level, supported on marble columns that seem spindly compared to the massiveness of their surroundings.

Selim II had paid for the mosque from the booty acquired from the conquest of Cyprus (1570–71). He waited impatiently for the great work to be finished, but died in December 1574 without having seen its triumphant completion. But we can agree with the judgment of the endowment deed of the building that "he built a paradise-like mosque which, in addition to being most beautiful, artistic, and novel, is unanimously judged by those who observe its four cypress-like minarets reaching the sky and its matchless dome as superior to the works of his powerful ancestors."

ABOVE
The use of Iznik tiles in the Selimiye is restricted to a few key panels, in order not to compete with the dominant decorative accents provided by painting. This tile displays tulips, carnations, and rosettes.

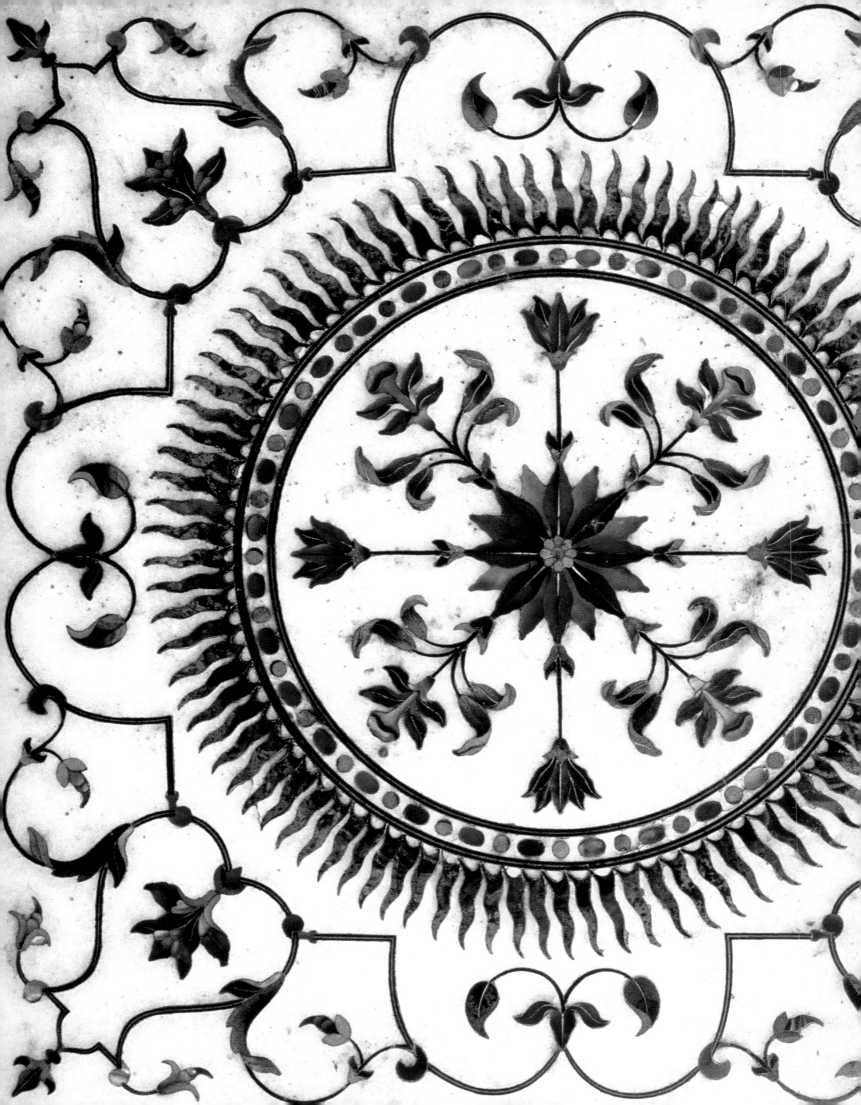

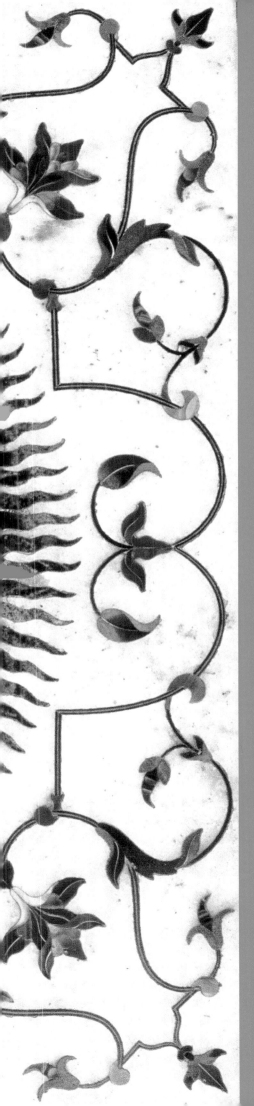

chapter **7**

OVERLORDS OF THE ORIENT
SOUTH ASIA AND THE FAR EAST

ISLAM IN INDIA

THE DELHI SULTANATE

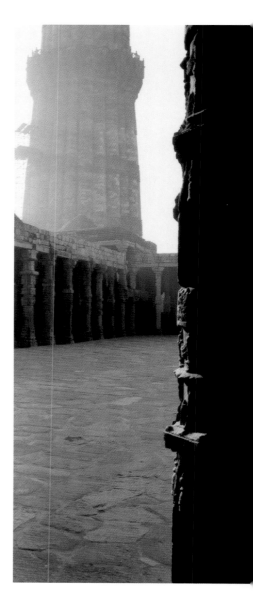

Muslim forces had reached Sind, in present-day Pakistan, by the early eighth century, and traders soon established bases along the western coast of India. However, it was not until the Ghaznavids and Ghurids (see page 112) invaded northwest India in the eleventh and twelfth centuries that there was a permanent Muslim presence in the interior. In 1193 Qutb al-Din Aybak captured Delhi for the Ghurids and in 1206 proclaimed his independence as sultan, beginning the Delhi sultanate (1206–1526). His successor Iltutmish reached Bengal by 1230 and cemented the Delhi sultans as rulers of most of northern India. The new dynasty balanced its military expansionism with a coherent civil administration designed to produce a steady stream of tax revenue rather than plunder.

Unlike most other major Islamic dynasties, the sultans controlled a largely non-Muslim population. As in early Ottoman times, an expansionist state confronting non-Muslims attracted many wishing to participate in holy war, such as a number of celebrated warrior Sufis who helped to spread Islam in the Deccan and eastern India. But there was also much accommodation with Hindus, many of whom paid regular tribute to the sultanate or were employed in the army and, from the fourteenth century, in government. In time Muslim and Hindu alike often venerated holy men of both religions. The language of administration and literature was Persian, and such was the distance of India from Arabic-speaking lands that Persian was used more than anywhere else—Iran included—on works of art of all kinds, alongside or even instead of Arabic.

PROCLAIMING THE FAITH: SULTANATE ARCHITECTURE

The first major Islamic monument in Delhi was the Quwwat al-Islam mosque, begun by Aybak and substantially enlarged by Iltutmish. The most striking feature of its construction is not the extensive use of materials from Hindu temples in the first wave of construction, but the virtuosity of the stone carving of the inscriptions and vegetal bands in the arched screen added by Iltutmish. This makes it clear that local craftsmen

BELOW

At the Quwwat al-Islam mosque, reused materials from earlier Hindu buildings have been incorporated into the arcaded style of the new Muslim conquerors, a message enhanced by the huge bulk of the Qutb minaret on the left. The minaret is still the tallest in the Islamic world, and, like the uncompromising Quranic inscriptions denouncing idolatry that decorate it, delivered a highly visible message of the domination of the new faith. Delhi, early 13th century.

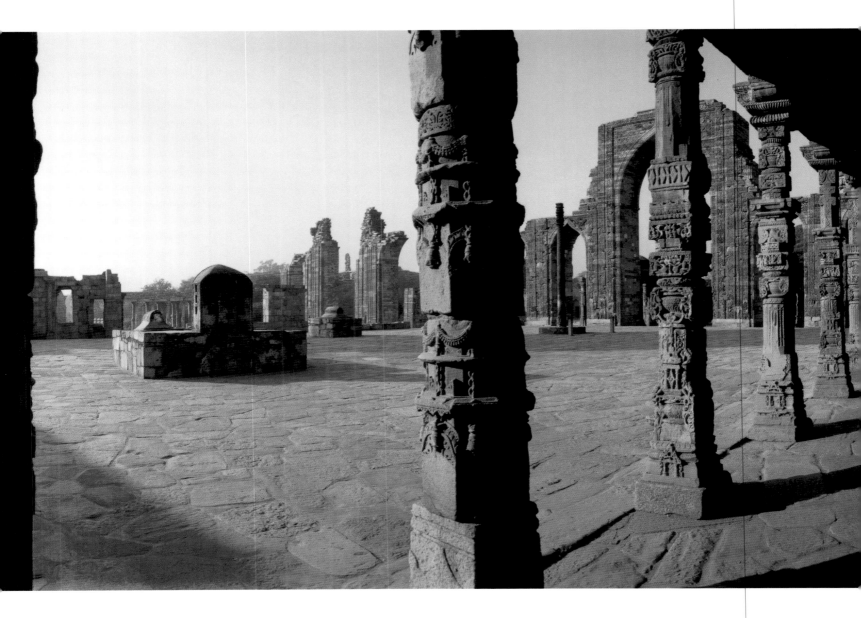

میانِ آن برنج را خوب شسته بیندازند یا آنکه رو

کندم که بسیار سفید باشد بیندازند یا سرو له آرد

بیندازند یا ماهیچهٔ باریک بیندازند و بالای آن کافور

و مُشک و کلاب واند گی عنبر اشهب بیندازند

و چون خوب پخته باشد فرو آرند نه بسیار غلیظ

باشد و نه تنک   موازنه بپزند

were involved, and such intricate handling of stone remained a hallmark of Islamic architecture in India. The subsequent development of architecture was an interesting amalgamation of Persian, Central Asian and indigenous themes and forms. The dome was one of these imported forms, and appeared almost invariably in mausoleums and frequently in the prayer hall of major mosques.

One of the largest dome chambers in India was built over the grave of the Sufi leader Rukn al-Din 'Alam (died 1335) at Multan in the Punjab. Surprisingly for such a splendid monument, it is uncertain, either from inscriptions on the building or from written sources, who funded it or exactly when it was constructed. Tradition has it that Ghiyath al-Din Tughluq (ruled 1320–25) built it as his own mausoleum while he was a governor in the nearby town of Dipalpur, but after he became sultan he built himself a smaller one in Delhi and it is unlikely that he would have forsaken such a magnificent monument. Rukn al-Din's order, the Suhrawardi, was one of the two most powerful in India, and it may well be that his followers caused the mausoleum to be built shortly after his death—it is known that he was buried temporarily in his grandfather's tomb.

The exterior of the Rukn-i 'Alam mausoleum is octagonal, its lower tier being distinguished by eight large buttresses that slope markedly inward. These are capped by turrets, perhaps echoing the minarets that graced the upper octagon of Uljaytu's mausoleum in Iran, built a few decades earlier. The upper tier of the mausoleum displays a profusion of tiles; although only in three colors, white, light blue, and dark blue, great variety is obtained through differences in relief and setting. The interior is relatively plain apart from the large *mihrab* of elaborately carved wood, a scarce material in India that underlines its place of honor. The spandrels feature six-pointed stars, the Seal of Solomon, a symbol that was popular all over the Islamic world but particularly in India.

Such was the prestige of this building that it was imitated for centuries in the area around Multan. Some of the finest examples, despite their ruined condition, are in the nearby town of Uchch. One of the most notable is the tomb of Bibi Jawindi; the occupant

OPPOSITE

The handlebar moustache distinguishes Sultan Ghiyath al-Din Khalji, ruler of Malwa in the Deccan (1469–1501). He was the patron of the *Ni'matnama* (*Book of Delicacies*), a royal recipe book with illustrations that combine features of Indian painting with the style of Shiraz in southern Iran.

died in 1402 but the mausoleum was not built until the end of the fifteenth century. It repeats almost exactly the form of the Rukn-i 'Alam, but differs in the greater use and variety of tilework, in particular in its extensive use of underglaze-painted tiles.

Very little of the decorative arts has survived from sultanate India; the decision of Sultan Firuzshah (ruled 1290–96) to replace figural scenes with vegetal ones on religious grounds may have led to the destruction of portable objects with figural decoration. Another reason for the lack of objects from this period may be the destruction and removal of booty that accompanied Timur's invasion of India and sack of Delhi in 1398–99.

THE CITY OF JOY

Timur left behind a considerably weakened sultanate, and many governors or local rulers formerly under central control declared themselves independent. One of these was the governor of Malwa in central India, who in 1402 founded a dynasty that lasted until the early sixteenth century. Its capital was Mandu, known as the City of Joy, in a beautiful hilltop setting on the edge of the Deccan plateau. In addition to fine buildings, the dynasty also sponsored book painting. Sultan Ghiyath al-Din (ruled 1469–1501) was famous for his hedonism, abjuring the cares of state in favor of his harem. Several illustrated manuscripts survive from this period, including a royal recipe book, the *Ni'matnama* (*Book of Delicacies*), which has many paintings that show Ghiyath al-Din with his distinctive moustache presiding over courtiers and servants (see illustration, page 184). The style, like that of sultanate architecture, mixes Indian and Iranian elements, with the simplified manner of Shiraz painting providing most of the inspiration.

The Lodi dynasty was able to restore sultanate rule over most of northern India by the end of the fifteenth century, but Ibrahim II (ruled 1517–26) managed to alienate the nobility and army commanders to the extent that they invited Babur, then based in Kabul, to intervene. The coming of Babur, a descendant of Timur, saw the inauguration of the Mughal dynasty.

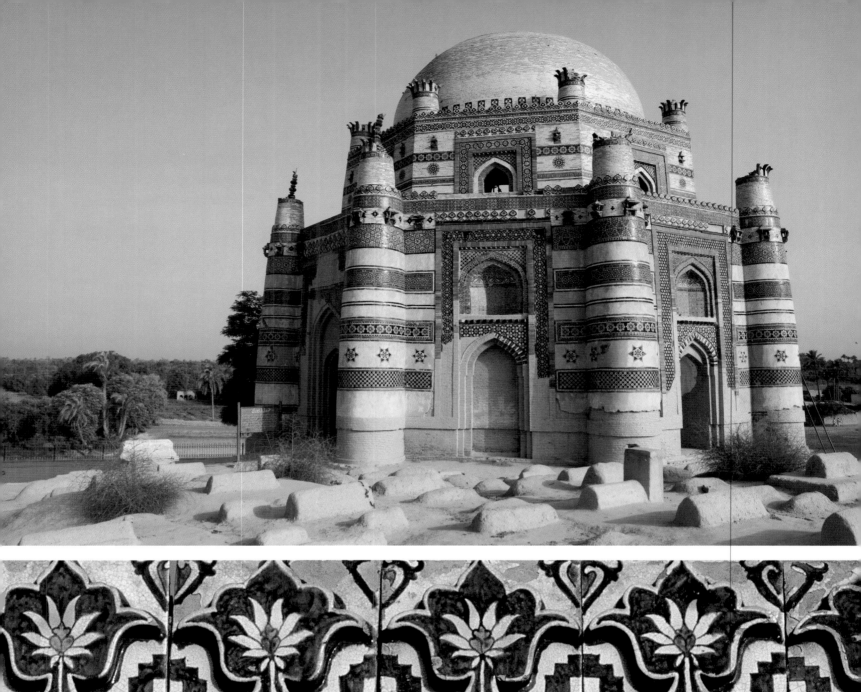

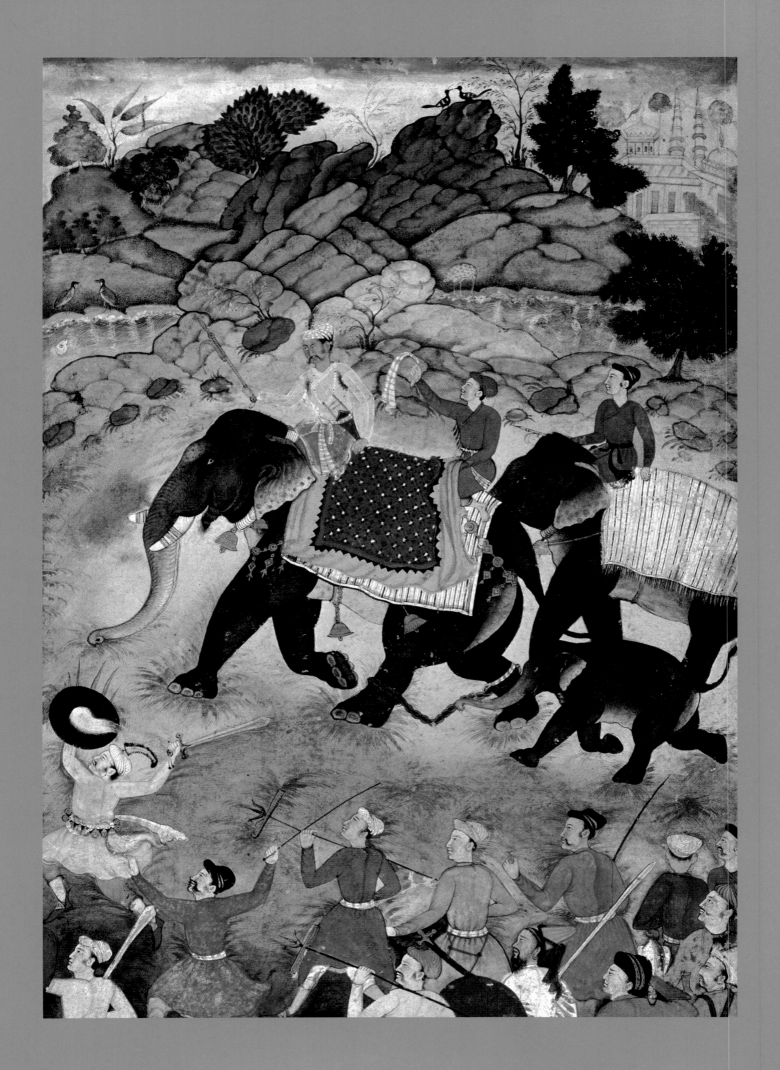

CONFLICT AND COEXISTENCE

THE MUGHALS

While known to European sources as the Mughals, the dynastic rulers who overthrew the Delhi sultanate thought of themselves as Timurids, since Babur was the descendant of Timur (Tamerlane). Although in origin "Mughal" or "Moghal" (or, formerly, "Mogul") is the same word from which "Mongol" is derived, in sixteenth-century India the term referred to the Mongolianized Turks who inhabited what is now Uzbekistan, where Babur had been raised and over which Timur had ruled. Babur's ambitions in his ancestral homelands had indeed been thwarted by the Uzbeks, and the Timurid dominions in Iran were overrun by the Safavids (see chapter 5). After his victory over the Lodi sultan in 1526, Babur lived for only another four years, and the continuing volatility of the struggle for power in northern India is underlined by the fact that a mere ten years later, in 1540, Babur's son Humayun suffered defeat at the hands of an Aghan federation under the leadership of Shir Shah Sur. Humayun was forced into exile, but with the help of the Safavid ruler Shah Tahmasp was able to regain control of Delhi and Agra in 1555.

AKBAR THE GREAT

A year later Humayun fell down the steps of his library and died, leaving the throne to his thirteen-year-old son, Akbar, who ruled for the next fifty years (1556–1605). It was in this period that the foundations of the Mughal empire were solidly established, owing to Akbar's abilities as a military commander and statesman. He re-established control over north India and Bengal, and gradually brought adjacent parts of the Deccan under his dominion, or at least forced their rulers to acknowledge his supremacy.

Akbar was exceptionally interested in religion, encouraging debates at his court between scholars of different faiths. The result was his promulgation to a select few at the court of the Din-i Ilahi, the "Divine Faith," which, while being rooted in Islam, combined mystical elements from many sources. This tolerance was reflected in Akbar's policies toward the Hindu majority of his subjects, who were exempted from the poll tax (*jizya*) that was normally obligatory for non-Muslims, and entered government service in much

OPPOSITE
Mughal artists often painted elephants and did so with great naturalism, as in this early 17th-century hunting party. The use of perspective for the buildings derives from European painting.

BELOW
Jahangir's court artist Mansur portrayed two captive cranes with calligraphic elegance. This is a 19th-century copy of the early 17th-century original.

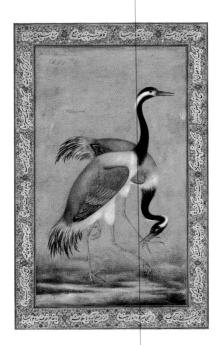

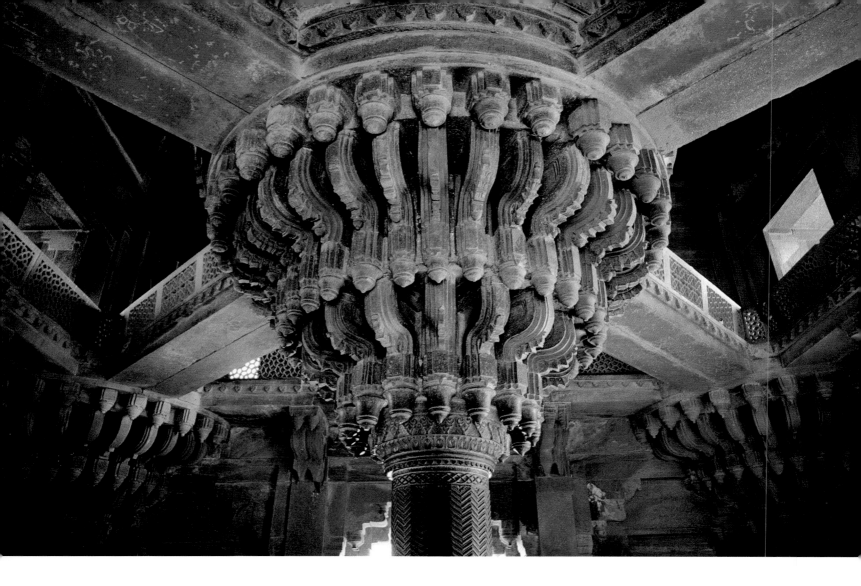

greater numbers than ever before. This may have served Akbar's interests in securing a more favorable balance of power between the Turco-Persian aristocracy and Hindus within the administration who owed their elevation to Akbar himself. Akbar established a new royal capital at Fatihpur Sikri, near Agra, but abandoned it in 1585 in favor of Lahore. In 1599 he returned to Agra, which remained the capital for the rest of his reign.

THE CENTURY OF THE THREE EMPERORS

The reigns of three Mughal rulers encompass the whole of the seventeenth century, bringing a stability that facilitated the expansion of Mughal power further into the Deccan. Jahangir (ruled 1605–27) was more interested in connoisseurship than military affairs, and commissioned paintings as a form of political propaganda. His inactivity was encouraged by his addiction to a daily mixture of wine and opium. The later years of his reign were marked by rebellions of his sons, of whom Shah Jahan (ruled 1627–58) eventually emerged victorious.

Shah Jahan was much more active, erecting Shahjahanabad, a new courtly city at Delhi (1639–48), which became his capital. The figure of 200,000 cavalry in his army gives an inkling of the vast wealth available to the empire at this time. Although successful in consolidating Mughal power in Gujarat and Sind, Shah Jahan's attempts to annex Uzbek territory achieved little beyond the temporary capture of Balkh in northwest Afghanistan. When he fell ill in 1647 another succession war broke out, in which the eventual victor was his third son, Aurangzeb (ruled 1658–1707). Aurangzeb favored a stricter application of Islam than his predecessors, and while he was just as successful as a general, he was much less interested than his predecessors in patronage of the arts.

A quick succession of rulers after Aurangzeb's death weakened the empire, as did the invasion of India in 1738–39 by the Iranian Nadir Shah, who sacked Delhi and carried off one of the most famous Mughal treasures, the sumptuous Peacock Throne. The subsequent expansion of the British into the interior completed the dynasty's eclipse, although it continued to exist in name until 1857.

MUGHAL PAINTING

As mentioned earlier (see page 186), in the period of the Delhi sultanate a new style of painting emerged that was based on a composite of Indian and Persian elements. To this mix the Mughals added a third element in the form of European-style shading and perspective (see illustration, page 188). Whereas in Iranian painting this innovation led to a decline in quality, Mughal painters applied it sparingly and produced a wholly new synthesis of Indian figures and primary colors, Persian perspective, and European realism that resulted in works unsurpassed by any other school.

BELOW

Akbar's reverence for the Sufi *shaykh* Salim Chishti led to his building of Fatihpur Sikri and, after the *shaykh*'s death in 1572, to the erection of his mausoleum. His tomb is famous for its *jalis*, pierced marble screens that give the appearance of weightlessness to the outer walls.

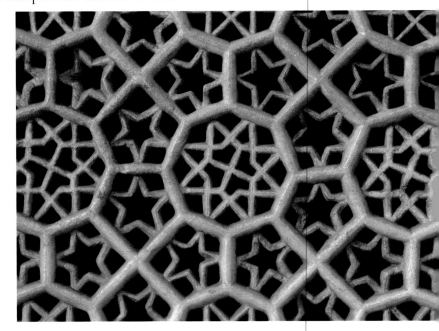

BELOW
The abundance of floral themes on this box is reminiscent of the dados and cenotaphs of the Taj Mahal, which were inspired in part by European herbals. But despite their apparent naturalism, the Mughal examples also display considerable stylization. Similar boxes were made in Sri Lanka and the Deccan, but the resemblances to imperial Mughal workshop designs suggest that this one was made in northern India, ca. 1700.

Two of the finest Mughal court painters, 'Abd al-Samad and Mir Sayyid 'Ali, were recruited by Humayun in his exile in Iran. They joined the atelier in Kabul in 1549, and both of them personally instructed the emperor Akbar in drawing. Akbar became an extremely enthusiastic patron of manuscripts, attending the court workshop regularly. His biographer, Abu'l-Fazl, devotes more space to Akbar's love of manuscripts than to his building activities.

The most extraordinary early manuscript of Akbar's reign was the *Hamzanama*, recounting the legendary exploits of Hamza, the uncle of the Prophet Muhammad. It took over fifteen years to complete (ca. 1557–73), not surprisingly in view of that fact that it contained around 1,400 paintings so large—ca. 28in by 20in (70cm by 50cm)—that they were painted on cotton backed with paper to add extra strength to the pages.

The text of the major manuscripts was in Persian, still very much the literary and spoken language of the court. Illustrated versions of Persian literary classics such as the *Khamsa* of Nizami or *Divan* of Hafiz were produced, but instead of the many copies of the *Book of Kings* (*Shahnama*), the Iranian national epic, that were typical of Iranian courts, the Mughal rulers preferred to commission illustrated accounts of their own lives, with themselves naturally portrayed in an equally heroic light. The autobiography of Akbar's grandfather Babur, translated from the original Turki into Persian as the *Baburnama*, is one example. The copy of Abu'l-Fazl's *Akbarnama* (ca. 1590–95) in London's Victoria and Albert Museum has some of the most vigorous painting of the period, depicting not just Akbar's successful battles, but also scenes of him

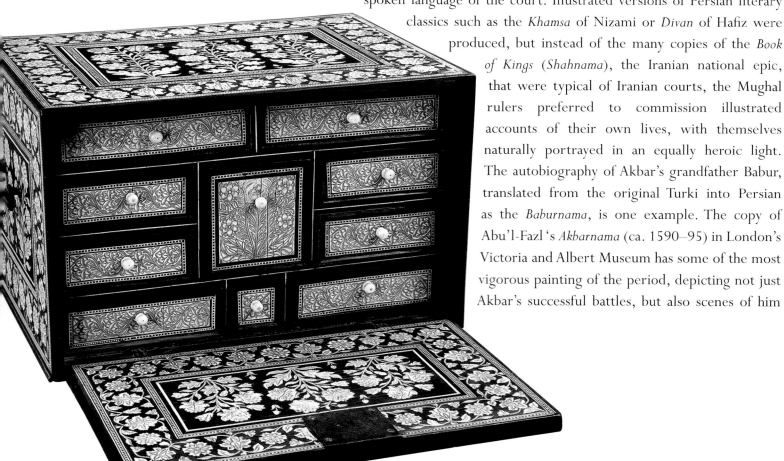

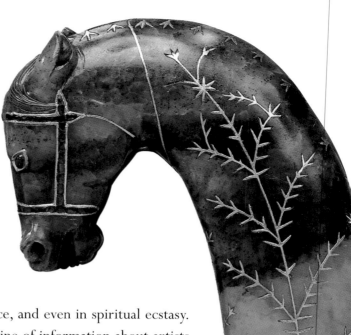

hunting, supervising construction, administering justice, and even in spiritual ecstasy. Like many contemporary manuscripts, this is also a mine of information about artists and workshop practice, as inscriptions on each painting name the person responsible for the design, the artist who executed the painting itself, and occasionally even a third individual who was responsible for the faces. To judge by their names most of the artists were Hindus, frequently from Gujurat or Gwalior in western India.

JAHANGIR: A ROYAL CONNOISSEUR

Jahangir was less interested in complete manuscripts than in individual paintings. He commissioned several allegorical paintings of himself, such as one that shows him comforting a diminutive Shah Abbas (the Safavid ruler and his sometime rival) on top of a globe. Jahangir was greatly interested in the natural world, and rewarded Mansur, the finest animal painter at the court, with the title Nadir al-Asr, "Rarity of the Age". The emperor's unflinching curiosity extended to ordering his court painters to record the skeletal appearance of one of his courtiers who was on the verge of death from opium poisoning.

In his autobiography, the *Jahangirnama*, Jahangir boasts of his connoisseurship in painting: "I derive such enjoyment from painting and have such expertise in judging it that, even without the artist's name being mentioned, no work of past or present masters can be shown to me that I do not instantly recognize." He was so proud of the court painters' abilities that on one occasion he borrowed a miniature from Sir Thomas Roe, the English ambassador, had five copies made by one of his artists, and challenged Sir Thomas to distinguish the original from the copies. Roe was able to, but only with difficulty, an outcome which Jahangir took as a triumph.

Shah Jahan was less interested in painting than architecture, as exemplified most magnificently by the Taj Mahal, the mausoleum he had built near Agra for his

ABOVE

The Mughals' love for jade is reflected in their many examples of wine cups and hilts of swords and daggers. Naturalistically carved animals such as goats, camels, or more often horses, as in this 18th-century example, are favorite subjects for hilts. Inlaid gold and rubies further enhance this piece's luxury.

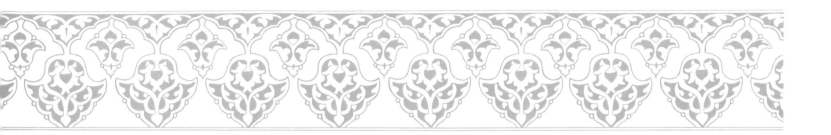

wife Mumtaz Mahal (see pages 200–203). However, he did sponsor one outstanding illustrated manuscript, the *Padshahnama*, a history of his reign. With his death and the accession of his son Aurangzeb the decline of Mughal painting quickly set in, as Aurangzeb's stricter interpretation of religion made him averse to figural arts.

A WEALTH OF JEWELS

The wealth of the Mughal court is also reflected in its patronage of the decorative arts. Jahangir took a keen interest in jewelry, recording an incident in his autobiography when the Safavid ruler Shah Abbas sent him a spinel as a gift. The gem was inscribed with the name of Ulugh Beg, one of Jahangir's Timurid ancestors, which Jahangir took to be a good omen. He had his own name and title inscribed on it and presented it to his son, the future Shah Jahan. Jahangir also acquired a jade wine cup engraved with Ulugh Beg's name and again added his own name and titles to it. Many jade objects were worked specifically for the court, such as another wine cup, this time for Shah Jahan. Dated to 1657, it has an extraordinarily delicate body in the shape of a Chinese gourd, tapering to a goat's head, resting on a foot in the shape of an Indian lotus. The Mughals' love of hard and precious stones could also be combined, as numerous jewel-studded objects show (see illustrations pages 193 and 199). Finest among these must have been Shah Jahan's Peacock Throne, completed in 1635, which was encrusted with the largest jewels in the imperial treasury (including Jahangir's inscribed spinel), as well as displaying enameling. Sadly, it was broken up after Nadir Shah carried it off to Iran.

However, one magnificent gemstone taken by Nadir Shah has survived. It bears the names of Jahangir, Aurangzeb, and a later Mughal ruler, Farrukh Siyar, as well as an inscription of Nadir Shah boasting of how it had been selected in 1740 from among 25,000 gems in the "Jewel House of Hindustan". This gem might also have a Timurid connection since there are suspicions that Nadir Shah's inscription might have replaced one of Timur himself.

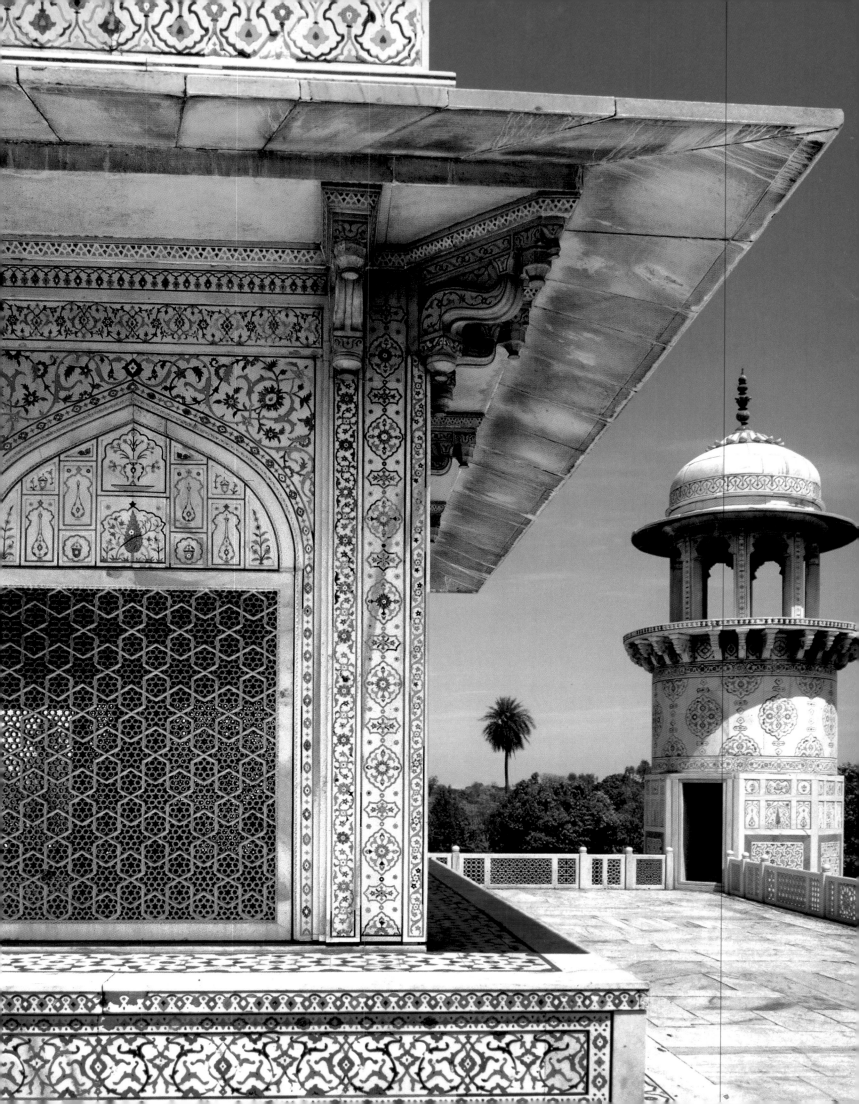

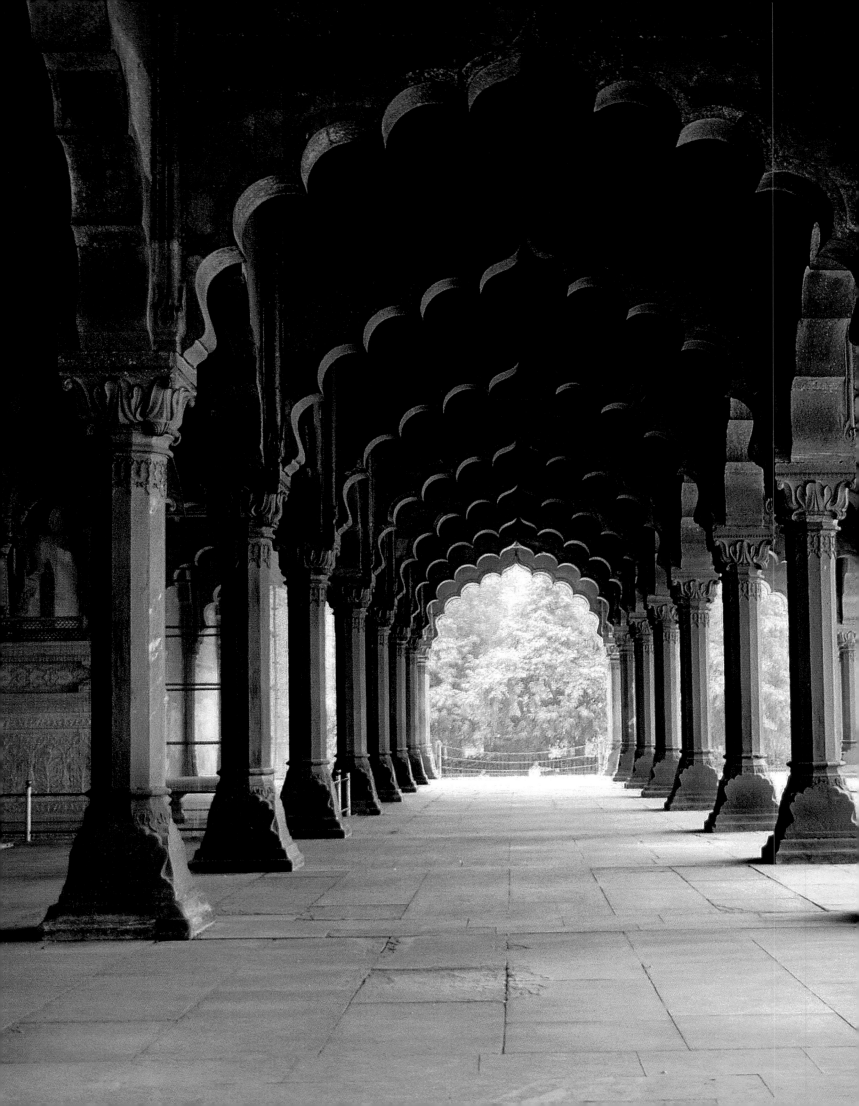

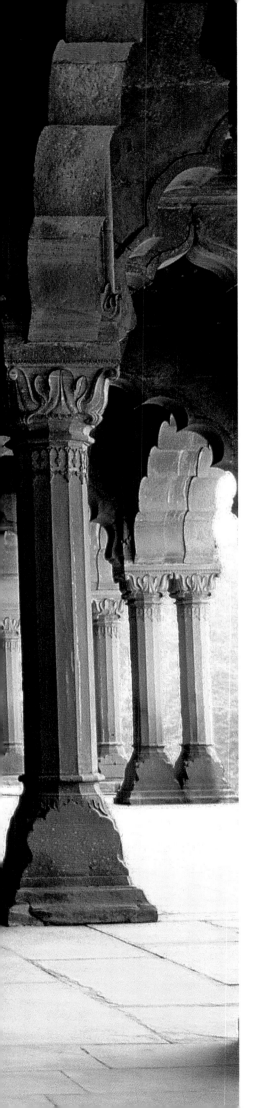

LEFT

Shah Jahan's public audience hall (ca. 1648) in the Red Fort, Delhi, is impressive for its network of polylobed arches of red sandstone. Visible on the left is the throne covered with a baldachin (canopy) from which the Mughal monarch would have presented himself to his nobles.

IMPERIAL GRANDEUR: MUGHAL ARCHITECTURE

The Mughals' link with their Timurid forebears is also emphasized in one of their first major monuments, the mausoleum of Humayun (1562–71). It was designed by Mirak Ghiyas of Herat who had earlier worked in Bukhara. It features the "Hasht Behesht" (Eight Paradises) plan, also seen in Safavid Iran (see page 146), of an octagonal base with four *iwans* supporting a double-dome on a high drum. Indian features include the broad arcaded platform which support the tomb, the red sandstone and marble materials, and the small domed pavilions above each corner.

Indian rulers had always had strong links with Sufism, and when a son was at last born to Akbar in 1569, supposedly following the intercession of the Sufi *shaykh* Salim Chishti, Akbar began the construction of a city, Fatihpur Sikri, adjacent to the saint's dwelling. The *shaykh* died in 1572 and work commenced on a tomb within the Friday Mosque that is one of the masterworks of Mughal architecture. Built entirely of white marble, it features a small central dome surrounded by an ambulatory, a plan of Gujarati origin. The outer walls consist of *jalis*, pierced screens of extraordinary delicacy (see illustration, page 191), and are linked to the deep eaves by serpentine brackets of equally fine workmanship.

Although the congregational mosque has the typical Iranian dome chamber preceded by an *iwan*, and an arcaded courtyard, all of the extensive residential buildings at Fatihpur Sikri are in the more traditional Indian style of flat roofs and wide eaves. One of the most mysterious buildings there is the Divan-i Khass, the private audience hall, which features an enormous pillar also decorated with serpentine brackets at the center, supporting a platform with a walkway connected to the four corners of the room (see illustration, page 190). This has been variously interpreted as a symbol of cosmic order and as a treasury for storing and inspecting jewels, but the traditional explanation seems the most likely: that Akbar used the central pillar as a throne when conversing with his ministers.

Akbar died without having built a mausoleum for himself, and his son Jahangir is mentioned in one contemporary text as the designer of the one that was built at

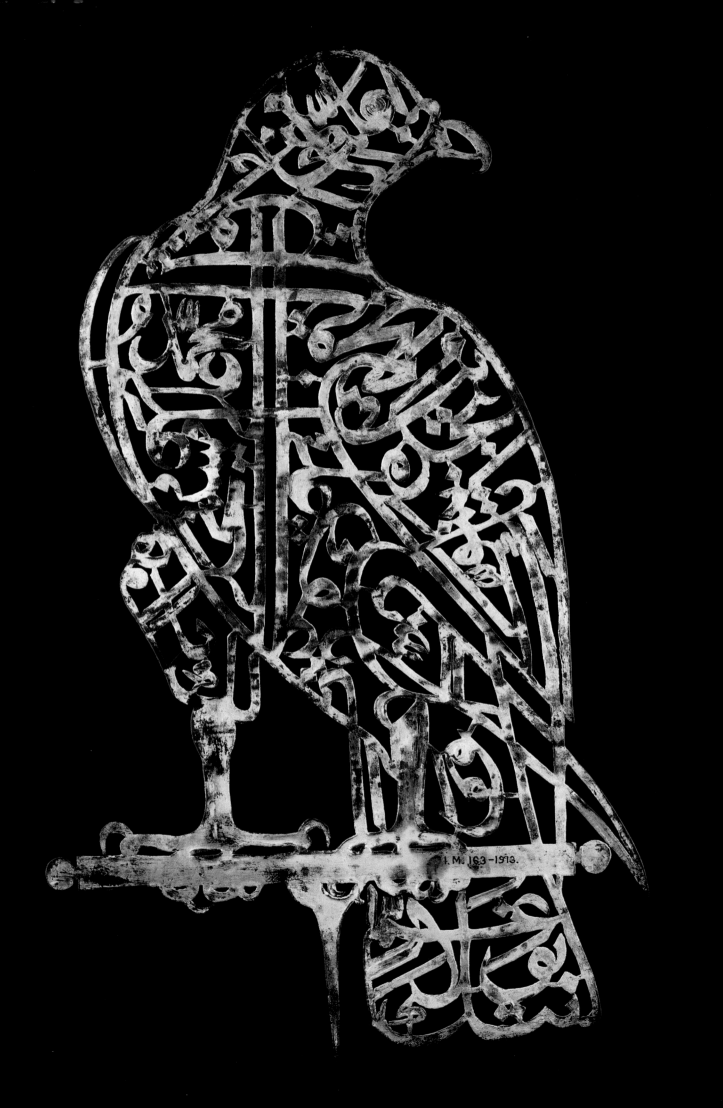

Sikandra near Agra. Although it resembles Humayun's tomb in being on a platform in the center of a garden, the upper structure is no longer the Timurid-inspired dome chamber but rather a fantastic version of a three-storey residence, loosely patterned upon those at Fatihpur Sikri. It is hard to disagree with a notable earlier scholar who described this ethereal construction as an anticlimax to the imposing substructure.

A similar combination worked better on a more modest scale at the mausoleum that Nur Jahan (Jahangir's wife) erected at Agra for her father I'timad al-Daula and her mother Asmat Begum (1628). Here there is only a single upper storey, a square chamber with a partly curved pyramidal roof. It is distinguished by the first extensive *pietra dura* (semiprecious inlaid stones) in Mughal architecture, used for the arabesques which appear not only on the outside of the building (see illustration, page 195) but on a surprisingly large scale on the floor of the tomb chamber itself.

THE RED FORT

Before the erection of the Taj Mahal, Shah Jahan's major architectural accomplishment was the building of Shahjahanabad, his new capital at Delhi (completed 1648). Earlier he had embellished the forts at Agra and Lahore, but these paled in comparison to the walled palace, now known as the Red Fort, that was the ceremonial centerpiece of the composition. Its public audience hall is impressive not only for the stateliness of its polylobed arcades (see illustration, page 196), but also for the *pietra dura* work behind the royal throne that combines local workmanship of lions with imported Italian depictions of birds and of Orpheus playing the lyre taming wild animals. This illustration of an ideal kingdom was intended to equate Shah Jahan with Solomon, the model of the ideal ruler in Islam.

BELOW

Both jade and rock crystal Mughal boxes were commonly inlaid with gold and precious stones such as the rubies and emeralds seen on this example. The silver mounts and hinges of the lid were added at a later date. Mughal, 18th century.

THE TAJ MAHAL

IMPERIAL MONUMENT TO LOVE

BELOW

A plan of the Taj Mahal. The tomb (1) is flanked by a mosque (2) and a guest house (3), with the Yamuna river behind (4). The garden (5) at the center is subdivided into quadripartite units. At the entrance to the entire complex is a courtyard with a monumental gate (6) with rooms for the tomb attendants and subsidiary tombs. Missing at the bottom (now built over) are four caravanserais (7) laid out around a central market square.

Although Shah Jahan had three lawful wives, his union with Mumtaz Mahal was altogether exceptional in the annals of courtly love. She bore him fourteen children, a telling comparison to the one child produced by each of his other two lawful wives. He was inconsolable upon her death following childbirth in 1631, aged only thirty-eight.

Mumtaz Mahal's tomb at Agra was begun almost immediately, although the whole complex was not completed until twelve years later. It is one example of Islamic architecture that has attained worldwide fame. With some monuments this might lead a visitor to experience a sense of anticlimax, but the exceptional majesty and serenity that the building embodies surpass even the highest expectations.

AN EARTHLY PARADISE

How is this achieved? The form of the mausoleum is the culmination of a series of centrally planned mausoleums with outer galleries, beginning in Iran and spreading from there to Central Asia and India, as seen for instance in the tombs of Uljaytu, Timur, and Humayun. Most earlier examples of this form that include a garden, such as the tomb of Humayun, situated the tomb at the center, but here, backed by the Yamuna river, the tomb is the culmination of a promenade through a fertile four-part garden, a layout chosen to represent the idea expressed by the chroniclers of the age that Mumtaz Mahal's mausoleum was an earthly version of her abode in paradise. In its day it was one of many plots filled with gardens and fine mansions that lined the riverside at Agra. The garden was originally filled with fruit-bearing trees and aromatic herbs.

This vision of paradise is reinforced by the exceptional care taken with the materials and the decoration of the building. The white marble chosen for the mausoleum was extraordinarily expensive, but its qualities of durability and translucence clearly recompensed Shah Jahan for his outlay. It both reflects and absorbs the changing light, varying its appeal throughout the day. It was also of symbolic import, being described by the court historian Lahuri as "pure like the heart of spiritual persons."

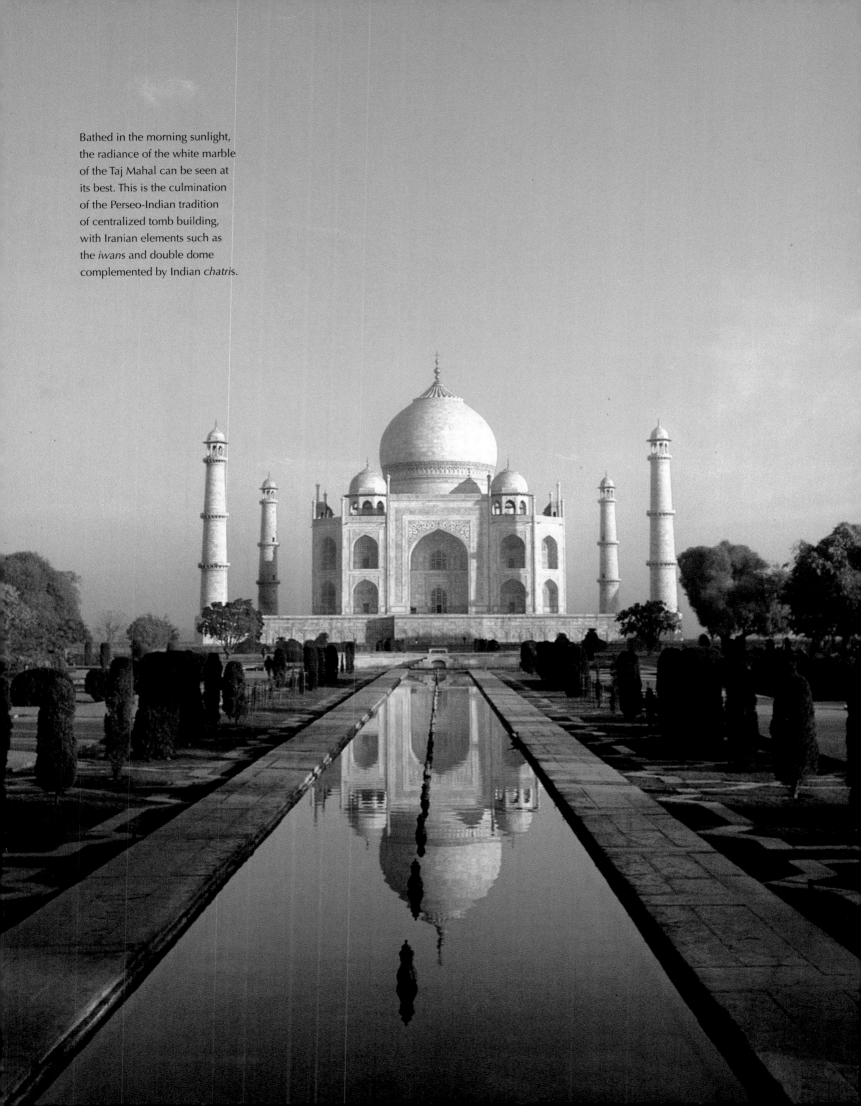

Bathed in the morning sunlight, the radiance of the white marble of the Taj Mahal can be seen at its best. This is the culmination of the Perseo-Indian tradition of centralized tomb building, with Iranian elements such as the *iwan*s and double dome complemented by Indian *chatri*s.

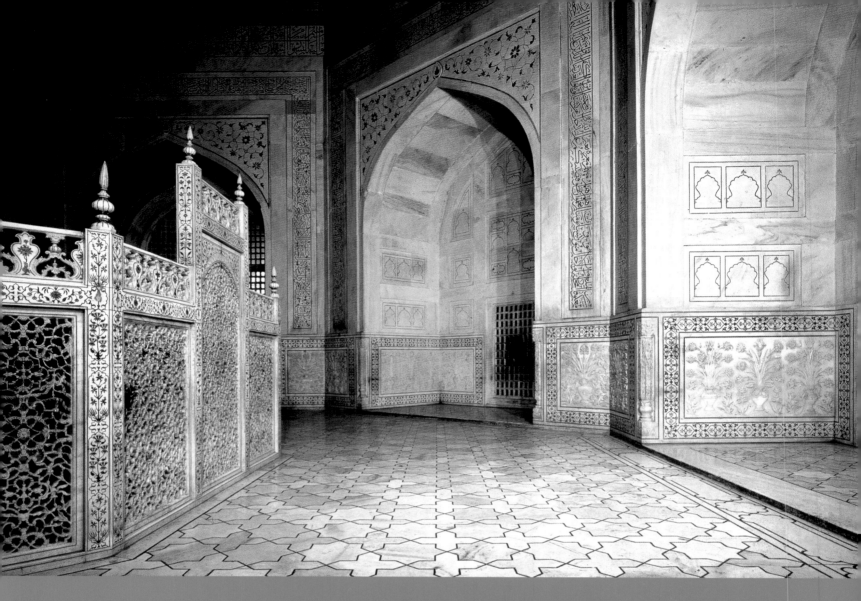

The decoration is remarkable for two features: the naturalistic representation of floral themes and the use of *pietra dura*, the art of inlay with semiprecious stones. All around the buildings are carved marble dadoes displaying floral sprays emerging from a naturalistic ground. Some flowers can be identified, but the majority are creations of the imagination. In the central chamber of the mausoleum the bouquets grow from vases and are even more finely carved.

MARVELS IN STONE

For the visitor to the mausoleum, the inner chamber forms the climax. Some initial disappointment is caused by the lowness of the inner dome, not unlike that of Humayun's mausoleum, rather than more impressive predecessors such as the tombs of Timur and Uljaytu. However, it is almost as if the designer tried to compensate by keeping the visitor's gaze at ground level on the most sumptuous screen and cenotaphs ever made.

First of all, the marble screen is carved, not with the more usual geometric grilles of earlier examples, but with an arabesque pattern that echoes the naturalistic flowers of the dadoes. Here the art of *pietra dura* is at its finest, and here too the floral theme is continued. The hyperbole of the court historian Lahuri, who wrote that it "causes the eye of the sun to be beautified," is entirely appropriate.

The cenotaph of Mumtaz Mahal is in the middle and that of Shah Jahan, added after his death in 1658, is to one side. However, Shah Jahan's is larger and, significantly, is decorated with *pietra dura* flowers where that of his wife has inscriptions, a measure of the prestige and paradisial connotations of floral motifs within the mausoleum.

The paving of the mausoleum carefully balances the naturalistic ornamentation of the dadoes, screen, and cenotaphs with a design of eight-pointed stars and crosses that reflect the axial octagonal plan of the building.

Although the sources identify two architects or supervisors of works, they also make it clear that it was Shah Jahan himself who was responsible for the major decisions regarding the layout of the monument. The rectangular entrance courtyard contains quarters for the servants who maintained the complex, and a bazaar on both sides. Through earlier plans and chroniclers' accounts we know that on the side of the entrance courtyard opposite the tomb was a commercial complex with four octagonal caravanserais whose outer walls comprised shops forming an even more extensive bazaar. This part has now virtually disappeared under more recent buildings.

Shah Jahan also added a garden on the bank of the Yamuna directly opposite the Taj, but this was not designed to house the legendary planned black marble replica of the Taj (which is never mentioned in contemporary sources). More likely, the garden was simply a place from which to view the mausoleum and its reflection in the river. One of the great pleasures of modern times is to view the Taj Mahal by moonlight, and the name of the garden, the Mahtab ("Moonbeam" or "Moonlit"), suggests that Shah Jahan enjoyed doing so himself.

BELOW
Shah Jahan's cenotaph dates from 1666. It is almost identical to that of his wife, but slightly larger, with *pietra dura* replacing a band of inscriptions, and with a symbolic pen case on top, representing his position as head of state.

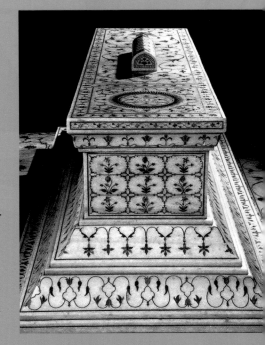

A WIND IN THE EAST

ISLAM IN CHINA AND SOUTHEAST ASIA

The Prophet famously enjoined Muslims to "seek knowledge, even in China." China was far beyond the Muslim world in his lifetime, but as early as 751 Muslim forces at Talas in present-day Kyrgyzstan defeated a Chinese imperial force and ensured that Transoxiana remained in Muslim hands. Further penetration in western China was blocked by Turkish tribes such as the Uighurs and Qarakhanids, but in the tenth century the conversion to Islam of the latter, ruling from Kashgar, brought China and Islam a step closer.

In his conquests of China, the Mongol leader Qubilai Khan (ruled 1260–94) employed armies with great numbers of Muslims recruited from earlier Iranian and Central Asian campaigns. He founded China's Yuan dynasty and appointed several Muslims to major government positions. Mongol indifference to religion enabled a considerable increase in the Muslim community in China, and the earliest significant extant buildings date from shortly after this. The most impressive mosque of this period is the Great Mosque of Xian. A stele there bears the date of 742, but this is clearly a forgery, probably attributable to the main period of construction in 1392. The plan

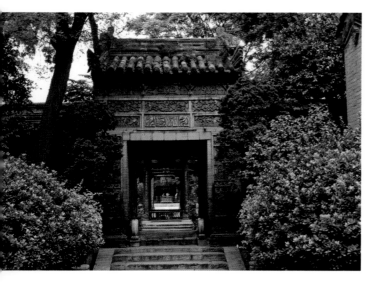

of the mosque is typical of traditional Chinese temples, consisting of successive courtyards, and the buildings and decoration are also entirely Chinese in style.

The open gateways of the first two courtyards lead to a third, at the center of which is a two-storeyed pagoda, dating from the Ming period (1368–1644), which served as a minaret. Along the sides of this and the next courtyard are extensive halls that show that the mosque functioned as a community center which included a library and rooms for the *imam*, for visitors, and probably also for teaching. The imposing prayer hall in the fourth courtyard could hold more than 1,000 worshippers. Its *mihrab* is of carved wood, with bands of Quranic inscriptions contrasting with the mandala-like square filled with large Chinese lotuses above the niche itself.

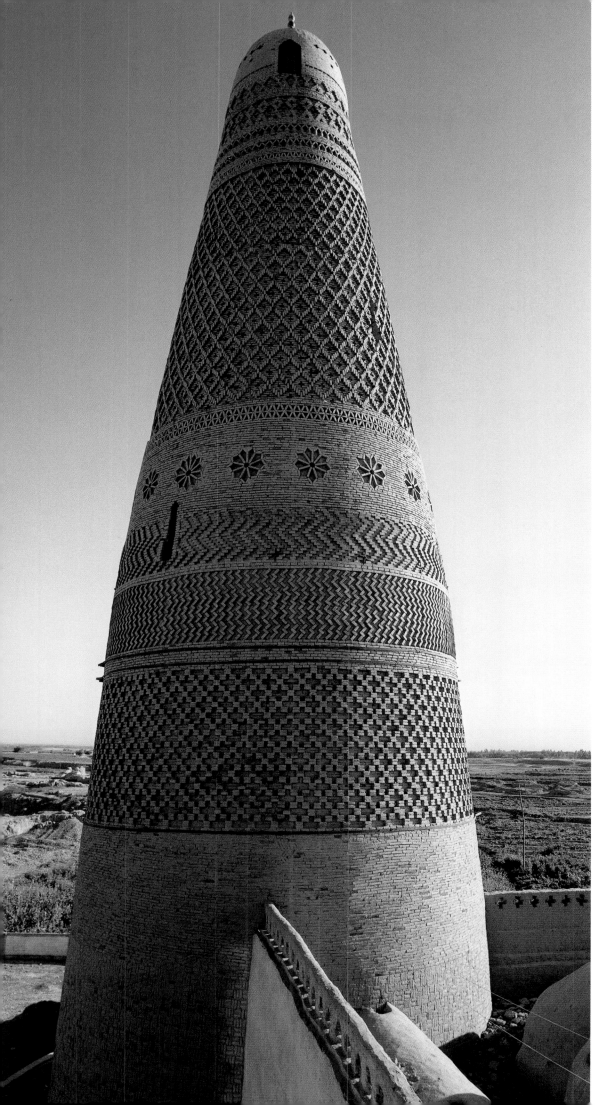

LEFT
The minaret of the Amin mosque in the Turfan oasis in western China has concentric bands of brick decoration and a pronounced batter, linking it to the most famous Central Asian minaret, that of the Great Mosque of Bukhara, dating from the 12th century. In the background can be seen the vineyards that provide the oasis with one of its main exports, raisins.

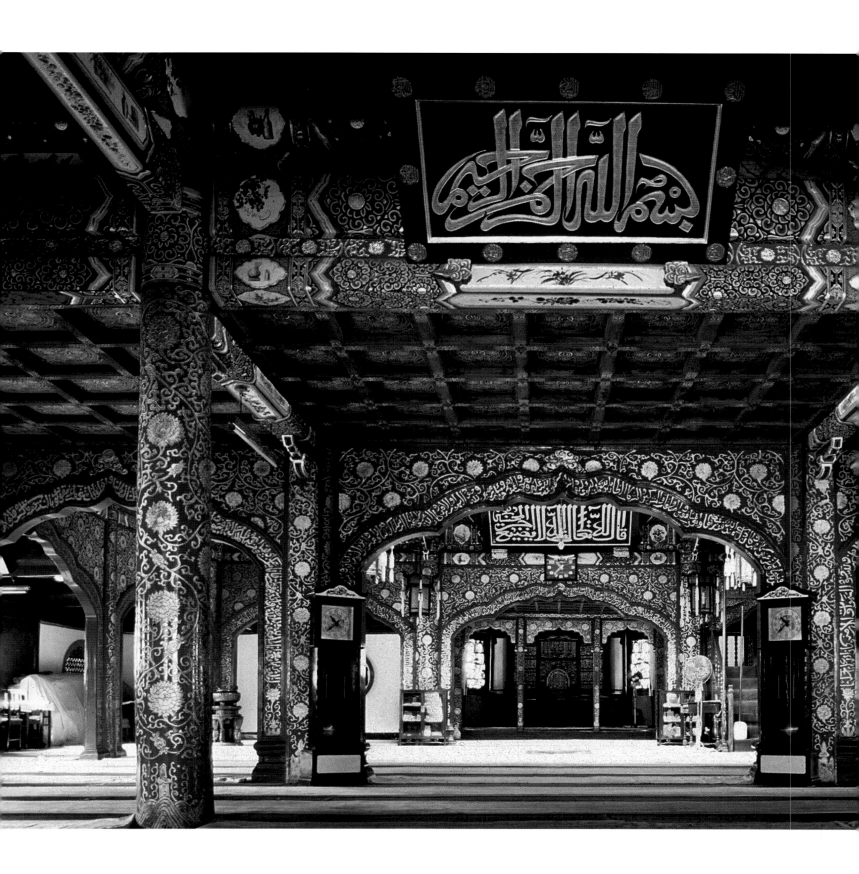

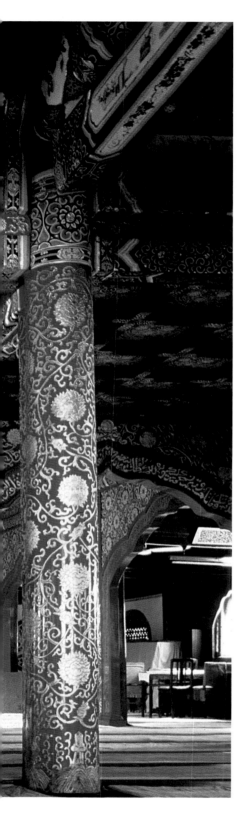

LEFT

The Beijing Mosque at Ox Street may date from the 14th century. The resemblance of its interior to that of the famous Temple of Heaven, in the same city, should not be too surprising.

BELOW

The brushrest in the form of stylized mountain peaks is a very Chinese object, so despite the Arabic inscription, this blue-and-white piece was probably not made for export. The porcelain mark indicates that it was made in the reign of the emperor Zhengde (1506–21) who was strongly influenced by Muslim eunuchs at court and may even have converted to Islam.

SOUTHEASTERN AND WESTERN CHINA

Islam also reached China along the coast, spread by seafaring merchants. The earliest mosque foundation in China may be the Huai-Sheng Si (Mosque in Memory of the Holy Prophet) in Guangzhou, where there had been a substantial Muslim community even in the eighth century. Its freestanding minaret, datable to the tenth century, is not pagoda-shaped but is in the form of a round brick tower, standing 118ft (36m) tall. Also unlike pagodas, it contains two brick stairways. Farther along the coast at Quanzhou are the remains of the Sheng-You Si (Mosque of the Holy Friend), which is distinguished by extensive inscriptions carved in ashlar masonry that date the building to the early fourteenth century. The wooden columns that supported the roof of the prayer hall have disappeared, but the regular disposition of blind niches topped by ogee arches around the interior give it a sobriety that differs from most other Chinese examples.

More typical is the Ox Street mosque in Beijing, the capital's largest. It too dates from the fourteenth century, although it was greatly expanded in the fifteenth century and had its interior repainted in the 1970s (see illustration, opposite). The resulting riot of color may not be too different from its original state. Like the Xian mosque, it has a two-storey pagoda as its minaret. The *mihrab*, now painted in gold on a striking black background, is interesting for the density of its calligraphy amid typical Chinese chrysanthemums.

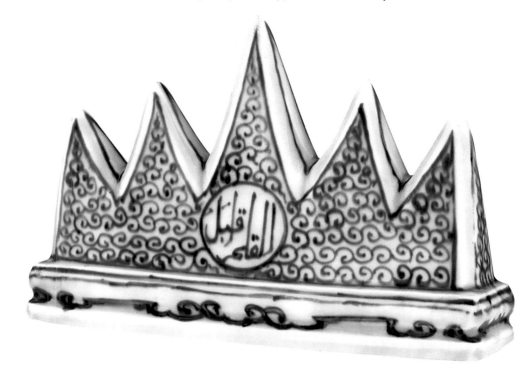

In western China mosques continued to be built in the Central Asian style. The Amin mosque (1778) in the Turfan oasis is an interesting example. Its massive 144ft (44m) minaret (see illustration, page 205) is set to one side of the rectangular building, although its extremely broad base gives it a military aspect that is only partly offset by its decorative brick patterns. The interior has an unusual combination of a central wooden-columned hypostyle area, without a courtyard, surrounded on three sides by domed bays. Light reaches the rather gloomy interior only through the windows of the *qibla* dome chamber and one open bay in the central hypostyle area. Its almost total lack of inscriptions perhaps reflects its geographic isolation.

Chinese pottery exports to the Muslim world began new phases of imitation there of Chinese styles, particularly in Safavid Iran and Ottoman Turkey. That some of these pieces were designed specifically for export to the Muslim market is suggested by the fact that they bear inscriptions in Persian or Arabic (see page 207).

ISLAM IN SOUTHEAST ASIA

The spread of Islam in Southeast Asia is closely associated with Arab and Persian merchants, following the lucrative spice trade. Initial contacts were limited to coastal towns, with an early major settlement recorded after a massacre of Muslims at Guangzhou in China in 878 encouraged many of them to move to Kedah on the west coast of the Malay peninsula. It was also on the Malay peninsula that Southeast Asia's first Muslim dynasty was established after the conversion of the Hindu king Parameshvara, ruling from Melaka (Malacca) in the early fifteenth century. The kingdom's wealth came from its ability to control the adjacent straits and to impose duties on passing ships, and many trading ports in the vicinity in Sumatra, Java, and Brunei at the same time either acquired substantial Muslim populations or had

BELOW
The links of the Chinese and Indonesian Muslim communities have long been strong, as symbolized by the Chinese style of the recently built (2002) Muhammad Chen Hoo mosque in Surabaya, east Java.

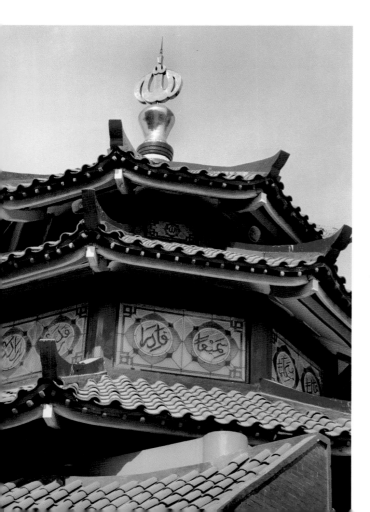

local rulers who converted to Islam. By 1478 the Javanese Hindu kingdom of Majapahit had fallen to Raden Patah, a vassal who founded the sultanate of Demak, a port in north Java that subsequently became a center for the diffusion of Islamic learning.

As in India, Sufis were instrumental in spreading the faith inland, and their message of accommodating previous religious practices within the new faith and a more personal approach to doctrine may have helped them find ready acceptance. One notable early Sufi saint, Sunan Kalijaga (active late fifteenth–early sixteenth century) used *wayang* (shadow puppet theater) and traditional gamelan music in proselytizing Islam.

ABOVE

A three-tiered hipped roof over a square base is typical of southeast Asian timber prayer halls. In contrast, the minaret is of brick and its form is inspired by Chinese pagodas. Masjid Kampung Kling (1748) at Melaka, one of the earliest Muslim settlements on the Malay peninsula.

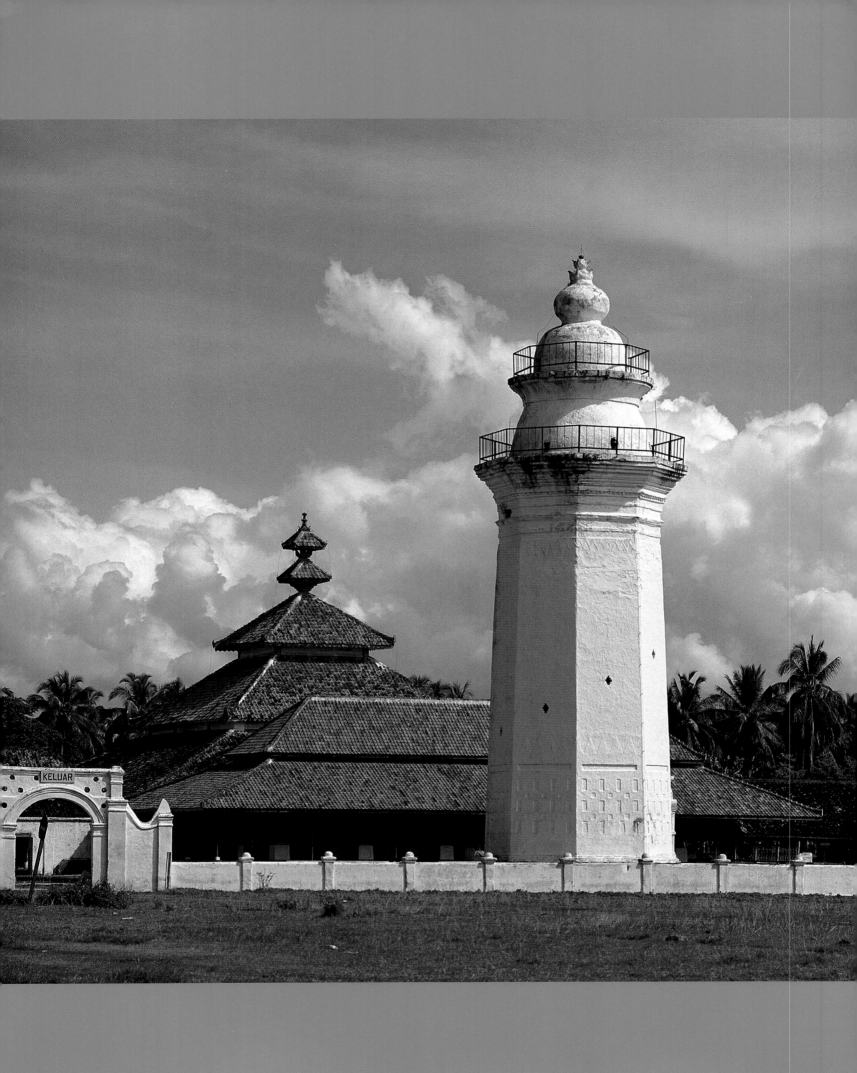

The lead taken by rulers in conversion to Islam is symbolized by the frequent juxtaposition of mosques with palaces, and the similarity of both can be explained by their common derivation from vernacular architecture. Like Chinese architecture, indigenous buildings were made of locally abundant wood with elaborate roofs supported by post and lintel construction that allowed for non-loadbearing walls. But there are considerable differences, the halls of Southeast Asia being usually square rather than rectangular, and with vertical tiers of pyramidal roofs (see illustration, page 209) rather than just one for each hall, emphasizing the symbolic importance of the space below.

One Chinese borrowing is the substitution of the call to prayer by the beating of large ceremonial drums; these could be at ground level, as in the Great Mosque of Demak (1474), the earliest extant mosque in the Indonesian archipelago, or raised in a gate pavilion or tower, as in the Menara Mosque at nearby Kudus, whose early sixteenth-century brick minaret (inlaid with Chinese ceramics) is also the oldest in Java.

The interiors of early mosques are usually devoid of ornament, although what little there is, often of carved wood, is notable for its continuities with earlier Buddhist and Hindu styles. A gateway in the Sendang Duwur mosque (sixteenth century) on Java is intricately carved with large stylized wings and birds; such was the layering of styles typical of early Javanese Islamic art that it is still uncertain whether it was made for the mosque or was reused from an earlier building.

The Great Mosque of Banten (1565) has an unusual minaret that may also have doubled as a lighthouse. The mosque itself is notable for its harmonious proportions, with the height of its five-tiered roof balanced by lower tiers which are of unusual width, in part because they accommodate the graves of local saints and members of the ruling family. The simplicity of its silhouette gives it a timeless elegance, very different from the intricacy that characterizes art from the other geographical extreme we have explored, the Maghreb, but a perfect illustration of the many and varied expressions of art in the Islamic world.

OPPOSITE

The Great Mosque (1565) of Banten in north Java has a five-tiered roof, built by Sultan Maulana Hasan al-Din. It is preceded by a rectangular veranda, slightly later but in the same style, and by an octagonal minaret which may also have functioned as a lighthouse. This was probably designed by a Dutch adventurer and convert, Lucazoon Cardeel, who in 1680 was employed by the king to fortify his new palace, adjacent to the mosque. He also built, in Dutch style, a two-storey brick pavilion next to the mosque, an example of the typically Javanese accommodation of styles of disparate origins.

GLOSSARY

amir a military commander, prince, or senior official

caliph (Arabic *khalifa*, successor) the successor to Muhammad as leader of the Muslim community. The title of caliph was claimed by the heads of several dynasties, including the Umayyads, the 'Abbasids, and the Ottoman sultans. Disagreement over the rightful succession to the Prophet lies at the heart of the differences between Sunni and Shi'i Muslims

caravanserai a large inn for travellers, in Anatolia often with a covered hall, a courtyard and facilities that sometimes included a mosque and a bath

chatri a small roof pavilion in Indian architecture

dhikr the invocation of God, in Sufi gatherings

Five Pillars, the five practices incumbent upon all Muslims (see pages 21–22)

hadith ("report") an account, or the body of accounts, recording the sayings, teachings, and deeds of the Prophet Muhammad

hajj the pilgrimage to Mecca

hijra the migration of the Prophet Muhammad with his followers from Mecca to Yathrib (subsequently known as Madina, or *Madinat al-Nabi*, City of the Prophet) in 622; the event marks the beginning of the Islamic calendar

imam the leader of the regular Friday communal prayers in a mosque, not necessarily a cleric

Imam (with capital) in Shi'ism, one of the persons regarded as the sole legitimate successors of Muhammad

iwan a hall closed on three sides, open on the other; a common feature of religious and secular buildings in Iran and elsewhere

jali a pierced stone screen

jami' a congregational mosque

khanaqah a residence for Sufis

khutba the sermon at the communal prayer on Fridays

Kufic angular script with a constant baseline

madrasa a college of religious education

Maghreb the western lands of Islam (corresponding to present-day Tunisia, Algeria, and Morocco)

Maghrebi pertaining to the Maghreb

masjid mosque

mihrab an arched niche in the *qibla* wall of religious building

minbar the pulpit from which the sermon is given at communal prayers

Mudejar a Muslim who remained in Spain after the Christian reconquest

muqarnas small segments of domes, arches, and brackets fitted together to make a composite vault

naskhi cursive script

niello black inlay material made of a variety of substances, including silver, copper, gold, and lead sulphides

pietra dura semiprecious inlaid stones, an art form copied from imported Italian work or developed from earlier Islamic inlay techniques

qibla the direction of Mecca, an orientation that influences prayer and burial

qal'a citadel

sabil public water dispensary

saz Ottoman decorative style with long jagged-edged leaves

shahada Islamic declaration of faith: *la ilah ila Allah, Muhammad Rasul Allah*: "There is no deity but God, Muhammad is the messenger of God"

Shi'i (or Shi'a) literally "party" or "faction"; belonging to or following the party of 'Ali, the cousin and son-in-law of the Prophet, who is believed by Shi'is to have been his rightful successor, or **caliph**

square Kufic a script in which the letters are placed at right angles

squinch an arch across the corner of a cube in the zone of transition of a dome chamber

Sufi an Islamic mystic; of or pertaining to Sufis or to Sufism (Islamic mysticism)

sunna the practice of Muhammad, and after him, that of the Muslim community

Sunni ("orthodox") belonging to or following the (non-Shi'i) majority of Muslims

ulama literally "learned men"; used of religious leaders

waqf religious endowment

BIBLIOGRAPHY

GENERAL

Brend, Barbara. *Islamic Art*. British Museum Press: London, 1991.

Blair, Sheila S. *Islamic Calligraphy*. Edinburgh University Press: Edinburgh, 2006.

Blair, Sheila S., and Bloom, Jonathan. *Islamic Arts*. Phaidon: London, 1997.

Blair, Sheila S., and Bloom, Jonathan. *The Art and Architecture of Islam 1250–1800*. Yale University Press: New Haven and London, 1994.

Ettinghausen, Richard; Grabar, Oleg; and Jenkins-Madina, Marilyn. *Islamic Art and Architecture 650–1250*. Yale University Press: New Haven and London, 2001.

Frishman, Martin, and Khan, Hasan-Uddin. *The Mosque: History, Architectural Development and Regional Variation*. Thames and Hudson: London 1994.

Hattstein, Markus and Delius, Peter. *Islam: Art and Architecture*. Könemann, 2004.

Hillenbrand, Robert. *Islamic Art and Architecture*. Thames and Hudson: London, 1999.

Hillenbrand, Robert. *Islamic Architecture: Form, Function and Meaning*. Edinburgh University Press: Edinburgh, 2000.

Holod, Renata, and Khan, Hasan-Uddin. *The Mosque and the Modern World: Architects, Patrons and Designs since the 1950s*. Thames and Hudson: London, 1997.

Irwin Robert. *Islamic Art*. Laurence King Publishing: London, 1997.

Jones, Dalu, and George Mitchell, eds. *The Arts of Islam: Hayward Gallery, 8 April–4 July 1976*. Arts Council of Great Britain, London, 1976.

Khalili, Nasser D. *The Timeline History of Islamic Art and Architecture*. Worth Press: Bassingbourn, Hertfordshire, England, 2005.

Watson, Oliver. *Ceramics from Islamic Lands*. Thames and Hudson: London, 2004.

1   ORIGINS

Herrmann, Georgina. *The Iranian Revival*. Elsevier-Phaidon: London, 1977.

Hodgson, Marshall G. S. *The Venture of Islam: Conscience and History in a World Civilization*. 3 vols. University of Chicago Press: Chicago, 1974.

2   THE EMPIRE OF ISLAM

Flood, Finbarr Barry. *The Great Mosque of Damascus: Studies in the Making of an Umayyad Visual Culture*. Brill: Leiden, 2002.

Fowden, Garth. *Qusayr 'Amra: Art and the Umayyad Elite in Late Antique Syria*. University of California Press: Berkeley, 2004.

Grabar, Oleg. *The Formation of Islamic Art*. Yale University Press: New Haven and London, 1987.

Grabar, Oleg. *The Shape of the Holy: Early Islamic Jerusalem*. Princeton University Press: Princeton, 1996.

Hamilton, R. W. *Khirbat al-Mafjar*. Oxford University Press: Oxford, 1959.

Hamilton, R. W. *Walid and His Friends: An Umayyad Tragedy*. Oxford Studies in Islamic Art, 6. Oxford University Press: Oxford, 1988.

3   IMAMS, PRINCES, AND SULTANS

Atil, Esin. *Renaissance of Islamic: Art of the Mamluks*, exhibition catalog. Smithsonian Books: Washington, D.C., 1981.

Barrucand, Marianne, ed. *L'Egypte fatimide. Son art et son histoire*. Presses de l'Université de Paris Sorbonne: Paris, 1999.

Behrens-Abouseif, Doris. *Islamic Architecture in Cairo: An Introduction*. Brill Academic Publishers: Leiden, 1989.

Ettinghausen, Richard. *Arab Painting*. Skira: Geneva, 1962.

Islamic Art in Egypt, 969–1517, exhibition catalog. Ministry of Culture of the United Arab Republic: Cairo, 1969.

O'Kane, Bernard, ed. *Treasure of the Islamic Museums in Cairo*. The American University in Cairo Press: Cairo, 2006.

4   FUSION IN THE WEST

Beckwith, John, *Caskets from Córdoba*. H.M.S.O.: London, 1960.

Dodds, Jerrilyn D., ed. *Al-Andalus: The Art of Islamic Spain*. Harry N. Abrams: New York, 1992.

Fernández Puertas, Antonio. *The Alhambra*. Saqi Books: London, 1997.

Grabar, Oleg. *The Alhambra*. Solipsist Press: Sebastopol, 1992.

Marçais, Georges. *L'Architecture musulmane d'Occident*. Arts et Métiers Graphiques: Paris, 1954.

5   SULTAN AND SHAH

Golombek, Lisa, and Donald Wilber. *The Timurid Architecture of Iran and Turan*. Princeton University Press: Princeton, 1988.

Gray, Basil, ed. *The Arts of the Book in Central Asia*. UNESCO: Paris, 1979.

Ipsiroglu, Mazhar S. *Siyah Qalem*. Akademische Druck- und Verlagsanstalt: Graz, Austria, 1976.

O'Kane, Bernard. *Timurid Architecture in Khurasan*. Mazda Publishing: Costa Mesa, 1987.

Seherr-Thoss, Sonia P. and Hans C. *Design and Color in Islamic Architecture*. Smithsonian Institute: Washington, D.C., 1968.

Wilber, Donald N. *The Architecture of Islamic Iran: The Il Khanid Period*. Princeton University Press: Princeton, 1955.

Welch, Stuart Cary. *A King's Book of Kings*. Thames and Hudson: New York and London, 1972.

6   PRINCIPALITY TO EMPIRE

Aslanapa, Oktay. *Turkish Art and Architecture*. Faber and Faber: London, 1971.

Atasoy, Nurhan and Çagman, Filiz. *Turkish Miniature Painting*. R.C.D. Cultural Institute: Istanbul, 1974

Atasoy, Nurhan and Raby, Julian. *Iznik: The Pottery of Ottoman Turkey*. Thames and Hudson: London, 1989.

Atil, Esin, ed. *Turkish Art*. Smithsonian Institute: Washington, D.C., 1980.

Necipoglu, Gülru. *The Age of Sinan: Architectural Culture in the Ottoman Empire*. Princeton University Press: Princeton, 2005, and Reaktion Books: London, 2005.

Roxburgh, David. (ed.) *Turks: A Journey of a Thousand Years 600–1600*. Royal Academy of Arts: London, 2005.

7   LORDS OF THE ORIENT

Asher, Caterine B. *The New Cambridge History of India: Architecture of Mughal India*. Cambridge University Press: Cambridge,1992.

Beach, Milo C. *The New Cambridge History of India: Mughal and Rajput Painting*. Cambridge University Press: Cambridge, 1992.

Bennett, James, ed. *Crescent Moon: Islamic Art and Civilization in Southeast Asia*. Art Gallery of New South Wales: Adelaide, 2005.

Koch, Ebba. *Mughal Architecture: An Outline of its History and Development, 1526–1858*. Prestel Verlag: New York, 1991.

Koch, Ebba. *The Complete Taj Mahal*. Thames and Hudson: London, 2006.

Necipoglu, Gülru. *The Age of Sinan: Architectural Culture in the Ottoman Empire*. Princeton University Press: Princeton, 2005, and Reaktion Books: London, 2005.

Seyller, John. *The Adventures of Hamza*. Azimuth Editions: Washington, D.C., 2002.

INDEX

Notes: Arabic names beginning with "al" are sorted according to the first letter of the word following "al". Page references in *italics* refer to illustrations, captions, and maps or plans.

ACKNOWLEDGMENTS
AND PICTURE CREDITS

Acknowledgments

I would like to thank Robert Hillenbrand whose forbearance led to my undertaking this project. It has been a pleasure to work with the conscientious team at Duncan Baird Publishers—Christopher Westhorp, Peter Bently, Julia Ruxton and Luana Gobbo.

Captions for the chapter opener images

Pages 12–13: "What God Wills" is the stylish inscription written on this 19th-century tile from Ottoman Turkey.

Pages 24–25: Arcades added in 862 to the Great Mosque of Qayrawan, Tunisia (836), by the Aghlabid client of the 'Abbasids, Abu Ibrahim Ahmad.

Pages 48–49: The Quranic inscription on the mihrab of the Sultan Hasan complex, Cairo (1361), was painted in a recent restoration, but is a reminder of how much more colorful most medieval buildings were in their original state.

Pages 78–79: "Here is the garden containing wonders of art the like of which God forbids should elsewhere be found." These words by the Nasrid court poet Ibn Zamrak begin the poem engraved on the basin supported by the lions in the Alhambra Palace, Granada, Spain (14th century).

Pages 106–107: Shah 'Abbas's Friday Mosque (or Royal Mosque, 1612–38) presented its best face to the square it overlooked: this detail shows the intricate floral patterns made possible with the smallest pieces of tile mosaic.

Pages 148–149: Gold, emeralds, rubies, and diamonds decorate the leather binding (dated 1588) of a manuscript of a *Divan* by the Ottoman sultan Murad III. Such opulence would have been inappropriate for a religious text like the Quran, but clearly not when flattering the ruler's poetic talents.

Pages 180–181: In this detail from the cenotaph of Shah Jahan in the Taj Mahal (1666) a solar halo surrounds the central medallion of *pietra dura*. When Shah Jahan appeared at sunrise every day to his subjects from his palace, historians wrote that they perceived two suns, a heavenly one and the imperial one.